MW00626442

The Water is Wide

A Rookie Cop's First 2 Years

By

Kevin M. Courtney

MARSHALL - MICHIGAN
800PUBLISHING.COM

The Water is Wide: A Rookie Cop's First 2 Years

Copyright © 2012 by Kevin M. Courtney

Cover design by Abbie Smith

Layout bby Kait Lamphere

Author photo courtesy of Author

The opinions expressed in this manuscript are solely the opinions of the author and do not represent the opinions or thoughts of the publisher. The author represents and warrants that s/he either owns or has the legal right to publish all material in this book.

ISBN-13: 978-1-935805-25-0

First published in 2012

10 9 8 7 6 5 4 3 2

Published by 2 MOON PRESS
123 W. Michigan Ave, Marshall, Michigan 49068
www.800publishing.com

All Rights Reserved. This book may not be reproduced, transmitted, or stored in whole or in part by any means, including graphic, electronic, or mechanical without the express written consent of the publisher except in the case of brief quotations embodied in critical articles and reviews.

PRINTED IN THE UNITED STATES OF AMERICA

To Eamonn, Erin, Ellen, and Kevin:
Only God's grace can explain how I ended
up with 4 such wonderful children.
You are my treasure.

From the Author

This book is written from my perspective and so of course there will be those who read it and wonder "what the hell is Courtney talking about?" All I can say is this is how I saw things and how they impacted on me, a new officer in a new town. I won't worry too much about any disagreements since no discussion of anything is much fun if everyone sees it the same way. One thing there is no disagreement on is the greatest blessing in my life besides the family I was raised in and the one God blessed me with after I got married, was becoming a Jackson Police officer and working with the finest bunch of men and women anyone could ask to be associated with. To those people I say thank you and God bless you. You are my brothers and sisters and enriched my life beyond words.

The names of the officers, with two exception, are their real names. Those names were changed as I did not wish to embarrass anyone with my "view." The names of most of the "innocent civilians" I met and made friends with are their real names. However, I did not use any real names in regards to the people I contacted in my duties or who I arrested. Those arrested surely deserve no recognition. Any connection of fictitious names to anyone living or dead is purely coincidental. The events described are true.

FOREWORD

It's been said that to truly understand someone, you must walk a mile in their shoes. Kevin gets you as close to walking in a rookie police officer's shoes as possible without actually doing so. He gives you an unedited, unrefined look into his experiences as a new officer and how his real life experiences are drastically different than what is portrayed on television.

Jump on for the roller coaster ride a new police officer enjoys starting with his first day on the job as a naïve young man full of enthusiasm with him quickly coming to the realization, as he stares at the body of a domestic assault victim, that the world is full of people who will do unimaginable things to each other for what seems to be incomprehensible reasons. Learn about the gut-wrenching fears officers experience on any given day, the disbelief as he is exposed to more and more horrendous acts of brutality, and the inner struggles as he must find a balance between his personal beliefs and values as they conflict with the "culture" on the street and trying to gain acceptance with veteran officers. Learn why officers become addicted to the adrenaline dumps the job produces, and the anxiety-causing encounters with the administration. Kevin hits the bull's-eye describing the extreme peaks and valleys officers experience as they learn the ropes while on their way to becoming a seasoned officer.

As Kevin takes you through his first couple years, you gain an appreciation for the level of responsibility that is vested in a 22 year old inexperienced police officer. Be it an officer that has been on the job for one day or 23 years, they all possess the authority to take away a person's freedom, or in a worst case scenario, their life. Experience the decisions that must be made in literally one or two seconds that could impact the officer, a citizen, or a community for years to come. Experience the level of professionalism most people often miss, and the media rarely covers, as officers make decisions at three in the morning on a cold February day, when no one is looking. Enjoy the camaraderie and lifelong bonds that are developed as a result of depending on your partners to "cover your back" and the isolation that is forced upon officers from society, because of their lack of understanding about what the job truly entails and the copping mechanisms that are developed, by the officers, that appear cold and callous in the public's eye.

Be it 30 years ago or yesterday, Kevin's experiences capture what every new officer encounters. The internal struggles, the emotional impact, the thrill of the job, the drunken debauchery off-duty, the alienation that occurs with the general public. America should be thankful young men, just like Kevin, are standing in line, willing to take on the burdens and make the sacrifices, to be one of the privileged to join the ranks and call themselves cops.

Matt Heins, Chief of Police
Jackson Police Department

CHAPTER 1

My dad used to say "There are two types of people in the world. Those that are Irish and those that wish they were." Some might say that's nothing but blarney but not me. Dad was fiercely proud of being Irish and I have followed in his footsteps. I never felt that pride more deeply than when I stood in the center of County Kerry, Ireland near the small village of Glencar, with my sister Cheryl. Cheryl and I were both police officers back in Michigan. I had been a Jackson police officer for almost exactly two years and Cheryl, four years my senior, had been working for the Saginaw Township PD for six years. She was, in fact, the first female officer to ever work as a regular road patrol officer anywhere in Saginaw County.

It was a fine soft day in May, 1981 that found the two of us in Ireland. We were enjoying the first half of our eight-day trip to the Emerald Isle, my first real "extravagance" since graduating college and getting a job, and the trip was most definitely the fulfillment of a life long dream for this Irish-American. We had just spent an hour or so visiting John Courtney and his wife, Bridgid, who lived just outside the village. My dad had found John by doing a little "research" from America, and we had hoped we were related. It turned out we weren't, but John and Bridgid, or Bridie as she was known, were gracious and friendly and John's last words as they stood waving good bye were, "And tell your Da I was asking after him." I truly wished that this kind and decent man was my kin. Thirty years later I'm still friends with his son, Pat, daughter in law, Maureen, and their daughter, Breda, and am blessed to say so. John must have thought I was OK too because once years later after I had visited him, Pat pointed out to his dad that we weren't really related. John replied unequivocally, "He's a Courtney." That was kinship enough for John and his words were like a Papal blessing to me.

An Irish folk song called the "Water is Wide" tells of the vast ocean that separates an Irish immigrant from his love back in Ireland: no matter how wide and deep the ocean, the man's love is greater and will keep the two together. I felt I had conquered that same vast ocean for a different kind of love. It was a love of my heritage, name, and people. I might not be much in the great scheme of things but I knew I had come a long way from the Courtneys who had left this beautiful island during the great potato famine more than a century earlier.

Cheryl had been to Ireland once before, so she'd planned out the trip and pretty much was running the show. This was nothing new for me as I had two other older sisters besides Cheryl, and all three were quite well practiced in telling me what to do. From time to time, they also took a run at my big brother, Stan, the second oldest, and they even had back up if needed as my Uncle Tom and Aunt Dorothy, who lived right across the road when we were growing up, had 7 daughters who ran roughshod over their only brother and never minded in the least helping out with Stan or I. I knew my place and it wasn't at the head of the line when any Courtney women were around.

As I stood looking at the countryside around me, I was flooded with a strange mix of emotions. I had an overpowering feeling that I was not in a strange place. Somehow, some way, deep in my soul, I recognized that "Courtneys" belonged to this place. I was also thinking about the fact that my great grandfather had left from somewhere near here, faced with persecution and starvation at the hands of the English. Now, just three generations later, two of his descendants had returned to this place with a level of education and holding positions of authority he would never have dreamed possible.

Tears came to my eyes as I realized what my people had suffered, and yet at the same time I felt tremendous pride at how they had overcome all that to make it in America. Just as important, they had never forgotten where they came from or who they were. It made me want to beat my chest and shout "Screw the Queen! We're still Irish and proud of it!" I also considered "mooning" England, but decided the distance was too great for the gesture to be effective so I flipped "the Royals" the bird instead.

I finally decided the right way to look at it was the Courtneys, like so many other Irish, had taken shit from the English here, and from damn near everyone when they got to America, but they never backed down or sold out. I decided I'd keep the tradition alive and do the same. I promised myself that if I were blessed with children one day, they would know these things as well.

All this reflection also made me consider just how I came to be a Jackson Police Officer in the first place. It was that opportunity that had given me an amazing ride for the last two years and the cash to come to the Emerald Isle. I also thought of the "water" I'd crossed in those two years as a new police officer and wondered if that wasn't actually the more vast distance. At least I'd grown up with knowledge of my family and its heritage. I didn't know squat about Jackson and not much more about being a cop when I started out in May of '79.

Kevin M. Courtney

CHAPTER 2

The sidewalk at Sacred Heart Catholic Church in Birch Run was perfect for playing cops and robbers on bicycles. It was a large horseshoe shape and was bounded on the sides by the church and rectory with the school at the top and the street at the bottom, custom made for "pursuits" and traffic stops. You just had to make sure that the priest, nun, or a parishioner wasn't walking between the buildings. Running one of them down was a sure venial sin, not to mention a direct ticket to parental wrath.

My buddies and I and our families were all members of Sacred Heart, so it was natural that we both feared and respected the moral forces it represented in 1960's America. I was no son of rebellion. Just the opposite, my heroes were the forces of law and order, and all I ever wanted to be was a police officer. Strange considering there were no police officers in my large, extended family. Not having a cop in an Irish Catholic clan was almost as shameful as no nuns or priests but my Aunt, Sister Rita Marie, (later Sister Gertrude Courtney) kept the family from complete disgrace. No, I came by my career choice from always identifying myself with the good guys from TV shows like *Gunsmoke, Bonanza, Paladin, Dragnet,* and later *Adam-12.* My buddies always wanted me around for the games because, as a future cop, I took making things authentic to heart. Fifteen years later not one of them was surprised to see me in a cop's uniform. Although they all busted on me about the apparent lack of any kind of background check being conducted before I was hired.

As I think about it, I guess one could make the case for ethnic background having something to do with it though, as along the

Saginaw/Genesee County line where we lived prior to moving into the Village of Birch Run when I was eight, five children from three Irish-American families became police officers. In the little more than one mile of road in question, there were probably only ten households total (most all Irish) and yet they produced 5 police officers. I also have two nephews continuing the tradition, so maybe the Courtneys were just late to the party this time.

My greatest hope growing up was to one day wear the uniform of the Michigan State Police. Birch Run was too small to have a real police force although they did have two auto workers who worked a few hours a week patrolling the community and harassing the long hairs that seemed to be sprouting up all over as the decade came to a close. However, there was a State Police Post just ten miles to the north in Bridgeport, and the sight of one of those distinctive blue cruisers made my eyes light up. I just knew that one day I would climb behind the wheel and be the guy locking up the bad guys. I didn't know exactly how it would happen; I just had faith that it would. That was one of the things that in some ways made me more Irish than American: Faith, that no matter where you were, you could somehow get where you needed to go.

My mother and father both graduated from high school in the Depression and came from the typical, poor, farm family background of that era. My mom, Helen, left home at the age of 16 to become a live-in babysitter for her room and board. Mom figured she got a pretty good deal. Little did she know that by today's standards she was being exploited. She finished high school and eventually put herself through business school in Bay City.

Her first real job was working at Dow Chemical in Midland, Michigan, where she met the founder and namesake of the chemical giant. She later took a job with Buick, where my dad was employed but gave that up after they got married and my oldest sister, Marcia made her arrival. Marcia was followed by brother Stanley and sisters Susan and Cheryl. Stan had the only German name in the family, as he was named after our maternal grandfather. My poor mother was 100% German but still only managed to produce Irish children, a phenomenon she never quite understood.

My dad, Laurence (Larry), was a hardworking autoworker who wanted nothing more than for his children to have things better than he did. That didn't mean he valued material things. Quite the opposite. He valued faith, family, character, hard work, and education in exactly that order. Laurence Courtney was fiercely proud of being 100% Irish Catholic and instilled that pride in his children. He made it clear to us that whatever we did, reflected on every single Courtney who ever lived, and so making an ass of yourself was not an option. His favorite poem was "Man in the Mirror." I used to laugh at the thought that Michael Jackson had made a musical version of it. Michael surely would have been the last person on the old man's play list.

The fact there were Courtney aunts, uncles, and cousins living in the same small community helped enforce Larry's view of responsibility. On a couple of occasions, a Courtney cousin got an earful from Uncle Larry about his or her behavior. Out of fear, respect, and love, they took the ass chewing and laughed about it when they were older. However, there wasn't much laughing going on when those blue eyes bore in on you. He never beat a child in his life, but the knowledge that he could was enough to keep us all mostly in check.

Like I said, Mom was a second generation German, and while the Irish side of the family overwhelmed her kids and she was forever reminding us we were half German, it was to no avail as we all saw ourselves as Irish through and through. It didn't help that most of Mom's family was living in Indiana and not around to back her up. She wasn't at all excited when I would snap off a Nazi salute and say "I am proud of the Germans" sounding like *Sgt. Shultz* from *Hogan's Heroes.* I thought it was pretty funny, but I think all she thought was Courtney humor ain't that funny even if it is your kid.

The bottom line is that Courtneys were hard working, honest folks who were maybe just a bit loud. Mom was a big part of teaching us to work hard but the loud came from the Courtney side. You didn't find any of our knives in your back. You found it in your chest and you saw us put it there. You couldn't ask for a better friend, but if you backstabbed us, you were more likely to win the lottery than have us forget your treachery. Not only that, if your actions were deemed bad enough every member of the extended family would then consider you scum and also hold a grudge; The Irish were world renowned grudge holders and we upheld that high standard.

Kevin M. Courtney

.

CHAPTER 3

I had no problem meeting all of the family expectations but education. I just couldn't seem to get my arms around the concept of studying hard to get good grades if the subject matter didn't interest me. As a result I was a barely average student throughout high school. It sucks to be a mediocre student, but it *really* sucks to be mediocre academically with four older siblings who were all excellent students and most of your teachers remembered them well. The only thing that saved me was I was an excellent English and history student, which made up for a complete lack of math and science skills. This had me thinking that maybe being a welder in a factory was more my lot than becoming a police officer. However, like many young people, I had the blessing of a teacher who saw in me more than I saw in myself.

Miss Chapel was a young journalism teacher with looks to make any teenage boy's heart skip a beat or two. It was her encouragement that got me to pick up my academic pace to the point where I had the grades necessary to get into college. She also genuinely liked me and my buddy, Henry, and as a result we listened to what she said. Besides listening to her meant you were standing next to her and that was *always* a good thing.

Added to that was the confidence I suddenly found in my senior year as a long distance runner. I loved to play basketball and decided running cross country would be good for two reasons. First, it would get me in great shape, and second, the cross country coach also was the basketball coach so the suck-up points would be helpful for a guy who was cut the year before. I did okay in cross country and by the end of the season was the number four or five runner on the team and was posting respectable times. I made the basketball team but didn't do much on the hardwood to impress anyone except the track coach, who talked me into running the two mile in the upcoming spring. It was the one and only time I was ever "recruited" as an athlete, and it was there that I finally connected effort with results and became the school record holder in the two mile run.

Running taught me discipline and gave me the confidence that I could be successful in college and become a police officer. Plus, for a guy who was hyper competitive, I finally got to WIN and I just could not get enough of the rush that comes from winning. I never smoked dope, but there was no freaking way that "high" could compare with the endorphin rush of winning. I didn't mind hearing my name announced over the PA system the next day in class during the daily announcements either.

CHAPTER 4

My four years of college seemed to fly by, and in the spring of my senior year I was considered by the Head of the Criminal Justice Department at Ferris State College to be one of his brightest students. Quite a change. I'm sure my friends from high school viewed it as something approaching the miraculous. I was even awarded one of two Alumni Association "Outstanding Student Awards." The other went to a classmate named, Denise who was a stone knockout. I enjoyed the $100 that went with the award but was far more appreciative of the chance to snuggle up to Denise for the photos. I hung out and talked with her after we got our awards and it made me wish I had made a move on her during our last year; now in the last 10 days of our college careers, I figured that opportunity was long gone.

I had started my college career at Siena Heights College, a small Catholic college in Adrian, so I could run cross country in college. I transferred to Ferris after 2 years because Ferris' Criminal Justice program combined the State's mandated police training with the regular classes needed for a Bachelor's degree. That meant, upon graduating, Ferris' graduates could go straight to work as a police officer in Michigan without attending a traditional police academy. Ferris also cost a whole lot less than a private school like Siena Heights, and I found I just couldn't dedicate the time necessary to become an elite runner at the college level so running was no longer a reason to stay at Siena.

My plan was still to become a state trooper as I neared the end of my senior year. I had taken the test for the Michigan State Police and was awaiting my interview with them. In February, Dr. Lawson, one of my professor's at Ferris, announced in Criminal Investigations class that the Jackson Police Department was hiring and had called wanting Ferris graduates to apply. I didn't pay a lot of attention because I was on my way to being a state trooper.

A week later, Dr. Lawson said, "Hey the lieutenant from Jackson called me again and wondered how come he didn't have any Ferris students apply. Now unless you geniuses all got jobs, you better not pass this up. Besides, Jackson's a good department and has always been good to us so don't make me look bad." I figured what the hell, it would be a good experience to go through, and so I called Jackson and got an application mailed up to me. I filled it out right away and sent it back, as did about a dozen or so of my classmates.

The Jackson Police Department written exam was given on a Saturday at Jackson Community College, and I was amazed to learn that there were more than 300 people taking it. I knew there were only eight openings, so I didn't really like the odds. The exam was pretty straightforward and appeared to be trying to measure one's aptitude to be a police officer. I felt like I did okay on it, but I wasn't too worried either way since the state police was where I was headed.

About 10 days later, the letter arrived from Jackson telling me I had passed the exam and was to call the Department and schedule an interview. I felt pretty good about that, and when I found out I was one of only two Ferris students to reach that level, I felt even better. The other was Gary Millar, (pronounced Miller) who was from Jackson. We both had to downplay our excitement a little since fellow classmates were feeling the sting of not making the cut.

Around this time, I was called by the State Police for my interview with them and I was very excited by that news. I decided to keep going with the Jackson process too, as I figured it couldn't hurt. My dad had suggested to me when I got my income tax refund I should buy a good suit for my job interviews. I was surprised a guy who only wore a suit to church, weddings, and funerals would think of this but had to admit it was a good suggestion.

I headed into Saginaw's Fashion Square Mall and went into the first men's store I came to, thus living up to the stereotype of how most men shop. I was hoping for one of those hot looking 20-something women who work in the mall to wait on me, but instead the salesman that approached was an absolute flamer. I thought, just my luck, I'm looking for Farrah Fawcett and instead I get Liberace. What the hell. I figured these guys do know clothes, so I'll just go with the flow.

Liberace picked out a nice, light-colored suit with matching shirt and tie pointing out spring was just around the corner so it would be perfect. He directed me to the dressing room, smiled, and said, "Let me know if you need any help." I said "thanks" but thought to myself I'd run through the freaking mall naked before I'd let you in a changing room with me sweet lips. The suit fit great and I was so pleased I even bought a new pair of shoes. All in all it was a good day for both of us. I got a new suit and Liberace got the commission on a $200+ sale, which in 1979 was serious coin.

I went down to Lansing for the MSP interview first, and other than being late after coming across 20 miles of ice covered highway near St. Johns I did fine on the interview. The lieutenant in charge of the recruiting and hiring process told me it might be six months before they ran an academy, adding that I'd be hired for sure but he just couldn't promise when that would be. That left me seriously concerned about my future. The common practice of college graduates goofing off for a summer before finding a job wasn't in vogue back in 1979, and sure as hell wasn't acceptable to good old Larry Courtney, who expected his kids to find a job NOW not later.

Kevin M. Courtney

.

CHAPTER 5

Next up was Jackson, and I felt I did a very good job on the interview until the last question. A civilian member of the interview panel asked me if I thought the job would be rewarding enough. I gave a run down of why I felt police work was an honorable profession and how doing such work could not be anything but rewarding. The questioner said, "No, I mean financially." I answered that I came from a working class family where we had a nice house and plenty to eat but no extras like motorcycles, fancy vacations, or snowmobiles. I was quite sure the salary Jackson offered would be fine in meeting my expectations. The interviewer explained that he was concerned because of the fine suit I was wearing.

I had to explain to the questioner that it was the only suit I owned and that I thought I had better have a nice suit when I went on interviews so as not to appear the small town boy I really was. The rest of the panel chuckled and gave me a nod so I figured I was okay on the fancy clothes issue. I was sure the old man would get a good laugh out of the story of what happens when the country boy tries to put on big city ways. My big brother, Stan, made a comment about pearls on a pig, emphasis on *pig*, when he heard about it. It is such a blessing to have supportive siblings.

I was still not really thinking that I was going to be hired by Jackson because I knew they were interviewing quite a few candidates. I did feel pretty good that I had gotten this far. I got feeling really good when, a week later, the Chief of Police's secretary, Marge Teske, called me and asked if I could come back down for an interview with the Chief. I asked if Gary Millar was also going to be interviewed, and

Marge seemed taken aback by the question. I quickly pointed out I did not have a car and was only asking for the purpose of getting a ride if Gary was going to be interviewed. Marge laughed and said Gary was on the list and that she would schedule the two interviews back to back to make it easier on us. I thanked her profusely.

Gary and I were aware that several of our classmates had tried and failed with Jackson, so we again kept our exuberance to ourselves around friends in the Criminal Justice program out of respect for them. All our buddies, however, congratulated us about reaching this step in the process. Up to this point, only two of the 70 or so people graduating from the program that spring had landed jobs.

The excitement really started to build as we were driving back to Jackson the night before the interviews. We started talking about what the interview with the Chief meant and, while we tried to stay calm and not get our hopes up, the only reason we could come up with for being called to see "The Man" was to be offered a job. We both agreed, however it was one more chance to step on it and blow any chance of becoming a Jackson Police Officer, so now was not the time to get cocky.

I went into the Chief's office both excited and worried, but I was by nature a pretty self-confident individual by then, so I settled down and went in standing tall, ready for anything. Chief James Rice was an old-school cop who had worked his way up through the ranks, and he looked more than a little intimidating to me when I sat down across from him. The Chief turned out to be pretty low key in the interview and he more chatted with me than questioned me. He even asked me if I went to church. That would be a big no-no in the future, but in the 70's it was no big deal. I figured the Chief just wanted to get a handle on who the hell the interview board was telling him to hire since he was the one who would bask in my achievements or suffer from my sins.

The only real reaction came when the Chief asked me if I ever smoked pot. Chief Rice showed a fair degree of surprise when I told him I had never smoked marijuana. The Chief raised his eyebrows and said, "You know a good Catholic boy like you can go to hell for lying." I chuckled and said, "I can go to hell for a lot of things I've done, Sir, but not for lying about dope smoking. I'm telling you the truth. I just had no interest in it." That was the truth, too, as I saw too many of my life long friends ruin their lives in high school by screwing around with that shit, and I wanted nothing to do with it. Once I got to college, I relaxed a little but still figured I didn't need any Mexican giggly weed in my garden. Besides, walking through the clouds of smoke in the hallway of the dorm my first two years gave me so many contact buzzes, I didn't need to light up. I felt like I was in a "Cheech and Chong" movie on more than one occasion.

Chief Rice said, "Well Kevin you're the kind of guy we want working here, so if you still want to come here the job is yours." I said yes without hesitation and shook the Chief's hand, saying the same thing countless other newly hired cops did: "I won't let you down Chief." It was April 7, 1979, and I had just gone from trying to achieve a dream to making it a reality. I was a police officer! That I would have to wait until after graduation to actually start working made no difference. I was a police officer!

The fact that I had only been in Jackson on 3 occasions counting this one--and knew a total of one person in the whole city of 40,000--didn't enter into my decision at all. Nor did the fact I was on the hiring list for the State Police. My upbringing told me if you don't have any money or a job, which I didn't, you have no business turning down honest work. That made my decision to say yes to the offer an inevitable conclusion. It might be the 1970's, but my attitude towards work was no different than the Courtneys of the1850's who came over on the boat.

In fact all I really knew about Jackson was it was home to the State Prison of Southern Michigan, which was where the adults of my childhood would say someone was headed if they didn't straighten up. I was sure at least some of the locals back in Birch Run would be getting perverse enjoyment about where Kevin Courtney had ended up.

Kevin M. Courtney

.

CHAPTER 6

The true realization that I was no longer just wanting to become a police officer but really was one hit me when I started to get dressed in the basement locker room at the police station. Putting on a Kevlar vest sort of clears up any confusion about what exactly you are about to get into. I was buttoning up my uniform shirt when a solidly built Mexican officer named Ricardo Cedillo came up and introduced himself to me. I knew enough Spanish from my college days to know the name was pronounced "Ce-dee-o" and not "Ce-dill-o." I liked Ric right off the bat and he is still my friend 32 years later. Ric used to joke he was Hawaiian, and I think about half the people on the street believed it.

I had come into work 40 minutes early on my first day but found out most officers were in the station and ready to go 20 minutes or so before the start of their shift. As such I was able to meet my first training officer, Roger Ramirez, and many of the other officers individually in either the locker room or the break room next door. I found most were not much older than I was and had anywhere from two to six years on the force. I would later learn shift picks were by seniority, and so days and nights had all the old timers, and the youngest officers worked afternoons.

With Cedillo and Ramirez, I had now met two-thirds of the Hispanic officers on the 90-officer force within my first ten minutes on the job. It was still the late 70's and in most departments it wouldn't have taken that long. Roger was a very good looking man, about 26 years old, with a quick smile and easy manner that I automatically liked. Roger told me that the first thing we had to do was go to "detail," after which he would get me all the stuff I would need to do the work of a Jackson Police Officer. Roger was impressed that I came to work with a hard briefcase since that was critical piece of equipment for any road officer, given all the forms we needed to carry.

I explained that my big sister, Cheryl, who was a police officer back in my home county, had taken care of that for me. Roger liked that and was even happier to find out Cheryl was a graduate of Michigan State University as was he. I gained even more points when I explained that while I did not attend MSU, I was a true Spartan fan and hated anything and everything having to do with the University of Michigan. Roger smiled as only a devout follower of a faith does when he meets another true believer.

Roger told me that detail started 20 minutes before the actual starting time of the shift, and, at detail the lieutenant or one of the shift sergeants would confirm what section each officer was working, provide department-related updates, and read the "desk cards." These were large index cards with the latest information, including areas to be given extra attention, particular problems to be addressed, suspect descriptions, and people wanted on warrants. The cards on people wanted on warrants or up to some type of no good would include a suspect photo when available. Officers were expected to carry a note pad and record this information so that they could refer to it during the course of their duties. Roger made it clear that being on time to detail was an absolute requirement and Lieutenant Johnson, our shift commander, was a real stickler about it. I had no idea what an impact this Lieutenant Johnson would have on me and my career, but I knew enough about "sticklers" to decide to not test the waters.

The next hour or so was a blur. I definitely was suffering from the fishbowl syndrome, as I was the only new hire to show up who had not been a cadet with Jackson PD and so I got all the "new guy" looks and comments. On top of that, countless procedures and forms had to be shown and explained, but Roger was by nature an easy going man and never once gave me the impression having me as a trainee was any kind of problem.

Once we got in the car to check in service, meaning we were on patrol and available to take calls, Roger asked me my badge number and not knowing any better I said "39" since that was the number on my badge. The station radio operator quickly corrected Roger and advised "your partner's badge number is "075." Roger explained to me that badges were catch-as-catch-can and didn't always match your true ID/badge number. That sounded reasonable but I still felt like a complete idiot and figured the rest of the shift, having heard the radio traffic, assumed the same thing. I even suspect there might have been a couple whose opinion never changed much. Once I made a few bucks, I bought my own badge with "O75" on it and eliminated the confusion.

That feeling left quickly when Roger pulled the car out of the rear of the station and headed out on patrol. I had been in patrol cars on many occasions but always as a ride-along. My heart raced with the thrill of being a real cop going out on real patrol. The fact that it was in a city completely new to me and that I had grown up in a very rural area, just added to the rush.

Kevin M. Courtney

CHAPTER 7

The section we were assigned to, David-24, was the south central portion of the city and traditionally the busiest. Our shift started at 4:00 pm or 1600 in military time which was the time used by the Department. Assigned areas were called "sections" at JPD, and David-24 was bordered by First Street on the west, Airline Drive on the east, Michigan Avenue on the north and the city limits on the south. It was split down the middle by "Francis," a street name that evoked the same response from area people as would the word "Watts" in Los Angles or "Harlem" would in New York. The fact those areas made Francis look like Chicago's Miracle Mile didn't matter. Like politics, perception of danger is all local. To some extent, Jackson had all the issues of those big cities just not with the same concentration or frequency.

The other unique aspect of D-24 at that time was that it was actually two sections. The area between First and Francis was really section Edward 25, and the area between Francis and Airline was D-24. Staffing levels at the time, however, had forced the brass to combine the two sections under D-24. Needless to say, officers working D-24 had to be someone willing to work hard or the call load would swamp them. Roger was a real worker and made it a point of pride not to have anyone else taking calls in his section.

The other sections were Frank 26: rich west side of the city, Adam 21: commercial, retail, fast food, and residential mix on the city's northwest side, Baker 22: the northeast corner of the city, which was primarily residential except for the Michigan Avenue corridor, which was commercial. The first few blocks off Michigan Ave. were low rent areas, but most of the section was quiet and with well-maintained homes. Charlie-23 was the city's southeast section and was a mix of owner-occupied homes, rental housing, a large industrial section, and a huge Conrail rail yard. Next to D-24, 23 was the City's toughest area. It was also home to a very large Polish population, including new immigrants from Poland.

Sections 21, 23, and 24 started at 1600 and 22 and 26 started at 1500 so as to create an overlap of coverage. Day shift cars started at 0700 and 0800 and midnights at 2300 and 0000 respectively to create the same effect over the 24 hours of the day. The Department had a minimum staffing level during all times of the day or night of five officers on duty. If they had more than five on a shift, the extra cars would either be assigned as "T" or traffic units, or as an Adam 30 car which provided backup on calls requiring more than one officer.

Each shift was lead by a lieutenant and had two sergeants. The schedule was set up so that Monday thru Friday, the lieutenant and one sergeant were on duty, and on the weekends, the lieutenant was off and both sergeants were on. Typically the lieutenant stayed in the station during the shift and a sergeant worked the road as "Sam 11" responding to calls that might require some oversight or just needed backup. Sergeants rarely took calls unless things got really busy. The street sergeant also collected paperwork from the officers on the street to cut down the number of trips officers made back to the station.

The section I was starting out in was an older part of town in which lived the largest portion of the city's black population. Housing included many neat, single family homes in the area east of Francis Street, owned by World War II-era, black, working class couples. Many of the men worked at the local Goodyear or Clark Equipment plant, and these folks had no intention of leaving *their* homes just because some young punk moved into the neighborhood. On more than one occasion, I was a bit shocked to hear one of those middle-aged black men ask me what I could do about those "niggers" living down the street.

There were also the dilapidated two story houses owned by absentee landlords and split up into multiple apartments. The section was home to two public housing projects that stood testament to the urban renewal policies of the late 60's and early 70's. The area was full of good people but had a rough edge and if there were a shooting, stabbing, or robbery, the odds were good it occurred on D-24's beat.

"So how much do you know about Jackson?" Roger asked.

"Hardly anything. This is my third day ever in the city" I replied. Roger laughed and said, "Don't let it worry you. I'll keep things simple and we will just go for direction to start with. Right now we're headed south and the street is Francis, so obviously a right turn is going to have us westbound and a left would take us east. You'll learn the area pretty quick as we're assigned here every night partner." The word 'partner' really affected me both because of the connotation and the sincerity with which Roger said it. "This is a tough area, but no matter what I want you to treat people with respect. There's only a small portion of them that are assholes. The rest are good people just trying to get along. Our job is to make sure the assholes don't make life tough for them." Again I could see the sincerity in Roger's face and hear it in his voice, and since that is what I truly believed about policing, I felt assured I was going to be all right.

I jumped at the sound of the dispatcher's voice calling "Central to D-24" and looked at the radio wondering what to do. Roger calmly picked up the mike and answered with "D-24," our location, and "go ahead." Dispatch gave us a family dispute call in the 100 block of W. Prospect involving the Garrett family. Roger acknowledged the call and told me this was a frequent customer. He reminded me to always give your location when answering a call so dispatch and other units would know how far you were from the call's location, which helped coordinate response in emergency situations. He then talked about being alert as we pulled up to a call, adding that you should always park a house or two from the location to give yourself room to react if something were to happen.

Roger pulled the car to a stop, and I got out only after Roger opened his door. No sense in being the first one out if you have no freaking idea of what to do. Roger walked up to the door and was immediately met by Jon and Dale Garrett, teenage brothers who came out on the porch followed closely by their mother, Sally. Roger greeted Mom with a friendly, "What's going on Sally?" Sally responded, "I'm tired of these two fighting in my house all the goddamned time and not paying any attention to what I say."

Right away Jon felt the need to clarify things, so he chimed in with, "you lying bitch, that's not what happened." Roger told him to pipe down until he asked him something. The whole time I, the country boy, was thinking I would have needed an ambulance and a priest if my Dad ever heard me say such a thing to my mother. Apparently Jon needed just such a male influence in his life because he told Roger to get screwed; he wasn't hanging around to listen to this bullshit. He then headed off across the small front yard and into Prospect Street using the "you can kiss my ass" step as he went.

I was truly amazed at just how fast Roger's demeanor changed and how quickly he caught up with Jon in the middle of Prospect Street. What followed was an ass chewing that would have brought tears to the eyes of the most hardened Marine Corps drill instructor. It started with, "You ever pull that shit on me again you little son of a bitch and I'll bounce your ass all the way to the jail" and ended with, "Now go stand next to the porch and be quiet until I tell you to move or open your mouth." In between were several direct comments about the need for improvement on Jon's part and "helpful suggestions" from Roger that carried with them a real threat of a first class Mexican ass kicking. Jon obviously felt the love because he went and stood like a whipped dog until Roger was ready to deal with him.

I stood along side thinking, *this is going to be a good job* because in my eyes what Roger was doling out was just what Jon needed. Well, actually I thought Jon could do with the ass kicking more, but rookie though I was I knew that wasn't going to fly.

Roger spent the next few minutes getting everyone's story and trying to create a little peace in the house with advice he knew would be ignored and arrest threats he knew would both eventually become reality and still cause little change. I was to learn that much of my work as a Jackson police officer would not be on true criminal behavior but rather dealing with much the same situations as this very first call.

Roger also ran checks on the people through LEIN and locally. LEIN stands for Law Enforcement Information Network, which is the Michigan computer system into which all law enforcement agencies entered their warrants, stolen property and vehicles, and other similar information. It also served as a means for agencies to exchange teletype messages. LEIN is also connected to the Michigan's Secretary of State Computer which contains all the identifying information on people's driver's licenses and all identifying information on any vehicle registered in Michigan including the registered owner. LEIN was also connected to the National Crime Information Center (NCIC) computer which gives an officer access to similar information found in LEIN from the other 49 states. Many a pain-in-the-ass complaint was settled by finding one half of a problem had a warrant in LEIN allowing responding officers to drag him or her off to jail and create a period of peace that would last until bond could be arranged for the person arrested.

A "local check" at JPD meant the cadet at the front desk would look in the actual department warrant file to see if there was anything there that might not be in LEIN. Sometimes very minor misdemeanor warrants like not filing a city income tax return would be in the file but not in LEIN. While it wasn't much of a charge, it did give an officer the authority to arrest the person, and even though the person arrested likely would be out on bond within an hour, it often was enough to settle them down for the rest of the day.

As we drove away and I was taking it all in, Roger realized the little respect chat and the last call were a bit at odds. He turned to say something to me and saw I had a big grin on my face. Roger started to chuckle and said, "All right, but the little fucker pissed me off." We both laughed and Roger added, "Just remember that is the exception, not the rule."

The rest of the shift went by routinely until 9:30 pm when the radio exploded with dispatch telling us, "Officers need help at 985 Chittock Street." Roger grabbed the radio and said "24 enroute" and in the same motion activated the lights and sirens causing an adrenalin dump unlike anything I had ever experienced. Roger and I had only been a few blocks away when the call came in and were in front of the house in less than two minutes. I saw a Sheriff's Department patrol car in front and was jumping out of the car when Roger, who was already on the sidewalk yelled, "Stick partner." I immediately thought, *oh shit, does he want me to stick with the car or grab my night stick?* I went for the action choice and grabbed my stick and raced after Roger. Once in the house, Roger went up the stairway three steps ahead of me, but the fun was over by the time Roger reached the top of the stairs.

It seems the local probate judge had issued a mental health pick-up order for one Jefferson Lincoln Jones, and executing those orders by law fell to the Sheriff. Two deputies had gone to give Jefferson his ride to the State Hospital in Ypsilanti, but he wasn't real interested in going and so the fight was on. Jefferson landed one good kick to the eye of a deputy before going down for the count and being hand cuffed just prior to the arrival of David 24. As Jefferson was carried past me and out to the county patrol car, he was screaming gibberish, frothing at the mouth, and from what I could see wasn't much worse for the encounter. The deputy however ended up with a black eye that would be talked about 30 years later. Back in the car, Roger would congratulate me for my rapid response to the "stick" command and let me know that next time he would use "stay" if he wanted me to wait at the car.

As I stood in front of my locker at the end of the shift, I was buzzing with a mixture of elation at being a real cop and gratitude that I didn't screw up too bad. Roger was in taking a shower and so I was alone with my thoughts. Roger came out of the shower just as I was leaving and said, "See you tomorrow, Partner," which further reinforced my view that the luck of the Irish had come through in getting me such a fine fellow officer with whom to start my career. I thanked the Good Lord for looking out for me and headed up the stairs to the parking lot. I never really gave a second thought to saying a quick prayer or about my regular attendance at Mass. Just like the St. Michael's and St. Kevin's medals I wore around my neck, and still do 30 years later, it was just part of who I was. If asked I would express my faith, but I was not a "witness" in the manner a fundamentalist would be. No, I respected them, but I figured I had enough to worry about staying straight with the Lord without getting into other people's business. If someone came to me with a question, that was a different story--but I was no "fisher of men."

CHAPTER 8

I reached the parking lot and jumped into my '71 Buick GS, a graduation present from Dad, to head home. The car was presented to me a month before I finished up my Bachelor's degree at Ferris State College. I was thinking the old man really got soft with the fifth of his five kids until the keys were followed up with a payment book covering the $900 Dad had invested in the car. Dad did not, however, request any particular amount per month and simply said pay as much as you can afford when you can. Not a bad deal from father to son.

The car had been owned by a lady from our neighborhood so it was clean, well cared for, and low mileage. It also had a pretty hot V-8 under the hood and ran great so all in all I was pretty happy with my ride. Plus it was my first car because Larry Courtney did not allow his children to own cars while they were in school. He had helped all but the oldest pay for college and had a simple theory: If you need my money for school, you don't have enough money for a car. He did keep a second car around most times for us kids to use to get to and from summer jobs, so Genghis Khan he wasn't.

I pulled out of the station and headed out onto Glick Highway to get back to Gary Millar's house. Since Gary had also been hired by Jackson PD at the same time I was, he offered to let me stay at his parents' house until we could move into an apartment we had rented in Pheasant Run on Springport Road. The complex was one of those standard apartment complexes you find scattered across America. They all had a pool, tennis court, and lots of young people trying to get started in their careers while trying to hook up with the hottie in the next building.

Gary's family lived about five miles north of town in a subdivision off Lansing Avenue so I wasn't worried about getting home. It was Lansing Avenue north to Cunningham Road, turn left, go down about a half mile, and there was the street Gary lived on. The only problem was I assumed Lansing Avenue came all the away down to Glick Highway because that was how I came into town. Wrong! Lansing Avenue was a two-way street until it got to North Street about ½ mile from Glick. At that point, it split into two separate streets. Steward Street was the southbound one-way that I came in on, and Blackstone was the northbound one way that I needed to turn onto from Glick, in order to get back on Lansing Ave near Foote West Hospital.

Unfortunately for me, I didn't catch that and so I made several laps of the downtown loop, which consisted of Glick Highway and Washington Avenue, fruitlessly looking for Lansing Avenue. I was in a sweat and panic when I finally pulled back into the station and walked up to the night shift lieutenant. I introduced myself and explained the situation and sought some help. The lieutenant seemed to take more than just a little pleasure in yukking it up over my situation before telling me of the street situation. I was happy to be on my way so I put up with the extra mirth.

Gary's dad was waiting up for me when I got home, and while slightly embarrassed about it, I liked it. It made me feel more at home, and I genuinely like Gary's dad Evlar. "Ev" was a retired State Police detective and polygraph examiner. We chatted for a bit before I headed off for bed.

The next day I went to Meijer's for a hair cut. Meijer's was Michigan's answer to Wal-Mart, and at that time all the stores had barbershops, beauty parlors, shoe repair, and a variety of other odds and ends types of shops. The store itself sold everything from hardware, to clothes, to groceries. My friends and I used to say, "If Meijer's doesn't have it, you don't need it." After years of having hair down over my collar by several inches, I thought getting it cut to the middle of my ear was pretty short. Nevertheless, the second shift sergeant had politely informed me my hair cut was not short enough for JPD and I should get that taken care of ASAP, so that is exactly what I did. As a result I walked out of the barber shop with my hair cut above my ears, off my collar and as short as it had been since I was in the seventh grade. I didn't really give a rip, though, as my hair length was never a statement of rebellion or even a fashion statement. It was a matter of economics. The less money I spent on haircuts, the more money I had for beer and chasing women--very serious matters for a single male college student.

Kevin M. Courtney

.

CHAPTER 9

My new look and I were in the station and ready to go a little after 3:00 pm; almost forty minutes ahead of detail time, but I used the extra time to meet more of my fellow employees and get a better feel for the station. It was a relatively nice building, except for the basement, and I was pretty pleased with my surroundings. I was, however, feeling that typical rookie cop sensation of *can I learn everything I need to know before these guys toss my ass out of here?* How little I knew would become crystal clear just 20 minutes after Roger and I went on duty that day.

Roger was just giving me some information on where block numbers changed and what streets served as the dividing lines between north and south and east and west streets in the city when dispatch broke up the lesson with the usual, "Dispatch to D-24." Roger had me answer and we were advised there was fight in the 600 block of Mechanic Street. I acknowledged the call with the standard "D-24 clear" and got a double adrenalin dump when Roger stomped on the gas and headed for the call. Clearly, Roger did not follow the "take your time and arrest a tired winner and battered loser" theory of fight call response. Roger was of the "Let's go kick some ass" school of thought. I definitely was cool with that.

As we pulled up to the address along with our back up, I could see several people up on a raised porch yelling and screaming and pushing and shoving--about what you'd see in front of the net in a good hockey game, but not really a fight. Roger, the back up officer, and I headed up onto the porch, and the senior officers started to break things up. The combatants were all transplanted Kentuckians who had come north to work in the local factories but had decided working for a living wasn't all it was cracked up to be. They instead chose to spend most days drinking and lying around.

They had spent today drinking and arguing so they weren't real interested in police community cooperation when Roger and the rest of us showed up. I found myself facing the dirtiest human being I had ever seen. The man's face was so dirt-covered that his eyes looked like a raccoon's. He looked like the kind of guy who would make a barn full of sheep real nervous. I was holding him off from the fun when I suddenly realized people behind me were getting tossed to the walls and handcuffed.

A second back up unit had arrived and so three of JPD's finest were handling the fur ball that calls like this can become, while I was basically keeping my dirty little man back from the whole mess, which he did not appreciate in the least, so he kept trying to get around me. I was very unsure what I could do beyond screening him off, so that's all I did. He must have figured out I was new and not sure what to do, because he kept pushing his luck. About the time I was getting pissed and feeling a need to smack the dust off the little jerk's ass regardless of legal restrictions, Roger stepped around me and said to the dirt ball "I heard this officer to tell you to back up so BACK THE FUCK UP before you end up in jail." Apparently these words didn't register any better than my screening attempt, so the dirt ball got his own set of cuffs and a ride to JPD.

I turned around to see that three other member of the original dance ensemble were in cuffs and being led to patrol cars. Roger told me to come on and so I jumped in the car. The dirt ball in the back seat was separated from the front by a roll bar and Plexiglas window, so while he could be heard and smelled he couldn't touch or spit on the officers in the front seat. I immediately started babbling about wanting to lock the dirt ball up but that I didn't know if I could and I was sorry Roger had to step in. Roger just laughed and said, "I'll book our prisoner while you go over the disorderly conduct ordinance."

I headed straight for the report room and found the recipe box where the disorderly conduct ordinance was laid out on 3 x 5 cards. There was just one general disorderly ordinance but numerous sub sections that prohibited everything from being "loud and boisterous" to doing anything to "resist, hinder, or oppose an officer" a real favorite, to "prowling" to "spitting on the sidewalk." The key is they all fell under the general heading of "contempt of cop." They were typically used on people too stupid, drunk, or brave to do whatever an officer had told them to do. Of course that worked out fine for the officer because most times a disorderly arrest solved whatever problem the officer had responded to in the first place. In the time it took Roger to book the prisoner, I had a good understanding of the disorderly ordinance and would be ready the next time some little dirt-covered gnome wanted to screw with me. Little did I know that before the week was out, I would hit the "arrest lottery"--and it wouldn't be a local ordinance charge.

Later that night, as we were patrolling through our section, Roger asked me if I had a girlfriend and I said no I really didn't get serious about anyone in college. Roger then remarked, "So you don't really know anyone in Jackson besides the guys you are meeting at the Department then do you?" I said, "That's about the size of it." Roger was quiet for a second and then said, "You know I've got a sister about your age I should introduce you to." I said that would be great and Roger smiled and said he'd see what he could do.

Kevin M. Courtney

.

CHAPTER 10

Friday May 25th was a gorgeous, warm, sunny day in Jackson. Roger told me when we got into the patrol car things would be hopping tonight. "You get warm weather and a Friday night and it'll get wild because people will start drinking early." I smiled, thinking to myself that was exactly the way it was back at college. Dispatch proved Roger right when just a few minutes into the shift they sent us to a domestic call on Warwick Court, a housing project just off Francis Street and notorious for all the things found in the typical federal housing project of the 1970s. Poverty, crime, violence, substance abuse, and people trying to get by in the middle of all of it.

Roger and I made contact with the cause of the call one, Calpurina Smith and her boyfriend, Earl James Gray. Earl J, as the male half was known, and Calpurina had been drinking all day and were exuding enough alcohol fumes to light a gas grill. If they quit drinking immediately, I figured they'd be sober about in time for services on Sunday. The complaint boiled down to "that worthless motherfucker hit me" and "you ain't nothing but a lying bitch." Unlike the enlightened 90's when domestic violence arrests would be made with probable cause, the `70's required an officer to witness a misdemeanor assault, which most calls like this involved. Since the odds of an officer getting lucky enough to walk up and see Daddy whuppin' Momma's ass were about as good as my dating a fashion model, officers were left with little choice but to give the parties the "if I come back, someone's going to jail" speech. Roger gave the two the standard pep talk and we cleared the call. For about 20 minutes.

Interesting to me was the fact there were three or four other people hanging around in the apartment when all this "confusion" was going on, but, they seemed oblivious to it. All they would tell Roger when he asked them if they saw anything was, "I stay out of other people's business so I don't know what was going on." Neat trick considering the room was all of 10 by 12 feet.

When dispatch sent us back to the apartment twenty minutes later, Roger was starting to show a little more temper and really reamed the two drunks out. His last words were basically, "I don't give a shit what the law is, if I come back here, you are both going to jail." I figured they heard the second speech as well as the first, and since it was still only about 5:00 pm there was more time for drinking and fighting before these two passed out. Dispatch proved me right when 30 minutes later they sent us back a third time, along with telling us Fire Rescue had been dispatched. Roger told me, "I've had enough of these assholes. We're taking somebody to jail." He was never so right in his life.

Roger had a certain "your ass kicking is here" walk when he was pissed off and he was using it as he strode towards the door of the Warwick Court apartment. I had to really hustle to keep up even though at 6'2" I was a good four inches taller than Roger. We were a short distance from the door when I saw Ken Hunt, a big firefighter standing by the door. As we got closer, Ken said to Roger, "She's gone." Roger replied with his head swiveling, "Where'd the bitch go?" Ken shook his head and said, nodding at the door, "No. She's in there but she's gone." Roger got the message and said "Oh shit." We entered to see Calpurnia sprawled in the chair with a huge pool of blood at her feet. Earl J. was sitting a few feet away, and Roger immediately told him to get up and he cuffed him. A pat down revealed a folding knife covered with blood. Backup officers arrived in a few minutes and Earl J. got shuffled out the door.

I was taking this all in and thinking to myself, *you ain't in Kansas no more Toto.* I had been a police officer on the street for all of four days and I was already at my first murder. I had heard stories about officers who worked a whole career and never were sent to a homicide. This on top of all the other crazy shit that had gone on in my first three days as a cop made me both a little nervous and at the same time I was stoked that I was doing real police work.

I found it strange to be in the room with someone who had met such a violent and immediate death. We had dealt with her just a short while ago and she was very much alive, but now she was dead. It somehow seemed wrong to just leave her there "as is" while the business of the investigation was done. Maybe it was because the sum total of my experience with the dead had always been in the environment of a funeral home where the person looked "good," like he or she was "just sleeping." Calpurnia neither looked good nor like she was just sleeping. She looked like she had been murdered. She was the first person I had seen in that situation, but she surely would not be the last.

The next several hours found me acting as an errand boy while Roger handled the mountains of paperwork that went with a major crime such as a homicide. I was not really afraid of paperwork as I loved English and writing classes, but learning all the correct forms and how to fill them out was a bit intimidating. I did listen to and soak up all I was hearing from Roger, the detectives, and other assorted players found at a homicide scene. Murder was still relatively rare in Jackson, with only an average of two or three a year, so it was treated as a major event and not with the "so what" you might find in a big city like Detroit or Flint, where they kill that many people in one crime, let alone in one year.

By 11:00 pm the detectives got done with the three witnesses who had been less than cooperative at the scene. I judged that by the fact that one of the three, Oscar "Popsicle" Samuels told Roger, "I didn't see a mother fucking thing" even though he was sitting in the apartment at the time of the homicide. Oscar got his nickname because he used to be the local equivalent of a Good Humor man and people got his attention by yelling "Yo, popsicle." Oscar didn't see work as a life long commitment, so he went back to hanging out, drinking, and who knows what which put him in Calpurinia's apartment at the time she "got dead."

Lieutenant Christner apparently decided to grease the skids of cooperation a little bit and told the witnesses that if they cooperated, told the detectives the truth, and quieted down a little while waiting in the station lobby, the rest of the night's drinking was on him and he'd give them a ride home to boot. Well the three held up their end of the bargain and so Christner grabbed me and told me to take a patrol car and give these folks a ride home. Great idea considering that just three days ago I had to ask him for directions to get *my sorry ass* home! He then handed Popsicle a twenty. Popsicle pointed out that "Jacks," the liquor store on Francis across from Warwick Court was closed so the lieutenant told me to take the three up to Amanati's Liquor Store on Cooper. Unfortunately it was also closed. Popsicle then said there was a store up near I-94 that was sure to be open.

Popsicle was being a regular Mr. Rogers in the Neighborhood to me since he needed me to be able to spend the 20. As a result, I got great directions to Cooper Street and I-94 on the north side of Jackson where we found the liquor store there open. I wondered what the locals thought about a patrol car pulling up to let a black man out to buy $20 bucks worth of Colt 45 and cheap wine, but I figured it ain't my worry since the lieutenant said to do it. Popsicle didn't turn over a completely new leaf, though, as he told me to drop him and the other two witnesses off on the north side of Warwick Court so the brothers didn't see him getting out of the patrol car like the snitch that he was. Of course, once Popsicle broke out the liquid goodies forgiveness would flow equal to the rate of the Colt 45 that warm summer night.

I made it back to the station in large part because I knew it was on the other side of the large Gilbert Commonwealth Engineering complex which I was now parked next to. On one hand I was a little embarrassed to have to navigate that way, but on the other I figured there were no points for style, just results. In this case, I helped with a murder case by taking a few of the locals to the liquor store, dropping them back off, and getting my green ass back to the station all without getting lost. I also earned my first hour of overtime, which based on my starting rate of pay was just about $10.50--serious jack for a guy who graduated college dead broke and often made it on just $5 spending money for a week.

I headed home that night both with the buzz of having been involved in a homicide case and also with the troubling image of a murder victim who one minute was drinking and raising hell with her old man like most every summer night and then next was dead as a result of an explosion of alcohol-fueled violence. It was a phenomenon that was anything but unusual in the urban areas in which most policing was done. I was not naïve, but for a man of faith who grew up in a small town I could not help but be troubled by it all. Even later, when I had seen more than my fair share, I would still feel it. Those nuns and priests did a good job of making me unable to ignore "sin" when I encountered it.

CHAPTER 11

"You ain't gonna believe this shit" starts many a police conversation in the United States and I guess probably all over the world. So I wasn't particularly surprised when Roger greeted me in that fashion when I reported for work on Saturday. That all changed when Roger said the pathologist had ruled Calpurnia's cause of death was cirrhosis of the liver. I figured my partner was yanking my chain so I didn't bite and said, "Yeah right." Roger looked at me and said, "I ain't shittin' you, the guy ruled cirrhosis of the liver so the murder charge is gone." I couldn't believe it and said, "So does the asshole walk?" Roger explained they had until Monday to formally charge the guy so he didn't know what would shake out.

A second pathologist from Lansing reviewed the body in the next few days and said Calpurnia might have been a boozer but cheap wine didn't fracture her skull behind the ear nor cut her femoral artery. He said the death was a homicide. The prosecutor decided he didn't want dueling Doctors on the stand, both of whom would be his witnesses, so he went with Assault with the Intent to do Great Bodily Harm, and Earl J. got 10 years a mile north of the City limits at the State Prison of Southern Michigan. Besides, neither Earl J. or Calpurnia were exactly pillars of the community, so nobody much gave a rat's ass how their business was dealt with by the Jackson justice machinery. All except me, who in that simple and very Irish view of right and wrong, saw a murderer getting a freebie.

The Saturday patrol shift passed pretty quietly and I was looking forward to making a quick run back to my hometown of Birch Run on my two days off which were coming up. I figured to catch the early

Mass at St. John's on Ganson Street between Cooper and Milwaukee and then head for home. I had a few things to pick up from home and I was looking forward to telling a few stories to the family and my buddies still living in the area. The nice thing about having Roger for a partner was days off were assigned by seniority and Roger had enough time on the second shift to get Sundays and Mondays off. As his trainee I, of course, got the same days.

The Jackson Police Department of the late '70's was very traditional in its approach to seniority, especially where shift assignment and days off were concerned. If you didn't have any, you weren't shit and ended up on afternoons. As a result of this, Roger with only four years' experience, could pull half the weekend as his days off by working the afternoon shift.

An officer with more than ten years on the force could easily take a spot on afternoons and get the weekends off, except none of them wanted anything to do with afternoons because you actually had to take calls the whole shift, you were surrounded by wild-eyed-crazy-assed rookies who wanted to lock up the whole goddamned city, and you were away from home when your kids got out of school. No, as long as seniority ruled, afternoons would be full of guys just like Roger and wild-eyed rookies like me.

I enjoyed the drive back to Birch Run as there was little traffic and I liked driving my car. The old Buick was my first car and I was proud of it. Plus, like all new cops, I liked the idea of going back to hang out with my buddies while packing a gun. This was in the days long before every idiot not drooling, barking at the moon, or pissing on himself was qualified to carry a concealed weapon in Michigan, so packing heat was some serious cool points. Granted, I was only carrying a .38 Chief's special, but when you had no money a $100 gun was fine. After all, it was still a gun and the feel of it in my waistband was exhilarating to a newly minted cop. After a few years it became a pain in the ass, but by that time you were paranoid enough that you didn't want to be without it.

The couple days back home did me good. I got to sleep in my old room and bed, eat some of Mom's good cooking, and shoot the bull with my buddy Dick Belill. Dick and I started kindergarten together, went to the Catholic school together, and graduated high school the same year. Dick had even made a couple of visits to Siena Heights

College where I spent my first two years. Another Birch Run guy, Bruce Ross, was also going to Siena so Dick's visits called for some serious boozing. Dick had started out to be a cop but decided it just wasn't for him so he took a job in a GM factory in Saginaw.

I got back to work feeling even more like a real cop and eager to learn more. I was especially cognizant that I knew very little of the streets in town and that was a serious limitation. Fortunately, Roger was very patient and that made learning easier for me but also made me want to do better. I had picked up a cross reference street guide at the local bookstore in Jackson and studying that was helping, but since it told you where a street was by referencing it to other streets, it wasn't exactly a Godsend for someone in my situation.

When I returned from Birch Run, Roger let me know that this was the last week we would be working together, as he was taking two weeks vacation starting at the end of this week but said I would be staying on second shift so I'd be fine. Roger also let me know there was a big party planned for Friday night at the local Fraternal Order of Police lodge. Roger was this year's "Officer of the Year" for JPD and tradition demanded a big blowout in his honor. I said cool, but all the time, I was thinking *how big a party can a bunch of middle-aged cops throw?* I was fresh out of college where parties routinely drew upwards of three or four hundred people, beer got guzzled like water, and even an average mutt like me could make some serious time with the women. I doubted a cop party could measure up to that.

Kevin M. Courtney

.

CHAPTER 12

The day on patrol went by pretty uneventfully as compared to the prior week. We did have one call on West Wilkins that bothered me. Alana Jefferson, a black woman in her late 20's with a couple of small children, was getting harassed by a local white dipshit named Harold Mores. Seemed Harold's 19-year-old brain thought standing in the woman's yard yelling, "Hey Nigger" and other pleasantries, was a good idea. Roger told the woman we would do the best we could, but unless we could catch the little bastard in the act it would be tough to prosecute him. We went looking for Harold but surprisingly enough his family hadn't seen him but assured Roger they would tell Harold to call when he got home. I thought, *right just as soon as he finishes filling out his application for Harvard.*

I sure wasn't a perfect person but that racial crap really pissed me off. I really did believe that everyone was equal. Growing up with stories about how the English spent 800 years screwing the Irish had two effects on me. First, I believed all problems in Ireland including the "Troubles" were the fault of the English, and second, that no one should have to take shit because of where they came from or the color of their skin.

Oddly enough the word "nigger" at that time was not the issue. It was how it was used. As a college student, many of my friends were black. In fact, I was the only white boy on a City league basketball team during my sophomore year. Those friends used nigger in their regular conversation all the time and referred to each other in that fashion without blinking. Richard Pryor had several hit comedy albums, all of which had "nigger" in the title. On more than one occasion I was even called "nigger" by a black friend.

I worked the front desk in the dorm my sophomore year, and a conversation there with a black buddy might go something like this. "Hey Kevin you seen that nigger James?" Or if a black friend and I were talking sports or politics and I said something my friend found too much to take, I would get a roll of the eyes and a "Oh, nigger, please" or "Nigger, you must be crazy." Now I was never comfortable enough to use the word on my friends but I clearly learned there was context to the word. Unfortunately, the little hemorrhoid Harold only knew one context, and for that I figured Harold needed a good ass kicking to, in the words of the warden in *"Cool Hand Luke,"* to "get his mind right"

At the end of the shift, Roger, a few of the other fellas from the shift, and I headed over to Evanoff's Bar, lovingly known as "Precinct 2" to all the local police. It was a cop bar owned by a first generation Macedonian who had taken it over from his parents. Most of the local pizza joints and Coney Island hot dog places in Jackson were owned by Macedonians. Evanoff's was nothing fancy, just a typical neighborhood bar with a pool table, juke box, and seating for maybe 60 people if you crowded them in. However, it had the key ingredients for a good cop bar. The owners liked cops, the locals knew it was a cop bar so acted accordingly, and it was convenient. A guy with a good arm could damn near hit it with a rock from the back of the police station.

Sitting in the bar and knocking back a couple of beers let me start to get a feel for my coworkers and become more a part of things. I found out that Howard Noppe, another new officer, was a former Marine, still had the jarhead attitude, and was a solid guy. I found myself liking Howard right away. Howard's favorite retort, if you busted on him about something like his shoes not being polished, was to grab his crotch and say, "polish this." You had to love a guy with communication skills like those.

John Stressman was a good sized man who was married to a nurse and had two years with the Department. He was quiet but had a dry sense of humor and an easy going manner that made him very likeable.

A relaxed atmosphere where you could get to know people and sort things out a bit is what has made the "pub" such a popular place world wide. I couldn't think of anything much more natural than an Irishman draining a few pints with his pals in the pub. I decided I was genetically predetermined to be here, and who was I to fight nature.

CHAPTER 13

The next day I happened to glance toward of the neighbor's house only to see a *very* attractive young woman sunning herself in the backyard. Once I managed to put my tongue back in my mouth and wipe the drool off my chest, I went and found Gary and demanded information. Gary wasn't all that excited and simply said, "Oh, that's Nancy. She's all right."

"Are you out of your mind?" I asked. "That's girl is hot!" I quickly followed that up with "how old is she?"

Gary chuckled and said "Eighteen but that ain't your problem stud. Her old man is the local State Police District Commander and one scary sumbitch."

I decided right then to put the hormones on a short leash, as I figured the last thing I needed as a probationary officer was to be messing with a command officer's daughter. Even though he wasn't one of *my* command officers, the guy likely knew my Chief's phone number and wouldn't hesitate to use it if some young JPD officer was sniffing around his daughter--especially one 4 years older than her. She was certainly a beautiful girl but I figured I needed a job more than a date. I managed to live next to the garden and just look at the forbidden fruit. What the hell, as long as I didn't pull out the binoculars there was no harm in some serious gawking. After all, she was sunbathing in plain view so I had the Constitution on my side.

Patrol that day was decidedly slow, except that the neighborhood pain in the ass was still making things rough for Ms. Jones on West Wilkins. Roger was really getting mad and typical of when that happened, his voice slowed down and his jaw got tight. "I've had it with that little fucker. Some how, some way his ass is going to jail." I was all for that and said it was too bad there wasn't a man in the Jones' house to whup Harold's little white ass. Roger pointed out if there were a man in the house, the little coward wouldn't come within six blocks of the place.

Another learning experience happened for me while we were handling a domestic on Morrell Street near Mechanic with Officer Dave Bachman as back up. All three of us were standing on the porch facing the front door while Roger was talking with one of the people involved in the complaint. Bachman slid up next to me and whispered, "Don't make a big deal but the babe I've got on the side just walked up behind us. Check her out when you get chance but don't be obvious."

I, being a man, was always ready to check out a hot female. I waited what I thought was a sufficient amount of time and slowly turned around as nonchalantly as possible. My reward for this smooth move was that I came face to face with a 200-pound toothless black woman dressed in men's clothing who smiled widely at me and said, "Hey baby cakes! How are you?" The shock on my face was a true Kodak moment. Fortunately for me no cameras were present.

Bachman could hardly stand up he was laughing so hard and the stupid look on my face only made things better. Once Bachman got control of himself, he said, "Martha, you better not be flirting with another man in front of me." Martha just laughed and said, "I like them young white boys." My face got beet red and Dave said, "Don't let me catch you cutting in on my time." He then broke up in more laughter. I had to admit Bachman had earned the mirth, and by the time we got to the car I was laughing along with him while muttering what a sick bastard he was.

CHAPTER 14

The next day, right after the start of the shift and taking a larceny complaint down on E. Mansion, Roger said, "Let's drive by Alana's house and maybe get lucky." I liked that idea and realized one could be proactive as a cop and not just run from call to call. I was beginning to understand why JPD used desk cards. They expected officers to go out and work, not wait. I was cool with that.

Roger told me as we were driving over to West Wilkins that we didn't want to come down Wilkins because if Harold was there he would have a chance to boogie before we could catch the little jerk. Roger wanted to know what street I would suggest we use. I was still pretty shaky on streets but I did know that Alana's house was in the 300 block, that was the last block in our district, which was bounded on the west side by First Street, so I said "First." Roger said that would work but we'll take Blackstone just in case he's walking around his house, which is on Blackstone. I saw the logic in that and immediately placed Blackstone on the map I was building in my memory.

Roger geeked me up as we started north on Blackstone from Morrell by telling me to look sharp because no matter where we saw Harold, he was getting jacked up for all the bullshit he was involved in these last few days. I was scanning left and right when we made the left turn onto Wilkins, and right there in the front yard of Alana's house was the little shit Harold yelling, "Hey you fat nigger bitch" at the top of his lungs. Roger shouted "Get him" as he slammed the car to the curb. With adrenaline flowing like water over Niagara, I was halfway out of the car before it came to a full stop. I was moving with a focus and purpose that was every bit as good as any police dog in

America. All I was missing was a collar and the ability to sniff my ass. Harold managed to turn in time to see a wild-eyed cop bailing out of the passenger side door with no kind of good intentions directed at his sorry little ass.

Harold, like every other little weasel in history, decided flight was a lot better than fight, so he hit the jets and started north down the alley that ran next to Alana's house. Bad choice when the cop coming after you is young, fast, and leaking adrenaline from every pore in his body. All running away does is cause even more adrenaline to rush into the pursuer's system. I exploded into a full out sprint eating up the distance between Harold and me like he was tied to a tree. I skipped the part about "Stop! Police!" or anything else and just felt the surge and confidence that running had always given me. This was the last kick of a 2 mile race and Harold was the finish line. I closed on him in about 50 yards and simply ran right into him. Harold did the right thing and face planted into the gravel alley, allowing me to drop right on top of him. I had the first cuff on as Roger came up behind us. Roger let me finish the cuffing and was smiling ear to ear as he patted my shoulder and said "Nice job, Partner." It was music to my ears. Sort of a human Milk bone. I especially liked the "partner" remark because I could tell Roger was sincere.

Roger also put his face up to Harold's and growled "Don't you ever run from us again you little asshole or I'll beat your ass. You're lucky my partner's a nice guy."

I was walking Harold back to the patrol car and had to pass right by the porch where Alana stood watching the proceedings. She was obviously very happy with the outcome and said, "Damn Kevin, you're fast!" The quick Irish wit kicked in and without even thinking I replied "Yeah and white too!" Roger about stroked out at the comment but all Alana did was burst out laughing and say, "Boy, you gonna get in trouble talking that trash" then she laughed even louder. From that day on, Alana would hear no bad mouthing of JPD in front of her because that "Kevin, and his partner Roger" took care of business just like she asked them to. She never failed to add the part about me being "one fast white boy." Many years later when I was Director of Public Safety in Big Rapids, I got a call asking me if I was still "the fastest white boy in Jackson." It was Alana, who was living in Grand Rapids and had seen me on TV. We had a nice chat and it really meant a lot that she remembered me after all those years. It also proved I was not mistaken in my belief that, as a police officer, I could make a difference in people's lives.

Roger allowed me to fill out the booking sheets on Harold, who was whining to the desk sergeant about police brutality because his palms and chin were a little scuffed up from the gravel. The sergeant dutifully asked him the circumstances and, after getting the story, told Harold next time he shouldn't try to run from an All American track star. I almost choked, but Harold was truly impressed and seemed to feel much better that he got rolled up by a star and not just your average white boy. In fact, I bet the little weasel bragged to his friends later that he outran an All American for 50 yards before he tripped. Screw the police brutality crap: Harold saw a chance to build his rep with the other little hoodlums in his neighborhood.

Kevin M. Courtney

CHAPTER 15

Surprisingly for a guy who loved English composition in school, the police reports were a challenge for me. Not the actual narrative of what happened but filling out all the individual boxes and making sure I didn't miss any. My problem was I wasn't methodical enough about it and jumped around the page. Roger got on my ass about it and pointed out that is why when encountering anyone, be they witness, suspect, or complainant, I should get their full name, address, phone number, and date of birth. That would make it much easier to find them later for court, interviews, or arrest since today's witness could be tomorrow's suspect.

Narratives of the reports came easy to me because JPD was advanced enough in 1979 to issue officers pocket tape recorders. This allowed officers to fill out the face sheet of the report with crime codes, times, dates, and the pertinent information on all the people involved while dictating the narrative of the report on to a mini-cassette which got stuffed in an envelope along with the face sheet for typing by the transcriptionist the next day. The only exceptions to this rule were short reports or an incident involving a felony arrest that needed to go to the prosecutor immediately in the morning. I certainly had the Irish gift of the gab, so talking was never an issue for me. Shutting up, yes. Talking, no. I did learn to make a short outline of important points to cover in the report before starting to tape it, which proved to be a big help.

As we were leaving for the night, I asked Roger if he was going to bring his sister to the party tomorrow night so I could meet her. Roger said, "No freaking way am I introducing you to my sister you pervert." I feigned offense and Roger laughed and said, "You're on your own partner. My mom would kill me if I let my sister date a guy like you." I decided that after all the usual banter that had gone on between us since Roger's offer, I couldn't really blame Roger for his change of heart. Too bad, too, because I later found out his sister was a real looker. Oh well, I'd just have to rely on my natural Irish charm, and the girl not having a brother on the Department, to find myself a date.

Roger took Friday night off since he was the guest of honor at the big FOP blowout, but I promised I would be there as soon as the shift was over. I was figuring I would make an appearance and then boogie to one of the local bars to check out the local female population. Anything but hang around a lame event with a bunch of middle aged guys on a Friday night. I spent the shift working with Dick Allen in B-22, which really messed me up considering I was just getting a handle on D-24, but Allen was a nice guy and treated me well. Dick liked to work traffic, which Roger wouldn't do at gunpoint, so it was a good chance to work on those skills. Plus, Dick was born and raised in Jackson and could give me a local's perspective.

Dick had been a hell of a football player in high school. He was big, fast, and as they say, he ran north and south. One of his old teammates remarked that Dick would rather run over a defender than around him. He got some serious interest from colleges but never played beyond high school.

The night in 22 went by quickly. Dick and I did get sent to a bar fight at the "Sugar Shack" across from the train station. Dick explained that is was a country western bar and, as such, fighting there on a Friday or Saturday night was about as uncommon as a U.S. Congressman trying to hump his office help. I could see several people standing around in the parking lot as we pulled into the lot. The way the bar sat surrounded by one way streets you had to go around the block to get into the lot if you came from the east. That is unless it was a really hot call, in which case you flipped on the lights and siren and said screw the signs. Two hillbillies wailing the shit out of each other at a CW bar did not, however, qualify as a "really hot call" in Jackson, Michigan, or anywhere else in the continental United States for that matter.

The crowd started to do the "Red Sea" and part for us and we could see the fight had progressed from the throwing punches stage to the tired wrestling one. I was thinking about jumping in and pulling the idiots apart when Dick simply stood over them and said, "You boys about done? Because if you ain't my partner and I are going to arrest you both for fighting in public and I don't give a rat's ass who started it." Now Jethro and Uncle Jed were both about to stroke out due to the fact they were equally overweight, drunk, and out of shape and the 40 seconds of real fighting and one minute of grappling was all they could handle. They were all for the quit option. Both were so tired they simply let the other guy go and didn't even talk shit after doing it. Dick told me to get Uncle Jed's story and he would talk to Jethro.

Based on the interviews, the brawl ensued when Uncle Jed bumped into Jethro and didn't offer to buy Jethro another beer to make up for the one Jethro dropped. That sort of complete lack of manners could not be tolerated, so Jethro gave Jed the option of taking an ass whipping in the bar or outside in the parking lot. Jed took option B and said it was a fair fight and that of course he was just about to finish whipping that stupid hillbilly when the cops pulled up. Dick sent the two on their way with the standard statement on how to seek a warrant if they so desired. We could have arrested both for fighting in public, but since they quit fighting when Dick told them to, did not force us to use physical force, and did not flap their mouths to either of us, they earned the right to avoid getting locked up. The general feeling among officers was if two nitwits want to beat the crap out of each other, God bless 'em as long as no cops or innocent citizens get hurt and no weapons are involved. Adding a weapon to the mix in most cases made it a felony which means someone's ass was headed to jail.

The law in Michigan at that time required officers to observe a misdemeanor being committed before they could make an arrest. Felony arrests could be made on probable cause. Standard procedure for JPD back then for misdemeanor cases, except those an officer observed and chose to make an arrest for, was to advise the parties that if they wished to press charges they needed to come to the police station, get a copy of the report on the incident, and take it to the prosecuting attorney who would review the case and decide whether or not to issue a warrant. Typically, most mutual combat situations never resulted in anyone seeking or getting a warrant, so if the cop didn't lock up the goofus delecti involved, nothing came of the fight.

Kevin M. Courtney

·

CHAPTER 16

I was in the locker room after going out of service, and every officer on my shift and every officer coming on duty for third shift had the same question: "You going out to the FOP Hall?" I made it clear I was and showed as much enthusiasm as I could, but bottom line I figured I would show my respect for Roger by showing up and then I'd blow a party that was surely going to be about as exciting as a funeral visitation. Figuring a bar with women was in the plan for the night, I had brought a pair of blue jeans and a t-shirt in with me. The usual JPD uniform pants and white t-shirt worn in Precinct 2 would not impress the women. I changed and headed out Airline Drive to South Street and the FOP.

South Street was Jackson's southern city limit and hence the name. The FOP hall sat on a small lot about quarter-mile east of Airline. Directly behind the Hall was the Department's outdoor pistol range. The hall itself was a fairly new building with its own private bar and small reception hall that could be rented. Most all cop parties were held there, along with assorted graduation parties, showers, and stag parties. The local Lodge was also staying open on some weeknights so members could have a couple of cold ones and help pay the bills.

I was impressed that the parking lot was full as I pulled in and even more impressed when I walked in the doors of the Lodge to a full-fledged blowout. As the song says, "I mean the joint was jumping." There was music blasting, booze flowing, food laid out and the place was full of cops, nurses, dispatchers, court personnel, prosecutors, defense lawyers and, most importantly, enough good looking women that I immediately tossed out the "leave to go to the bar" plan. Even if a majority of the ladies at the party were wives and girlfriends, I still liked my odds. In the corner was a handmade wooden coffin that threw me for a loop, but I was told that was for "the ride home."

The ride home was an Officer of the Year tradition started by the Department's underground group known as the "B.O.A.S." Several officers got together to poke a little fun at the Department's formality, policies, and general attitude and came up with the group name, Benevolent Order of Aides and Sickies, or BOAS, which was pronounced like the snake of the same name. The term "aide" came from the fact that if more than 2 officers were involved in an arrest, the primary officer's name went in the booking log along with the term "aides," which denoted there was more than one assisting officer. So you had stars and you had aides. Members of the BOAS consider it a badge of honor to be among the aides.

The ride home was started for the practical reason that the Officer of the Year in most cases was too drunk to find his ass let alone his car and to poke a little fun at the recipient. The ride was always tailored to something in the honoree's background that was either well known or well hidden, the later of which was even better. Roger got the coffin and hearse because, a) he was always a little creeped out by that stuff, and, b) he had studied for the priesthood for a short time.

I started to think I might have to reconsider my image of the members of JPD. Any group that could come up with a party like this and the whole "ride home" concept had some real potential. I was working on my second beer and meeting more and more of the Department members who, because of shift work and leave days, I had not seen before. All of them were exceedingly friendly and welcoming to me by nature, but, it also didn't hurt that the beer was being consumed at a rate that would make any frat boy proud.

I found myself talking to a couple of the local ER nurses when Roger came up and goosed me, telling the nurses "to back off ladies, he's mine." I jumped a good three feet, giving everyone a good laugh, and even though my face was bright red I had the presence of mind to call Roger "a cheap tramp." Roger was genuinely pleased to see that I had made it to the party, and after talking with the nurses and me for a few minutes, he wandered off to mingle with more of the guests. My new friends introduced me to a few other people, and I was having an all around good time tossing back a few more beers and socializing.

I held off on "getting numbers" as I didn't want to be too aggressive and I also wanted to find out who was available and who wasn't.

I was sweet talking a lovely young thing who worked in District Court when I heard quite a commotion. It had come time for Roger to head home. Roger was good and drunk and wasn't too excited about going in the coffin, so five or six of the boys had a hold of him and were trying to stuff him in it. It was a pretty good battle for about two minutes and then Roger gave in. He was then "prayed" over by the "Right Reverend James T. Henly," a Department Lieutenant who, while a good Catholic, was really a tele-evangelist at heart. Once the Right Reverend got through, Roger was carried out of the FOP to a rousing chorus of the "Great Amen" sung in true southern Baptist tradition. Once outside they stuffed Roger in the back of the hearse which a local Funeral Home was dumb enough to let a cop borrow, and somewhere between eight and twenty-three additional officers jammed in to make sure Roger didn't make the last ride alone. I could still hear the singing when the car was a good three blocks away from the Hall.

The party kept right on rolling and so I hung around for another half hour or so and then headed for home. I felt pretty good about the evening, the ladies I had met, and that I was starting to become a part of the Department. I was smart enough to have not gotten so loaded I couldn't drive. The attitude towards the whole drinking and driving thing in the late 70's was infinitely more relaxed than it is today but still I tried to keep things under control in those days when it came to partying and driving. Back in college it was never an issue since I never had a car and all the parties and bars were within walking distance of my dorm. There were a couple of times I was really too drunk to stagger, but back in those days as long as I stayed reasonably close to the sidewalk I figured I'd be OK.

I remember one night when my buddy Eric, better known as "Bubbles," and I had a real problem staying on the sidewalk after a stag party on Ives Street just north of the Ferris campus in Big Rapids. Getting home turned out to be the easy part. Bubbles was supposed to get up early the next morning and meet his fiancé for breakfast, but since he slept till noon that plan went the way of Elvis' diet. Bubbles could think of only one way to get back in his squeeze's good graces, and that was to blame the whole situation on me. The approach worked as Bubbles' fiancé had me pegged as a dog right from the start and knew eventually, worthless bastard that I was, I would try to corrupt her Bubbles. So Bubbles dutifully nodded when she explained to him what a low crawling piece of shit I was, and now that Bubbles knew that he had better stay clear of me. My take on the situation was that Bubbles had absolutely no backbone and was in for a long, tough road if he didn't man up pretty damn soon. Easy to say when you're single. After getting into a serious relationship, I gained a lot more sympathy for Bubbles.

CHAPTER 17

I decided to head for my hometown right after the shift ended the night after the party so that I would get an extra day with my parents and start gathering up the stuff I was going to need in the new apartment. Gary and I would be allowed to move into the apartment on Monday, so this trip home was to get as much of my parents stuff as possible and thereby avoid having to buy things. My brother-in-law was going to let me use his pickup, and my next door neighbor and lifelong friend, Marty Doll, was going to help me out. Marty would drive the pickup down, help me unload, and then bring the truck back to my brother in law.

I pulled into my parents' driveway about 1:00 am and immediately felt the comfort and relaxation that only comes from being "home." I was already really liking my life in Jackson, but in my mind you only ever have one hometown. I figured that was part of the reason I was so in love with all things Irish. It was because ultimately Ireland was the "home" of the Courtneys. Of course that attitude confused many of the Irish in Ireland, but since it brought in bucketfuls of American dollars via the tourists, they weren't exactly trying to change anyone's mind about it. I didn't care either way: I was determined to make a trip to Ireland one of my first fruits of my labor.

I was quiet as I walked into the house through the kitchen. My old dog, Omar, thumped his tail at my entry and got up off his rug to greet his best buddy. Omar was a medium-sized white mutt with hair like a Brittany Spaniel, but otherwise he was a true mixed bag. Omar walked my paper route everyday for almost two years starting when I was 14. The two of us were a fixture in the small town and it broke the poor dog's heart when I got "too old" to be a paper boy. Unlike a "jilted" human, however, Omar couldn't hold a grudge and thus welcomed me back home.

I spent ten minutes at the kitchen table fussing with the pooch and just enjoying the pleasure that comes from sitting quietly with a good dog. I wondered if tough cops did this sort of thing but figured this was just one of the ways I would maintain my humanity. Like every true Irish Catholic, I not only thought I could make a difference but felt an obligation to do so. If I gleaned nothing else from the nuns and lay teachers, I learned that the Catholic faith was one of action and not the door-to-door Bible thumping that drove me crazy. I really believed that as a police officer I could and should make a difference in the situations I would encounter and that I had to do my best, as Roger said, to respect the folks with whom I interacted. Not only that, but treat them with compassion. Well, most of them anyway.

I was clearly a man of strong beliefs and passion, and while that made me a natural leader it also got me in trouble because "keeping your mouth shut" in the face of an injustice was something I couldn't do. Police supervisors, commanders and politicians loved patrol officers who spoke their minds about as much as cats like to swim, as I would find out. It wouldn't quiet me, but it would make me wonder if some of the people I worked for had ever read the Constitution they took an oath to uphold.

My old bed and bedroom were quite a comfort after two weeks of being a guest in someone else's house, and I fell fast asleep with dreams of a home cooked breakfast dancing in my head.

Mom's breakfast was a perfect way to get the morning started before heading off to Mass. I was looking forward to seeing people I had known all my life and enjoying not being a "stranger in a strange land," even if it was just for a day. I really enjoyed the friendly banter and visiting after Mass and speaking to Father O'Sullivan who I had always liked. The priest was a quiet, sincere man who made you think instead of doze when he gave a sermon. He also had gotten me started as a lector, the lay person who does two of three Scripture readings that are part of most all Catholic Masses. Not only that, he once set me up on a date with his niece who was visiting from Ireland. Now how many guys can say they had a priest rep'ing for them?

I was clearly blessed with the Irish gift of gab and loved to talk, so I was in no hurry to walk the two blocks back home. My Dad once remarked that I didn't need to waste any time kissing the Blarney stone if I ever went to Ireland. He said it would be overkill. That gift of "Blarney" was a major asset for a cop if he wanted to avoid brawling every other day which clearly was one of my goals.

That afternoon I got a shock when I answered my parents phone and heard a deep voice ask for Kevin Courtney. I said, "This is Kevin," and the caller replied, "This is Lieutenant Hall of the Michigan State Police Kevin, and we are starting an Academy next week and would like you to be in it." I couldn't believe it, the job I had always wanted was mine for the taking. The problem was I already thought of myself as a Jackson Police Officer and no way could I just up and quit on them after only two weeks. No, JPD gave me a job and I owed them an honest effort in return. "Lieutenant, I really appreciate the offer but I'm sorry. I have been working for Jackson PD for the last 2 weeks and it just wouldn't be right to quit." Lieutenant Hall sighed and said, "You know Kevin I would have been a little surprised and disappointed if you had said yes. See I had heard you got hired by Jackson and from what I've learned about you, I knew you would honor your commitment to them. You're working for a good Department and I want to wish you good luck. If you ever decide you want to work for us, give me a call."

I thought things over after the lieutenant hung up and as much as I had wanted to be a state trooper in my heart, I knew I had made the right decision. I was pleased that Lieutenant Hall had said the things he did and that I had not created any bad feelings by turning the job down. I told my Dad about the call and my decision and, even the old man said in his best Irish brogue, "You did the right thing me boyo." I figured I was golden once I got the old man's seal of approval.

Kevin M. Courtney

CHAPTER 18

Marty Doll came across the yard to meet me in my parents' driveway on Monday morning as I started loading things in my brother-in-law's pickup. "Man, you should be ashamed of yourself the way you're ripping off your parents," Marty yelled. I replied, "Jealousy is an ugly emotion. Now get your ass over here and help me complete the burglary." Marty was a short, square-built guy who would never be considered handsome, but I was truly amazed at the number of stone-gorgeous women who literally threw themselves at him. Marty would simply grin and say, "What can I say? These women have great taste!"

After the loading was completed we headed south for Jackson with me leading the way in my car. It was a two hour trip and when we pulled into the lot at Pheasant Run, the first thing we saw were some babes next to the pool. I figured Marty would dump the truck right in the middle of the drive and go over to start working his magic, but he actually restrained himself and followed me to the new apartment. It was truly the equivalent of a dog walking past a new fire hydrant without giving it a sniff and taking a whiz.

It didn't take long for us to unload my stuff into the new apartment. It was a nice two bedroom, basement-level apartment so the bottom of the windows were at ground level. This made it convenient to check out the women as they walked by without being too obvious. Being at basement level also made it cooler, which in the heat and humidity of a Michigan summer would be nice. People from warm-weather states seemed to think because Michigan had snow and cold in the winter, summers wouldn't be all that hot. Wrong. Ninety degree days were not at all uncommon. I used to get a kick out of the fact it could get to -20 degrees Fahrenheit in February and four months later in June it would be 110 degree warmer with temps at 90. A common adage in Michigan was "If you don't like the weather, wait 10 minutes it will change." It was not a state for people who didn't like variations in their weather.

Marty and I sat around drinking a cold pop and bullshitting for a while before Marty headed back home with the pickup. I thanked him and said I owed him one. Being a warm and caring friend, Marty answered by saying, "You're goddamned right you do. And if my back stiffens up, I'll sue your ass for workers comp." We both laughed and Marty headed off. I looked around the apartment and again realized that the tie to being a "kid" was becoming more and more undone. One minute you're in college drinking beer and chasing women, with no responsibilities to speak of, and the next you got a full time job and you're living on your own with rent and utilities to pay.

CHAPTER 19

For the next two weeks I bounced around between Fitzroy Douglas, a Jamaican immigrant, and Dick Allen. Fitzroy turned out to be a big Detroit Tigers fan, as was I, so we spent a lot of time talking baseball. The time passed pretty uneventfully, and I found myself learning the streets much better each day. I was still staying primarily in sections D-24 and B-22, but generally I always knew what direction I was going and most times I could navigate to the address of the call when I drove. Typically, however, the senior officer drove the car about 90% of the time because I was still so new to the City.

Fitzroy was easy going and helped me learn a lot about defusing situations with a more low key approach. Between talking baseball and learning more about who was doing what in the city, I really enjoyed working with him. A lot of the women we came in contact with loved hearing Fitzroy talk with his heavy Jamaican accent, and I got a kick out of watching how Fitzroy handled the attention. I also liked the fact that I was treated like a fellow officer and not just a dumb-ass rookie. Another Irish trait was being very sensitive to any type of slight.

The only exceptional thing that happened during this two week span was I met the "voice." All Jackson County was served by a centralized 9-1-1 center at that time. In fact, it was the first consolidated central dispatch ever attempted in Michigan and became a model for many other counties that followed suit. All reports of fires, medical emergencies, and requests for police came into central dispatch where they were answered by one of the 4 operators usually on duty. Operators were assigned to one of 3 separate radio consoles which provided communication with fire departments and ambulance services, city police, or all police working in the county outside of the city. During the busiest hours the extra person was usually assigned to do the computerized checks of people and license plates that police officers routinely request and to help with answering phones. On a summer Friday night, the place could get jumping pretty good.

Supervision of the center was provided by sergeants from the city, state, and county as part of the cooperative agreement that created Jackson County Central Dispatch. Overall it worked pretty well and was an example of how jurisdictions could work together to provide better and more efficient service. Naturally, the cops, deputies, and fire fighters were constantly bitching about Dispatch but cops, deputies, and firefighters bitch no matter what you do. If you gave them free beer on a 100-degree day, they'd complain it was the wrong brand, so hearing them yang about Dispatch really didn't create many waves.

Most of the dispatchers were well known to the local cops because their shifts were similar and they'd stop by Precinct 2 on a regular basis. The dispatch work force was primarily female, so naturally the testosterone-fueled cops were definitely scoping out the talent whenever possible. The boys' radar definitely came on when they heard the newest voice on the radio. It sounded so nice it could only belong to a young and beautiful woman. God would not waste tones like that on a fat broad, nor could ugly ever sound so sexy.

Ed Hey, one of my college buddies, was a police officer in Albion, a small city on I-94, right on the western Jackson County line. Albion had its own dispatch, but monitored Jackson county radio traffic since it was not uncommon for something from Jackson to spill over into Albion. I swear that to Ed, the new voice was like phone sex, except he didn't have to pay. He would go crazy every time he heard it and was close to driving lights and siren from Albion to Jackson dispatch, to profess his undying love.

All the buzz about the new "voice" had me chuckling to myself. First, while I was as big a dog as the next guy, before I went off like a beagle chasing a rabbit, I wanted a look at the rabbit, even if I had to admit that was one fine-sounding rabbit. Caution told me, however, a voice that nice just might be attached to a face like Godzilla and a body like Dick Butkus. Besides, a man had to be desperate to act like this over a voice. I even went so far as to tell a couple of the guys on the shift that I'd bet she had a beard and weighed an easy 200. She probably used to be a lumberjack in the Upper Peninsula of Michigan.

CHAPTER 20

Gary and I decided that since we had been in our apartment for two weeks, a party was in order. We invited a bunch of JPD officers, dispatchers, and nurses over to the apartment on a Sunday night since that happened to be when we were both off. Gary had worked his way through Jackson Community College as a dispatcher so he knew almost everyone down there, and they were all happy to see one of their own make good.

The party was the typical low key get-together with everyone bringing his or her own beer or booze and the hosts providing munchies. People mostly just talked and told war stories while knocking back the alcohol without having to worry about non-cops pissing and moaning about double standards. Plus, you didn't have to listen to "how a cop screwed me over" stories.

The party was rolling along nicely at about 11:00 when Margie Carpenter, one of the dispatchers, walked in with the "voice." Her name was Julie Sykes. She was 24 and a knockout. I decided at that point that every rule had an exception and Julie was the exception to my "no voice that nice could be attached to a beautiful woman" rule. I also decided a woman like this would never talk to a guy like Ed, but since he was my friend, I'd lie and tell him she was fat and ugly.

Now Margie, who was born, raised, and still lived on Jackson's south side, was a matchmaker at heart. She had brought Julie to the party with the express intention of introducing her to Gary, whom Margie figured had been single far too long. Gary, on the other hand, viewed being single as a good thing and so reacted like Superman to kryptonite when it became obvious what Margie was up to. I was nothing if not opportunistic, so I jumped right in with my best stuff and the party kept rolling. I made a few bonus points when Julie spilled a beer on the carpet and I jumped to clean it up telling her not to worry. Gary helped out by saying I did a lot worse than that on the rug when I had been drinking. How could I not impress a woman with that kind of support?

By about 2 am, most everyone had split for home except Julie, Margie, Fitzroy, and Gary Hudson a black JPD officer. Jackson had 7 black officers at the time which wasn't bad for most departments their size. Unfortunately, that number would drop in a few years due to resignations, and it took a long time to get it back up again.

Since this was Michigan and beer was being drunk, a euchre game had broken out. No true Michigander can drink beer with friends without playing at least one hand of euchre, the official card game of the State. More than one lousy exam grade at a Michigan college or university was a direct result of an all night euchre and beer drinking party.

Critically important elements of euchre in Michigan include accusing your opponents of cheating, expounding on why your strategy is better than theirs, and blaming all lost hands on something other than your own lack of talent. Fitzroy pointed out at one juncture that it was hard for him to play with white people since he had been raised to believe they were the devil. No one took any offense to that any more than they did when I pointed out that since Jamaica was home to voodoo I wasn't all that comfortable with Fitzroy either. Gary Hudson settled things when he said, "I think both you mother fuckers are cheatin' and I don't care where the hell you came from." Shortly after that Gary began referring to me as "Ya-Clark-Kent-lookin' motherfucker" and the nickname stuck with him, and later Howard Noppe.

Finally at about 3:00 am, our party goers said their goodbyes and I did a quick clean up of the apartment. I had decided that Julie was going to be worth some follow up so I determined I had better get busy. After all, it wouldn't take long for the rest of the dogs in blue and brown to start working the same track, and I wasn't crazy about competition. Once, while in college, when I discovered that a classmate and I were trying for the same young lady's attention at a house party, I went and grabbed the phone and yelled to the guy, as he was talking to the target of our lust, that his fiancé wanted to talk to him. Needless to say, that boy ceased to be competition as soon as he got up to answer a call that wasn't there. He did have a fiancé, she just wasn't calling right then.

CHAPTER 21

At the start of July, right after the party, I found myself assigned to work with Officer John Stressman. John grew up a military brat following his dad from base to base until his family later settled in Mount Pleasant where his Dad took an administrative position with Central Michigan University. John was pretty serious and more of a Joe Friday "just the facts" kind of cop. He had only been with the Department for a couple years and he was ready to help out a new guy. He was also very interested in ensuring that any rookie had the same work ethic he did. John had a dry sense of humor and was really a pretty easy guy to get along with, even though his reputation was that of a real hard ass. I couldn't keep from thinking how lucky I had been to end up on a shift with the types of officers who graced JPD's afternoon shift.

John was primarily assigned as a relief officer, so he covered sections when a regular assigned officer was on his leave days. This gave me a chance to learn even more of the city streets and gain more confidence. John was a good teacher and seemed genuinely concerned with helping me out. This paid off when I mentioned meeting the new dispatcher and John said "well call her up and get a date." Not exactly wisdom from the mountain stuff, but I had to admit it was a good idea. John then came up with a better idea and found a reason to stop by Dispatch.

Dispatch was located in the basement of the County Building and had all the charm of a sixth century dungeon. There was no outside light, no fresh air, and since smoking was allowed it stunk of stale cigarette smoke. John and I walked in, and John immediately started an easy banter with the on-duty dispatchers while I said a casual hello to Julie and decided she looked even better the second time around if that was possible. I decided I would ask her out but this visit was not the time, so I just chatted with her a bit and then John and I left.

John was letting me drive most shifts and was encouraging me to try and get at least one self-initiated ticket or arrest each day. No one on the shift that I had worked with so far was big on traffic enforcement; in fact, Roger was proud of the fact that he rarely wrote a ticket, so I was glad for the new experience. I knew the bosses liked to see some "biscuits" along with other examples you were doing something other than simply taking calls.

Catching someone in the act of committing a crime was a real plus, but there were plenty of people wanted on warrants to pickup. Additionally, Jackson was a busy enough city with enough serious crime that an officer working the busy sections could count on a couple of felony complaints where a probable cause arrest could be made. The bottom line was there was no need to do any "creative" charging to get the stats needed to keep the shift lieutenant happy. All you had to do was stay busy and keep your head out of your ass.

John was overall pretty happy with the progress I was making on all facets of police work, but my driving was leading John towards getting a prescription for tranquilizers. I had a habit of following the car in front of me too closely and driving a bit faster than John preferred. A common position for John when I was driving was both hands on the dashboard while shouting, "Don't get so goddamned close Kevin," or "slow the fuck down." Whenever asked by other officers on the shift how I was doing, John would answer, "Fine except he's going to give me a heart attack with his driving." I really didn't mind because John always said it with a chuckle, and I knew it was John's way to both pat me on the back and remind me I *was* following cars a little too closely.

I was leaving work the first Saturday night after starting to work with John and was headed straight home for a change. I pulled out of the rear of the Department and headed west towards Francis Street where I would make a right and head for Glick Highway. I was pretty relaxed and not really thinking about anything until I looked up and saw that a car was stopped in the intersection and there were people milling around it. I immediately started to slow down and was trying to figure out what was happening up ahead before I drove into the middle of something.

It became pretty apparent to me that some type of dispute had broken out so I pulled to the curb behind the car and got out. As I approached the people, I realized there were two men and a woman present and they had been scuffling, so I asked "What's going on." One of the two males on the scene said, "Nothing man we're all right." so I badged him and said, "I'm a cop and it doesn't look all right to me." I then looked at the woman and said, "Are you all right ma'am?" She gave me the typical non-committal, "It's okay officer," which meant "NO, it is not all right." I was starting to get a little nervous, and about that time John pulled up on his way home.

Nothing makes a cop by himself who is starting to worry about his situation feel better than the arrival of backup. John changed the whole dynamic of the situation and he and I were able to figure out that an argument had started in the car and spilled out into the street about the time I pulled up. Nobody had been injured in any way, and it was apparently more pushing and shoving between the two men than anything else. Based on that, John decided to send the three on their way with the admonition to use a little better judgment on where and how to settle disputes.

I was starting to wonder if I had made a good choice in stepping into this mess, but John made a point of telling me I did a good job of intervening and that I handled myself very well. It is always a tough spot for an officer to be faced with whether or not to get involved in something while off duty, but John told me I'd made the right call. He then told me about Dale Kreh, a JPD officer who was back home in Flint standing in line in a drug store when a guy robbed it. Dale pulled his gun and ruined a perfectly good day at work for one armed robber. I figured I would stick with breaking up domestics for now, but catching an armed robbery in progress off duty is damn near nirvana for a young cop.

Kevin M. Courtney

.

CHAPTER 22

I wasn't really big into "working out" at this point in my life, but I still did like to go running and to head downtown and play hoops at the local YMCA. As this was my day off, I spent a couple of hours at the Y playing ball with a collection of 20 and 30 year old guys in the typical pick-up games you find at a gym. I was a pretty good player and my stamina from years of running gave me a little edge, but my biggest advantage was being left-handed. Most players were right-handed so guys had a hard time defending a true southpaw and I worked hard at switching from right to left to get a step up on my opponent. My experience playing pick up games in college with and against kids from Michigan's inner cities didn't hurt my game either.

Once I got back to the apartment I decided it was time for some domestic duties. Specifically, I needed to do some laundry. I had thought about throwing on my swimming trunks and heading out to the complex's pool, but most of the women I had talked to by the pool on my past visits were married so I had decided that was not worth the effort. Instead I picked up my laundry bag and headed across the hall to the conveniently located laundry room.

I could hear a machine running as I stepped into the laundry room, and I was brought to a dead stop by an absolutely gorgeous blond of about 23 standing in front of one of the machines. She had beautiful long legs and was wearing a pair of short running shorts that accentuated them perfectly. She also had on a light white t-shirt that showed off her bronze tan and kept me staring. She was also wearing make up, along with perfume that was enough to drive a monk nuts.

Juxtaposed with this vision was good old me, who looked and

smelled like I just fell out of a dumpster. I was wearing basketball shoes with no socks, a pair of ratty cut off sweat pants, and a t-shirt I had bought in high school. I wasn't wearing makeup or perfume, but I did have a day's growth of beard and my "scent" was that of the first place winner at an Armenian goat wrestling festival.

Just as I was thinking, "This shit isn't happening" the beauty spoke to me: "Hi, I'm Becky from next door," and she held out her hand and smiled such that I almost forget my name. I politely wiped my hand on my sweats and said, "Nice to meet you, I'm Kevin." I thought her name was perfect since one of the many women who turned me down cold back in high school was a blond beauty named Becky. My guess was I was going to be two for two in the "how not to impress Becky" category.

Funny thing was Becky seemed quite pleased to meet me and was chatting away while I was unusually quiet because of my embarrassment. I found out quite quickly that Becky and her husband, Ron, who was a new Doctor in town, had been living in the complex for just a little longer than Gary and I. Knowing I had absolutely no chance of getting anywhere with this woman allowed me to relax, and I explained my appearance and odor. Becky laughed and said, "Don't worry I work out all the time and know all about smelling bad." I thought, *No, you know about not smelling good, I know about smelling bad. There is a difference.*

I went about loading two machines with my laundry and Becky seemed impressed that I knew enough to sort whites and colors. I joked I did my delicates by hand in the bathroom sink and hung them on the shower rod. Becky liked that, and liked it even more when she found out Gary and I were cops. She said she was home alone a lot at night due to Ron working long hours at the hospital, and the complex could be a little creepy. I said if she ever got worried about something or someone to just come next door and pound on the door. Either my roomie or I would likely be there and would be glad to help her out. Since she was married, I was truly being a nice guy. Had she been single, I would have been the one pounding on her door. I did think the Lord might have gotten a little confused since I often prayed not to be lead into temptation and it certainly appeared that some serious temptation had moved in next door. I'd just have to be strong. Real strong.

Becky hung out in the laundry room for quite a while and I really did enjoy her company. She finally wandered off to her apartment with her laundry and I thought it was pretty cool to meet her even if I wouldn't be able to hit on her as would have been my normal method of operation. I filled Gary in on the meeting later that day, and Gary remarked about what a knockout Becky was. Seems old Gary had been scoping her out for the last week or so and holding out on his roommate about her living next door. Typical rotten stunt I would have pulled had I been in Gary's spot. A damn shame when your roommate is as low crawling as you are.

The second week John and I worked together we were in D-24 and noticed a beautifully-restored old Pontiac double parked just off Morrell Street. I pulled up behind the car and John said, "This guy needs a ticket." I wrote it out and John said he'd put it on the car. He walked up to the car just as the owner came out from one of the houses. I really wasn't expecting much since parking tickets were only a few bucks and didn't involve any "points" on one's driving record. Apparently that didn't compute with the owner of the car, one Elroy Charles, because he went into a screaming tirade, and in a matter of about 15 seconds, he and John were involved in a full-fledged wrestling match. The amazing thing is one of Elroy's arms was missing from the elbow down, but he was still a handful to say the least.

I couldn't believe what I was seeing, but I jumped out of the car and sprinted towards the fight. I never thought of myself as a brave man or even a fighter, but I did not hesitate to go to the aid of my fellow officer. It was a weird sensation; I was scared but at the same time the adrenaline from the old "fight or flight" response was kicking, so I was geeked to be going into battle. Elroy had the bad luck to be facing away from me as I came running up so I used a cop's best friend and slapped a high grade choke hold on Elroy's sorry ass. Elroy initially struggled even more but while he was doing pretty well one on one with John he wasn't able to overcome the 2-on-1 advantage and within less than ten seconds the choke hold had taken the fight out of him.

"Choke hold" was actually a misnomer because I wasn't choking Elroy. I was using the pressure of my forearm and bicep against Elroy's carotid arteries to cut the flow of blood to his brain. Done properly this resulted in unconsciousness in a matter of about six seconds and took the fight right out of the biggest bad asses around. It also prevented all sorts of lumps, bruises, and lacerations since night sticks, saps, fists, and flashlights were not necessary. Cops loved the choke hold, so of course civil libertarians and every other left wing nut job hated them. Easy for them to do since they were never faced with 6'4" 250 pound whack jobs who had to be taken into custody. Eventually choke holds would be outlawed except in the most dire circumstances, but for now they were in play and a quick way to end most serious physical confrontations.

I was coming into law enforcement just at the time the whole use of force issue was swinging towards more restraint on officers' actions and more litigation of police brutality complaints. In the "good old days" criminals who fought with the cops expected a thumping and took it like men. Now it seemed like any physical contact with a suspect set off howls of brutality. It wasn't that long ago that a criminal running from the scene of a felony was likely going to hear the sound of gunfire, but those days were going quickly too. I was not interested in beating suspects, but at the same time figured if you start a fight and come in second place it doesn't make you a victim.

The valuable lesson for Elroy that day was the Cops don't fight fair, they fight to win. We got him cuffed and stuffed and called for a wrecker to impound his car. Once that car was on the hook, Elroy got hauled into the station and booked on a "resist, hinder, and oppose" charge which was part of the disorderly conduct ordinance. I would learn that although there was a state statute that made assaulting a police officer a felony, most scuffles like this were handled as misdemeanors. The attitude was that this kind of stuff was simply part of being a cop and didn't deserve felony charges. Sort of like most hockey fights only draw a five minute penalty, but every once in a while there will be a game misconduct assessed.

The other benefit to me from this little dust up was that John retold the story several times, emphasizing how fast "Kevin jumped right in and slapped a choke hold on Elroy's sorry ass." That got me some points from the other officers as a guy who wouldn't hesitate to jump in when someone needed help. Most guys could forgive a lot of failings but they would never forgive any form of hesitation to jump in when the shit hit the fan. I was still somewhat of an unknown quantity, but I was headed in the right direction in terms of officers trying to figure me out.

As we sat in the report room doing paper work, John was on my ass again about not getting a date with Julie, and asked what the hell I was waiting for. I came up with the lame excuse that I didn't have her home phone number and with shift work it was hard to find the time to call. John rolled his eyes and said she was working right now so call the non-emergency number and ask her out. I realized this was one of those situations where if I chumped out and didn't call, the word would spread like wildfire and I'd never hear the end of it. Plus I was also thinking that if I kept screwing around someone else was sure to beat me to the punch. That maniac Ed might even try. I looked at John and said, "Anything to get you off my ass."

Julie seemed a little surprised by the call but agreed to go out with me. The conversation was short and to the point and I was more than a little pleased with myself when I hung up. "You happy now mother?" I asked John. He replied, "You'll thank me some day, you ungrateful prick, but I'm a big enough man to wait." I had to laugh at that but had to admit I probably wouldn't have acted without John's boot in the ass.

The month spent on patrol with John flew by and I was feeling pretty good about things. John had become a good friend over the beers we drank at Evanoff's after going off duty and I had even gotten to know John's wife, Beth, who was very pretty, and a real live wire who made any gathering more fun.

Kevin M. Courtney

Chapter 23

I had started to get to know a lot of the officers better and had begun hanging out with Howard Noppe and Gary at Howard's house on Lake Columbia in the southern part of the county. Jackson County had lots of lakes, much like the northern part of the state, and I had always enjoyed being on the water.

Howard had a nice little house along a channel that fed into the lake and most importantly he had a slick ski boat. That of course attracted not only Gary and me but usually some of the ladies that Howard knew. It was hard to find a better way to spend your days off during Michigan's hot summers than drinking a few beers and water skiing. Howard, for all of his gruff "I don't give a fuck" exterior, was a great host and liked to see his friends have a good time. There was an easy, friendly banter among the people that hung out at Howard's, and it helped me feel even more like I was with my "boys."

Of the eight people hired when I was, four of them had been cadets with JPD so were well known and part of the Department when they became officers. This gave them a tremendous advantage over us outsiders. The four former cadets included Howard, Carl Rice, Tom Bernardon, and Scott Rogers. Carl was the Chief's nephew, Scott had been a township cop for a year or so before coming back to JPD and he was married to a JPD officer named Gail, who had been with the Department for a couple of years, and Tom was a big, strapping farm boy from Concord, a small town in the south-west corner of the county. The other four hired included Gary, Karl Ankrom, Dave VanSteempvoort, and me.

Karl, the oldest member of our group, was a U.S. Navy veteran, married, and with a son. He had been working as an officer in the village of Brooklyn, home to the Michigan International Speedway, along the southern border of the county when he was hired. The brass at JPD assumed he had been through the police academy since he was working as a police officer; unfortunately that wasn't the case. Michigan law at that time did not require officers working for agencies with less than three people, like Brooklyn, to attend an academy. Well, JPD didn't get the bargain they thought they were getting in terms of not having to pay for him to attend an academy, but Karl was still a good hire so he was sent off to the academy at JPD expense while earning his salary and getting his benefits. He also got an April hire date and a higher seniority position than I did. I didn't come on the payroll until I graduated college and received my police certification. As Karl and I became friends, Karl would bust on me about being junior to him, and I would remind Karl that I had more time on the streets and therefore was the more experienced cop.

Dave VanSteempvoort, called "Van," was a poster boy for his Dutch ancestry. He was a tall blond who was very quiet and reserved. He had grown up in Michigan's thumb area working on his family vegetable farm and had attended Michigan State University. Van was also married. His wife was not at all comfortable with his new job or the idea of him stopping at the bar for a couple with the boys but he managed to make it out a couple of nights. Van was a likeable guy and eager to learn his new job and city just like I was.

All eight of the new hires were brought together for two days of in-service training that summer after we all were on board with the Department. The training was good and covered a lot of Department policy and procedure, report writing requirements, and general "how to be a member of JPD" kinds of things. The real benefit for the eight of us was to get to know our fellow "rookies" better. We all got along pretty well and the two with no ties to Jackson, Van and I, fit right in and didn't get any bad vibes about being the outsiders.

We were all sitting together in uniform in the McDonald's on Prospect Street having lunch on the second day of training and getting more than our fair share of stares. Most people had never seen that many cops in one spot. Three or four people of course had to come up and ask if anyone was protecting the city. Each time, one of us would politely explain we were new officers and in training so the city was safe. I was starting to figure out that wearing a uniform was not always going to be a benefit.

Eventually a guy in a suit walked up smiling and asked, "Hey, can one of you pigs tell me how to get to the Cascades?" which was Jackson's lighted manmade waterfall. I was wondering what this idiot's deal was when Gary answered, "You have to go to Ann Arbor for that." This got a good laugh from the citizen and the local boys at the table. Howard looked and Van and me and said, "This jerk is Detective Brunk." Brunk then introduced himself to us and turned out to be quite a friendly guy. I would later learn he was a key member of the BOAS and part of its ruling council. Aside from the fact he rooted for the University of Michigan, he turned out to be one helluva of a guy with a great sense of humor.

The only real drawback to my first two months on the job was being assigned to work at the Harness Raceway. Normally this assignment was done by officers on overtime, but in an effort to save money the Department decided to use on-duty people to cover the detail. One of the command officers had the bright idea that you could send rookie officers down there and save taking an officer off the street. Besides, there would always be a couple of senior officers on the detail and there was little chance the new guys would get into any problems at the track watching people piss their money away betting on the trotters and pacers. As a result, I was pulled off my regular shift numerous times to work the track, which to put it bluntly sucked.

Standing around in the area under the grandstands, watching the crowd, and chatting with the locals was cake duty, but it wasn't where a young crime fighter wanted to be, especially not on a Thursday, Friday, or Saturday night. The only semi-exciting time came at the end of the night when the officers escorted the nights take, usually over 50,000 in cash, to the bank. Once the radio code was given that the money was en-route to a local bank, radio silence was observed by all units until the money was safely in the bank. This, however, did not make up for the fact I was missing out on real police work.

About the only compensation that I could find was the track had great grilled kielbasa on a bun and they were cheap. Being single, I wasn't cooking much unless you consider pouring cereal in a bowl cooking, so dinner was whatever I got while at work. The truth was until I got married I rarely saw a meal that didn't come out of a fast food bag or box. The other good thing was that shifts at the track were eight hours and many nights the track detail was done in around six hours or so. That meant we could go out snooping around without having to take calls, or we could run as backup on every exciting call and not have to worry about doing any paperwork, every cop's dream. Of course if you were working with Brunk, you had to slink through Sharp Park and harass the parkers just a little since the park officially closed at 10:00 pm. The truth was Brunk just liked ruining a night's romance.

CHAPTER 24

Starting at the end of July, I was assigned to Dave Bachman, another two year veteran of the force, and a former cadet. Dave's dad had been a sergeant with JPD before dying young, and Dave was happy to follow in the old man's footsteps. He had the reputation of being one tough s.o.b although he was an average-sized man. He also was very hard working and went out and took care of whatever problems there were on his beat. In short, he was a Cop's cop and well respected by his fellow officers on second shift.

Just as impressive as Dave's arrest record was the number of citizen complaints that were made against him. Tact was not his strong suit, and he had no patience with anyone who challenged his authority. The result was he had more than his fair share of scuffles and less than satisfied customers who wanted to complain. This created the age old dilemma for his bosses. How do you sand off the edges but still keep the hard charging attitude? The Department had enough non-controversial officers who did the minimum necessary to stay employed, so the brass wanted to keep those who went above and beyond and really did try to earn their salary. Bachman was clearly part of this group.

I had a little bit of an advantage when I started to work with Bachman. First, he had been watching me for the last two-and-a-half months and generally liked what he saw, and second, John Stressman had bragged me up for my willingness to jump in when John got in trouble. All of this carried weight with Dave. I would still have to earn my bones, but I was coming in with no baggage and a little boost.

Dave was assigned to section C-23 the southeast side of Jackson.

It had traditionally been the Polish enclave of Jackson and was still very heavily Polish. The local Catholic Church, St. Stan's, had a Polish-speaking priest, the local markets had Polish-speaking employees, and the area was home to several Polish fraternal halls such as the Polish National Alliance and the Polish Legion of American Veterans. The Department even had two Polish speaking officers. On the north edge of the section along Michigan Avenue and the adjacent streets lived a large number of black residents, and there were also quite a few whites who had come north from Kentucky to work in factories in the city.

All in all, Charlie 23 was a mixed area with a decidedly downward spin to it which made it a great place to do police work if you wanted to stay busy. Dave had grown up in the section so he knew it like only a true local could. He was a good teacher and right away I was glad I was assigned to work with him. Dave was intense, but I was ready to learn so I didn't let that bother me.

The first couple days we worked together things went pretty smoothly. There was nothing too difficult to handle and I spent a lot of time just trying to learn the streets. It didn't help that there was a bunch of sewer work being done and several streets in the section were tore up. Still, I felt a whole helluva lot better now than I did back in May when it came to getting from point A to point B.

The first Sunday I worked with Dave was hot, and as I drove into work I figured we would be busy. I had all ready been a cop long enough to know that the only real slow time in the rough districts on Sunday in a city like Jackson was the morning. People were either sleeping off Saturday night or they were in Church. Once the afternoon rolled around, either the hangover had been forgotten enough to start drinking or the good Christian behavior had been put away until next week. By five or six o'clock in the afternoon, the fights and squabbles started. It wasn't so bad when the weather cooled off, but 85 degrees required multiple 40 ounce Colt 45's for residents to get through the day, and stupid coupled with alcohol was never a good combination.

Right around dusk, dispatch called C-23 and B-22 and advised that the State Police had ended a pursuit just north of Michigan Avenue in B-22's District and could no longer be contacted via the radio. This was not a good thing and so Dave headed the patrol car in that direction in a hurry. As we pulled up, I could see that two troopers were pinning a man against a car parked in front of the patrol car and that two additional people were draped over the troopers. It looked like to me that these individuals were trying to yank the troopers off. Naturally there was all ready a crowd of onlookers gathering to see what was going on. Live entertainment in areas like this usually involved police cars, fire trucks, ambulances or any combination of the three.

Dave yelled at me to go help the troopers, so I ran directly to them. As I was coming up I yelled at the guy on the trooper farthest from the patrol car to get off the trooper. The man said "I'm helping," and I said "We're here and we'll help now, Get off the trooper." I figured this was the best bet because if the guy wasn't helping I needed him out of the way, and if he was helping it was better to have the cops and not citizens wrestling with suspects. The helper complied with my request, and I grabbed one of the suspect's arms to try and get him cuffed. It was pretty obvious the trooper was gassed from the struggle, and once I got a grip on the suspect it looked like we were going to be okay. How wrong I was.

Dave and his "helper" did not have the same positive contact that my buddy and I did, and the fight was on. I managed to look over and see Dave down between the patrol car's front bumper and the rear bumper of the suspect's car which were almost touching. The helper was over top of Dave, and Dave had been yelling for me to help him but I hadn't heard any of his calls. About the time I realized what was happening, more officers were arriving so I was able to let go of the suspect and jump to Dave's assistance along with a sheriff's deputy who had rolled on the call. The deputy and I grabbed the helper, one Juan DeRosa, and started pulling him off Dave. During this group grab, Juan took one in the chops from Dave's nightstick and got some chipped chompers for his trouble. Things were finally brought under control and the state troopers left with their prisoner and Dave and I left with Juan.

Dave was really smoked as we got in the sally port of the station. The sally port was basically a two car garage attached to the booking area where officers parked when bringing in a prisoner. The doors were automatically controlled from the front desk and so it provided very good security. Because Dave was so wound up I wasn't sure what was going to happen, and I already didn't think it was a good thing that Juan was bleeding from the mouth. As we started to walk the prisoner from the car to the booking area, Dave grabbed Juan by the throat and started to give him hell for attacking him. I figured one "grade A" top-of-the-line melon thumping was about to commence, so I immediately stepped between the two to provide a little whuppus interruptus.

I realized that rookies didn't go around telling senior officers what to do, but this was a bad situation about to get worse so I had no choice. I used every bit of charm I had and soft talked my way into getting Dave to release his grip on Juan, who was then taken into booking where the sergeant. took over. Dave was still pissed about the whole situation and I wasn't too sure some of his anger wasn't directed at me, so I kept my mouth shut. The two of us finished our paperwork in about time to go off duty and by that time Dave had wound down. I was still pretty upset by the whole situation and was invoking my right to remain silent for the most part. Dave really wasn't doing anything to dispel my concerns about what he thought of me.

I decided I had really bagged the pooch on this one. First, I hadn't come to Dave's assistance fast enough and, second, I had overstepped my bounds as a rookie by telling Dave to let Juan go. I was literally sick to my stomach over the whole mess. The terrible thing was I knew it was the right thing to do, and Dave likely knew it too, but it still came down to junior telling senior what to do. Neither Dave nor I could be comfortable with that at this time and maybe we never would. How we handled it in the coming days would likely decide our relationship for the rest of our careers. That was assuming I had a career after tonight. I was nothing but a dog shit probationary officer and knew as such I had no protection at all from getting fired. A bad report on a single incident like this could be enough to send me packing, and I didn't figure Bachman saw this as a shining moment in my short career.

I had a date that night with Julie to meet after work and I told her the whole story over a couple of beers and a burger. By the time we got together, I was convinced my career was over and I would be branded as an officer who let his partner get beat on. Julie did her best to cheer me up as she tried to understand all this macho cop stuff. She was becoming a good dispatcher but hadn't been around cops long enough to get a handle on this stuff. She was, however, a very caring and perceptive young woman and so understood I wasn't just worried about a bad evaluation.

She apparently did like me enough to give it her best shot, but at this point I was thinking I was headed back home in short order and nothing else mattered. Not even the fact that Julie was obviously quite concerned about me, which any other time would have pleased me immensely. I finally tossed in the towel and told Julie it was just a lousy night and I had to go. I had no idea how lousy things were going to get in the next few days.

Kevin M. Courtney

I got the additional good news when I came into work on the next shift. The Department had started an "internal investigation" into the incident. The Jackson Police Department did not have an Internal Affairs unit but they did, however, take allegations of wrongdoing very seriously and had an administrative lieutenant assigned to investigate all serious complaints against officers such as excessive force resulting in injury. Lesser violations, like being rude, were dealt with by the officer's lieutenant or sergeant.

The administrative lieutenant at this time was David Locke. He was a clean cut soft spoken local from the western part of the county and had been quite a good amateur boxer both in the Golden Gloves and Army. Oddly enough his younger brother Ralph was a high school classmate of Julie's. Lieutenant Locke was without a doubt was the last guy on the Department you wanted to throw hands with, yet was probably the guy least likely to lose his temper and give a dirt bag the slapping around he so desperately needed. I'd had little contact with him other than he was the person who had done my background investigation as part of the hiring process.

I got the word I was to report to Lieutenant Locke's office the next day in the morning to be interviewed regarding the incident. The knot I had been carrying around in my stomach did a quick doubling and I broke out in a cold sweat. That I had done nothing wrong was beside the point. I had the same emotional response to the order every other honest cop did: Fear. Good cops only want to do the right thing and be a good cop so naturally when they were questioned about their actions they initially started doubting whether what they had done was right, or they assume the Department is going to throw them under the bus to satisfy some asshole citizen.

I lacked the life preserver that most cops grabbed on to when they were on the hot seat: a union contract and representation. I was a probationary employee and would be for 12 months from the date of my hire. During this time, I was for all intents and purposes dispensable. The Department did not have to give a reason for dismissing me. They could just send me packing, and unless I could show the dismissal was based on a protected class like race, ethnic background, or gender, I was road kill. Clearly the Supreme Court wasn't known for taking cases involving 22 year old Paddys who got the boot, so I was on my own. I feared the Department would decide to fire my ass and not waste time finding out if I did anything wrong.

My mind was not eased when Lieutenant Locke started the interview by reading me my Miranda warnings and asking me to sign a waiver. I might be new to police work, but I knew you only got the Miranda warnings when you were the focus of a criminal investigation. I was having visions of losing a job while at the same time adding to my family's pride by getting charged with a crime in my first three freaking months on the Department. I was sweating like a coal handler on a steam locomotive and having a hard time getting a grip on myself long enough to sign the waiver.

I never once considered not signing the waiver. My upbringing said if you did something, own up to it like a man and take your medicine. A rational person in my shoes would be an idiot not to seek legal advice first, but since I was scared shitless, rationale wasn't an issue. I probably would have signed a pledge of loyalty to the freaking Queen of England I was so scared.

Lieutenant Locke got right down to business and asked me to lay out what happened. I gave it to him gospel, and once he made some notes Locke got down to the questions. Following a few preliminaries, the interview went pretty much like this: Did you hold Juan DeRosa so Bachman could wail the hell out of him? No. Well did you hold him *while* Bachman wailed the hell out of him? No. Did you wail on Juan? No. Did you see anyone else wail on Juan? No. How many times did you see Bachman hit Juan with his nightstick? I didn't see him get hit. How can that be if he was right in front of you? I was on his back. Tell me again exactly what you did see, Officer Courtney, and don't leave anything out.

Things got so much better when Lieutenant Locke said he knew how tough it was and how I felt I had to be loyal to my partner, but telling the truth would be so much better for everyone. I figured that was a polite way to say, "I know you're lying you worthless rookie piece of crap so cough it up; you two beat the shit out of this guy and after we fire you, you're likely going to jail." I figured in the 110 years since my people got off the boat, my going to jail would just about be the most embarrassment a member of the Courtney clan had ever caused the family. I could only imagine how pleased my Dad would be to hear this bit of news.

Locke changed gears again and wanted to hear about the ass-whipping interruptus that took place in the sally port. I tried to downplay the situation but it was obvious that Bachman was in the crosshairs. I laid out what happened but tried to show it was my perceptions that caused me to act, and since I was so new you couldn't really trust my judgment. Locke wasn't buying it, and by this time I was starting to wonder whether I could get out of my apartment lease and if my big brother could get me a job at the Buick Plant in Flint.

Finally the interview wound down and I felt like I had just taken a 10-round beating from Joe Frazier. Locke told me I was free to go and that I would be contacted later regarding the outcome of the investigation. Locke was about as warm as Charles Bronson when he said that, and so I left his office figuring the loss of employment was simply a matter of when, not if. I would have had to cheer up considerably at this point to be considered clinically depressed. I later became great friends with Locke and we can laugh about the "interview" now but I wasn't laughing back then.

I went back to the apartment and just sat and stared at the TV. I wasn't even aware of what was on. I needed to talk to someone but who the hell would I call with this little gem? Jesus, Mary, and Joseph, I hoped to hell no one ever found out about it. Normally in a situation like this I would have prayed, but I was so shell-shocked I never even thought to call for the big backup. Finally it came time to head into work and a new wave of dread hit me since I would have to face Dave.

Kevin M. Courtney

CHAPTER 26

For the first time in three months, I was not excited to be coming to work. It was as if a black cloud had descended over JPD and it just wasn't going to move. Well, there was no sense being a sissy about it; after all I thought, *you're gonna be fired anyway.* I walked into the locker room and there was Dave putting on his vest. He greeted me with no hint of anything between us and so I said nothing and just went to my locker. Dave made small talk and I cautiously answered him, wondering where this was all leading. Probably trying to get my guard down so it will be easier to cut my throat.

I found out fairly quickly that while Dave had a fearsome temper, it was also very short lived. He did not hold a grudge about the other night and talked to me about it with no animosity. He actually laughed when talking about hollering for me and my not hearing him. I was feeling a lot better about things but still was worried about the internal. Dave told me not to worry; you work hard and lock folks up, you end up with internals. He pointed out that we didn't do anything wrong, so we had nothing to fear. He was right about nothing to fear as we were cleared of wrongdoing although when he said it I wasn't so sure he was right.

The next week passed pretty uneventfully for us. We did come across one of the local winos standing in the middle of Milwaukee Street just past Michigan Avenue one afternoon. The wino, one Brinkman Bronson, was drunk enough to be standing in the street but still sober enough to want to make life difficult for anyone with whom he came in contact. In this case, that would be me, because Dave had said, "Get his dumb ass out of the road before we have to take a fatal accident report." I got out expecting to just escort Brinkman to the sidewalk and then get back to crushing crime and dodging danger. No such luck.

Brinkman took one look at me who was still about 10 feet away and opened the negotiations with, "What the fuck do you want?" I kept my cool and said, "Why don't you come over here to the sidewalk and I'll explain it to you." Brinkman had a better idea and explained it to me by saying, "Why don't you kiss my ass you stupid motherfucker" and I noticed he was also balling up his fists. Now I was hung up between whether to continue to show my patience or to show that I don't take shit all day from drunks standing in the middle of two lanes of traffic on a busy street. Dave was standing off to the side, letting me handle the situation, so I knew what I did would matter a LOT.

I went with "no more shit" and told Brinkman, "You need to get out of the street or you're going to jail." Brinkman having heard that before said, "Well then come and get me you big asshole." Now I was not quite so interested in what Dave thought but rather was real interested in bouncing this fat-mouth drunk onto the sidewalk. My Irish temper was coming up and I was sick of getting fronted off, so I took a few quick steps toward Brinkman and reached out for his arm to pull his sorry ass out of the street. Brinkman decided that wasn't happening and pulled away telling me "keep your fucking hands off me."

That hit the ignition button on my temper and before Brinkman was really clear on what was going on, he was sprawled across the hood of the patrol car getting his arm twisted behind his back and handcuffs put on. I was mad now and said, "I tried to be nice to you, but no, you got to get a case of the ass with me. So now you can go to jail and tell all your bunkies what an idiot you are." Dave just lightly touched me on the shoulder and said, "Be cool, just stuff his ass in the car." I immediately chilled out and thought, well, I guess that makes us even, although I really wasn't planning on thumping on Brinkman anyway.

I completed the booking sheet and carefully typed out the disorderly complaint and warrant, not wanting to make any mistakes, and Dave made a point of telling me I'd done a good job. That was important, and the incident seemed to wash away any lingering tension over the whole DeRosa fiasco. We headed over to Evanoff's after our shift that night and things were nice and relaxed. A couple of the other new guys were there also, so it was a good night all around.

CHAPTER 27

The next shift Dave gave me crap about being so worried about the incident at the pursuit. I had forgotten that Dave's wife worked at dispatch and so of course the word filtered from Julie to Dave's wife to Dave. Dave seemed to appreciate how serious I took the whole situation and showed it by yanking my chain. We were both testosterone-filled cops, so we weren't going to light some incense and get in touch with our feelings. We did what men do in situations like this: we make light of it and abuse each other so we know things are cool between us.

I had been doing a pretty good job of staying on Julie's social calendar, and we had a date to go to the county fair on our upcoming days off. Central dispatch assigned shifts and days off in much the same manner as JPD, so from a social standpoint it helped my cause that she got the same crappy shifts and days off I did. I picked her up at two in the afternoon and we headed down to the fairgrounds, which were located in the city along Ganson Street just east of Blackstone. I loved fairs for a couple of reasons. Even though I was a skinny 150 pounds at the time, I had the appetite of a 200 pound lumberjack and loved all the junk food fairs produced. I truly believed anything that started with "deep fried" was worth trying at least once. Plus, when I was a kid, I never had the money for such luxuries as fair food. Now that I had a job and money, I was free to indulge.

The second reason I loved fairs was to look at the draft horses, especially the Belgians. I'd grown up with stories of how my grandfather had farmed with horses right up until he died in 1943. That was 14 years before I was born, so all I had to connect me to my

Grandfather Courtney were the stories my dad and aunts and uncles told. I especially loved to hear about the horses. My grandfather had owned Percherons also, but his favorites were the Belgians so those were the ones I had to check out. I used to tell people that some day I would have a farm and own Belgians, but when a 22-year-old says that it really doesn't carry much weight. I didn't care; I knew I would do it just like I had known I would become a police officer.

The only negative to the whole fair experience was I could not ride a carnival ride much faster than a merry-go-round. If there was any spinning or flipping involved, I was going to hurl. I simply couldn't handle any of the typical gyrations of most fair rides. I always blamed it on the fact when I was eight years old I had gotten sick at Birch Run's little summer fair and ended up getting my appendix out. Regardless of the cause, a man could not impress his date if he blew lunch on her lap. It was always touchy when explaining the "no ride" policy to a date, though, as one's manhood could be challenged.

Julie didn't seem too worked up about the issue, so I was looking forward to walking around the grounds with her on a bright, sunny afternoon. I had money in my pocket and a beautiful girl on my arm, so things were definitely looking up compared to the start of the month. We wandered around the fair and I managed to put a curb on my usual "eat a stray dog" appetite while still getting my share of Fair staples like elephant ears and French fries with malt vinegar. Julie and I tried a few of the carnival games, and each time we did I had a real urge to file check the carnie running the game, as I was sure most would have outstanding arrest warrants from somewhere. Looking at a couple of them, I wouldn't have been surprised to learn farm animals were involved in their crimes.

Julie didn't seem to mind when I dragged her off to the horse barn to check out the draft horses. I even managed to chew the fat with a couple of owners while we were walking through. All in all it was a pretty good afternoon indeed. Julie and I had headed out on to Ganson and started walking west to where we had parked when I happened to look across Ganson at eastbound traffic.

I saw a car with several young Mexican males in it just as the passenger behind the driver saw me. The man immediately pointed at me and said "That's him" so clearly I could hear him. All heads in the car turned to look at me, and I immediately reached under my t-shirt for the butt of my gun. I told Julie to "keep walking and if I tell you to run, you run like hell away from me." Julie was oblivious to what was going on and was clearly thinking "What the hell is this whack job talking about?" I was fixing my eyes on the car and apparently my move under my shirt sent the universal message of "I've got something for your ass" loud and clear because the car kept driving east bound and made no attempt to turn around.

I explained myself quickly to Julie and then didn't waste any time getting to the car. I was thinking this girl is going to toss my ass to the curb so fast it'll make my head spin for all the crazy shit I'm putting her through. Still, she appeared to be handling things pretty well, so I wasn't completely without hope. We went on to grab something to eat and she really didn't make much of a fuss about the incident. I wasn't used to this but, then again, I had never dated anyone for more than about two weeks so my frame of reference wasn't all that good. My buddies at college used to joke that they never bothered to learn my girlfriend's name because they'd only see them once more anyway. It wasn't quite that bad, but I did have a little attention deficit problem.

I decided to not report the fair incident since I really wanted the whole situation to go away, but I didn't think that was all that likely. In fact, things got a lot worse when the prosecutor dismissed the assault charges against the guy Dave smacked. It seemed that the two state troopers made it very clear that the people the city officers pulled off them were indeed there to help the troopers and were not interfering with the troopers at all. To say Dave was not pleased was like saying Nixon had issues with telling the truth. I took a little different view. I figured the troopers were telling the truth, but I also rightfully assumed that the two "helpers" still had had a legal obligation to step back when told to and so Dave's arrest was good. Of course I was just a dumbass rookie, so my opinion was not exactly highly sought after in the court house, or any where else for that matter. In fact, for the first six months on the job, most people in the court system looked at rookies with a "who the fuck are you?" expression on their faces when the new hires showed up for court or to sign a warrant.

Kevin M. Courtney

CHAPTER 28

The Jackson Police Department had a cadet program that employed several young people between the ages of 18 and 22. These cadets worked the desk, wrote parking tickets, handled very minor calls, and did a variety of non-critical services for the Department. In return, they were paid a salary and had their tuition and books paid for up to the completion of an Associate's Degree at Jackson Community College. The idea was that they would be hired as full time officers when an opening occurred, provided they had the two year degree and had performed up to standards while a cadet.

Each shift had a couple cadets assigned to it, and one was always assigned to cover the desk, answer phones, and handle non-emergency radio traffic such as keeping track of lunch breaks, looking up warrants the Department held, and making the occasional phone call for an officer on the street. If a second cadet was on duty, they went on the street to write parking tickets and handle very minor complaints. Unfortunately for me, in late July and August there were several days no cadet was available to work the desk so I got stuck there. I was not at all happy because I would not be on the street doing real police work, and the desk bored the hell out of me. I would also have to deal with Lieutenant Johnson who scared the crap out of me. Although normally the desk job was boring, it would be anything but on August 6th. This would be one Monday I would never forget working the desk.

Just a minute or two after 10:00 pm, I heard dispatch send units to the Tastee Freeze on Prospect for an armed robbery and kidnapping that had just occurred. At the same time, there were a couple of officers in the booking area with Lieutenant Johnson processing minor arrests. I immediately got on the building PA and advised them of what was going on. The two uniforms did the hot foot boogaloo out of the station and Johnson came up to the front after quickly stuffing the prisoner in one of the two holdings cells in the booking area.

I gave Lieutenant Johnson an update of what I knew as soon as he got up front. Almost at the same time, the first unit, Det. Jim Conant and Howard Noppe, who was working with him that night, arrived on the scene. The two quickly learned that two suspects, described as black males in their 20's, had forced their way into the Tastee Freeze at gun point. The victims also described the suspects as carrying drawstring bags. In the shop at the time were the owner, a male employee, and 17 year-old Paula Samuelson. The robbers quickly took the males' wallets and asked where the money was. The owner did not hesitate in telling them where to find it, but for whatever reason the robbers did not go get it.

The two suspects, one armed with a sawed off shotgun and the other with a .38 caliber revolver, walked all three people from the Tastee Freeze out of the store and to one of the employee's cars intending on kidnapping all three. Paula was placed in the car first, and at this point the other two intended victims saw their chance and made a true run for their lives. Both managed to escape screaming for help every step of the way. An employee of the bar across the street from the Tastee Freeze, alerted by the screaming, saw the car the suspects had stolen go north with its lights off, and he jumped in his car to give chase but his car stalled several times and he lost sight of the suspects as they fled north.

The suspects must have realized their plan was in the toilet as they fled with Paula, a high school girl from Vandercook Lake, a small town just south of Jackson. She was a beautiful girl with all the hopes and dreams of any 17 year old living in a safe community, working at the typical teenager's job, when without warning she was swallowed up by pure evil.

Det. Conant was the first officer on scene and as a result became the officer in charge of the investigation until relieved by a higher ranking officer. Conant quickly relayed the basic information about the suspects, vehicle, and victim, and requested a blockade. The only problem with this request is that it had to go to the State Police Operations Center in East Lansing, known as ELOP, via JPD

Headquarters and not central dispatch. JPD HQ at that time was relying on one Kevin Michael Courtney, who three months ago couldn't find his way home and now was expected to handle a critical request in the middle of a major crime. I had a real feeling for how Custer must have felt at the Little Big Horn.

A blockade was a police tactic that had been around since the 1930's, and the plan was to place officers at likely routes away from the city where a crime had occurred at a sufficient distance from the crime scene so the blockade could go up before the suspects reached that location. The idea was that offenders fleeing from a given area would likely follow the same main routes the average person did when driving from one city to another. As a result, blockades requested by Jackson went up closer to places like Ann Arbor, Lansing, Battle Creek, and Adrian. Blockade points in and around Jackson in return went up when serious crimes occurred in those communities. The decision to implement a blockade and which points to employ was made by the State Police and used officers from all the agencies in Michigan. It was one example of everyone being on the same page and working together in an emergency.

Blockades were not very effective and rarely resulted in the capture of criminals but they did on occasion work, and when a 17-year-old girl had been kidnapped, any and all means to find her and return her safely to her loved ones would be employed. Besides, much of police work involved failure and using tactics that weren't guaranteed to work, but in the absence of something better the cops would continue to do what they had always done the same as in every other profession known to man.

I told Lieutenant Johnson that the unit on scene wanted a blockade requested and that I didn't have the vaguest idea of how to do it. Johnson snapped at me, "Get the LEIN manual from behind you and look it up." LEIN was the state wide computer system used by police to send messages between agencies and to run checks to determine whether someone was wanted, to check vehicle license plates, and to verify whether someone had a valid driver's license. How to actually use the machine was not something that had been part of my training to date. I only knew how to give the information to a dispatcher via the radio and have the dispatcher run LEIN for me. Little or no training on desk duties was provided for new officers; we were simply a warm butt to throw in a chair when no cadet was available.

I wasn't exactly getting applications from Mensa but I knew that Lieutenant Johnson snapping at me meant he likely didn't know a goddamned thing more than "it's in the LEIN manual." I already had developed a bit of an attitude towards him for an earlier incident when I was stuck on the desk. The cadet from day shift had left a novel on the desk and when I found it, I picked it up and was in the process of marking the page it was left open to when Lt. Johnson saw me and jumped on my ass about wasting time on "extraneous junk" when I could be studying work-related items. I pointed out the book was not mine and I was simply clearing it off the desk. He later tried to justify his response but I wasn't buying it. The funny thing was that Lieutenant Robert L. Johnson eventually would become Chief, promote me to sergeant and lieutenant, and become one of my greatest mentors, role model, and a trusted friend. At this point, however, he was just a miserable s.o.b. that I could do without.

I grabbed the manual and found the phone number for ELOP because now was not the time to try and show how smart I was by doing things step by step, as though I were assembling a freaking Christmas bicycle. It was time to get things done and if the hard ass lieutenant did not like my methods, well then he could stick some other poor bastard in here the next time there were no stupid cadets working.

I dialed the number and a civilian State Police employee answered. I gave it to her straight; the Jackson Police Department had just had an armed robbery and kidnapping and I was a rookie with not even three months on the Department and I didn't know if I was on foot or horseback when it came to running LEIN let alone getting a blockade order issued. That might not be the best thing for maintaining one's pride, but all I wanted was to get the freaking blockade issued and not completely screw the pooch at this critical time. The lady at ELOP got the message and didn't screw around with proper procedure and simply told me to tell her all the information I had regarding the crime, suspects and victim. She copied that down and said, "Stay on the line. I'm going to get the blockade issued and then get back on with you."

I was relieved I had made the call and lucked into a pragmatic, common sense person and not some by-the-book jerk. The MSP employee came back on the line and she walked me through sending a message via the LEIN, so all the "I's" got dotted and the "T's" got crossed. We were both happy. I got the blockade issued and she had an official teletype message for her records. I thanked God for putting at least one practical thinker at a state agency.

Once the blockade was taken care of things quieted down in the radio room a bit, and I had time to consider the situation. I said a prayer for Paula but I had a sick feeling in the pit of my stomach that this night was going to get worse. It made me both angry and sick that something like this was happening. I didn't give a rat's ass about all the psycho babble that so called experts and apologists used to try and explain people like the men responsible for this crime. I knew, as maybe only an Irish Catholic taught by nuns can know, that the two assholes who did this were evil in every sense of the word. They were proof to me that true evil was not just an imagined entity but a force that motivated acts that were so reprehensible there could be no other explanation. I didn't give a shit either what anyone thought; they could tell me it wasn't the bad guys fault until they were blue in the face, but I knew these people were evil and chose to follow that path just as I and every other good cop in the world knew it was our job to take them out of society.

It only took a short time before the magnitude of the crime brought all the Department brass into the station and for the phone to start ringing off the hook with calls from the local media. I stayed busy telling the media nothing and pissing them off which really didn't bother me in the least. I might only have been a cop for three months but I knew as well as a 30 year veteran that given the slightest opportunity the media would do all they could to make the cops look bad. There were also a variety of requests from units in the field for phone calls that I needed to make since "cell phone" in 1979 meant the pay phone you got to use just before getting locked up.

Kevin M. Courtney

CHAPTER 29

I was on the desk when the early cars for the midnight shift started filtering in for the start of their shift which was 10:40 p.m. and they began asking me for the scoop on what was going on. I gave them what I had along with the suspect information so they could join in the search. I was struck by the obvious distress the news of the robbery and kidnapping had on one veteran officer named Ed Casad. I figured Ed must have known the family or something because the news of the crime obviously bothered him a great deal. I asked one of the other officers if that was the case and the reply was, "No. It's just this kind of stuff really hits Eddie hard." I decided right then a guy that cared that much for strangers was okay in my book any day.

Finally, at around 1145 p.m. another of my fellow rookies, Scott Rogers, reported finding the car used by the suspects to make their escape in an alley in the 100 block of West Wesley. Scott had been searching for the car in his marked unit but had been called back into the station to switch to an unmarked car so that a third shift officer coming on duty could have the marked unit. Scott stayed back from the car, which he thought was empty, and waited for back up thinking the suspects might be in the area. Scott was all ready on solo patrol because of his prior experience as an officer.

Additional units swarmed to the location and the decision was made to begin searching the houses in the immediate area. As the officers moved forward, Scott saw the lifeless body of Paula in the back seat of the car. She had died instantly from a single shotgun blast to her heart. She was also shot a second time, although it was completely unnecessary. Finding her dead was a kick in the stomach to all the officers involved. Most all of them had seen victims of senseless violence and, to be blunt, often times those victims were not much different than the suspects when it came to lifestyle and behavior. That was not the case here. Paula was truly an innocent victim who had done nothing to deserve this.

The news of finding Paula dead took the air out of the station and although I had never met the young woman I felt a sense of loss. She was only five years younger than I was so I could still see myself at that age. Not only that, I had grown up in a loving and supportive extended family and could only imagine the pain and heartache that her murder would cause.

When Paula's parents, who were waiting in the station's historical room, were given the news, the cries of anguish I heard that night pierced my very soul. It would not be the last time that I would hear such pain in my career and on more than one occasion I would be the person to deliver the news. I could not possibly begin to understand the loss Paula's parents had suffered, but hearing what they were going through left a lasting impression on me. I realized what an enormous responsibility officers had in making sure those responsible for such a terrible crime were held accountable and, if at all possible, in preventing these acts from happening in the first place. I was just a dumbass rookie and not really part of doing that now, but I would be soon and I would not forget the lesson this night had taught me.

The Department threw every resource it had at the investigation into the murder. State Police assistance was also requested in the form of a tracking dog, and more importantly, the Michigan State Police Crime Laboratory, which at that time was one of the best in the country and would respond to the scene of major crimes anywhere in the state. The Jackson County Sheriff's Department was also helping, and their Detective Sergeant John "Stubby" Southworth was a major asset to JPD investigators because of his extensive contacts and knowledge of local criminals.

This crime was not some local druggie getting done in by a thug associate, nor was it a domestic dispute gone bad; those are crimes the general public can understand and in most cases, not really fear since they pose no real risk to them. This crime was different. It *did* present a risk to community members and their loved ones. It wasn't someone who "had it coming." It was an innocent young girl with her whole life left to live. The community was shaken and many a police chief has found the unemployment line for not properly responding to situations just like this. No community can accomplish anything if its people don't feel safe, and the only ones who can maintain or restore that feeling are the police. Politicians know that and so don't hesitate to toss a chief out on his ear to show the public they won't let the community's security and safety be compromised.

Chief Rice was not about to drop the ball on this case, and he made it abundantly clear to his command staff he didn't want any excuses. He wanted these assholes locked up and didn't give a shit what it took, but everyone, had better understand there was NOTHING that took precedent over this case. The Chief was known to be blunt and to have a short fuse, so no one on his staff was confused about what would happen if they did fail. Fortunately for the Chief, JPD was a very professional department with hard working street cops and some excellent detectives so he was turning loose a pretty good pack of hounds on the trail.

Kevin M. Courtney

.

CHAPTER 30

The next day I came on duty looking for updates on the case and was not disappointed. Fairly quickly the investigation focused on Timmy Mays and John "Skeeter" Williams, two local criminals. Detective Sergeant Southworth had contacted JPD officers early in the investigation and advised them that he was looking at the two as suspects in the armed robbery of the Mr. Steak Restaurant outside the city a few weeks earlier. Other tips had come in and the most promising was from the owner of the riding stable located in Sharp Park, which was just south of the Tastee Freeze. The owner told detectives that he was leaving the stables about 8:00 pm when he observed two black guys acting suspicious near the Stable. He looked them over very good and recognized one of them as Timmy Mays. The other guy hung back near some trees and the owner did not recognize him. His description of the guy matched the victims' and the owner also noted the two were carrying drawstring bags similar to those the robbery victims described.

At around 5:00 pm, Bachman, Scott Rogers, Stubby, and I were detailed with information that the pickup of Mays and Williams had been authorized. All four of us were assigned to go pick up Timmy on East Mansion at his parents home. My heart was literally beating out of my chest. I was headed out to arrest a murderer who was not some drunk who went off and killed his woman, but was a cold blooded killer who I must assume to be still armed and willing to harm me or anyone else. I'm not ashamed to admit I was scared, and I said a prayer as we headed south from the station. This was the first time in my brief career I truly believed that I might become involved in a shooting.

Many people have the wrong impression about fear. They assume it is paralyzing and makes the person experiencing it a coward. That can happen, but in truth it is fear that kicks in the "fight or flight" response in all animals including man. Fear causes the senses of hearing and sight to actually become more acute, blood to flow to the major muscles used for running and fighting, and for the person to become more attuned to his or her surroundings. I was experiencing that phenomenon completely as we headed for Mansion Street. The brave man is the one whose fear creates the fight response, and I was hoping that would be the case with me. It was comforting to know that I was still in great shape if the "flight" response won out.

My trepidation was largely unwarranted. Timmy was at his parent's house and we arrested him with little fuss or fanfare. Bachman and I took custody of him and transported him back to the station. It was a very strange sensation for me to think that this guy in the back seat had less than 24 hours earlier snuffed out the life of a completely innocent young woman. It was very unnerving for someone who had grown up like I did to be in such close proximity to such evil.

We weren't at the station very long before we were sent looking for John "Skeeter" Williams. He had apparently called and talked to one of the detectives and made it clear he wasn't coming in to talk to nobody about nothing. It struck me as pretty stupid of him to not haul ass out of town after committing such a crime, but clearly these two were not criminal masterminds who had done a great deal of planning. They were just ordinary street thugs who with little thought committed a despicable crime and then had nowhere to go but the same places they always went. They weren't even smart enough to get the cash bag from the Tastee Freeze before they left.

The first place we headed to was the apartment of Skeeter's girlfriend in the 900 block of Maple in the south central section of town. Along with Bachman and I were Roger Ramirez and Scott Rogers. There was no one at the apartment when we arrived but a guy sitting on the porch of the house told us the girlfriend, Carol, had just run to the store and would be right back. We waited for a few minutes before Dave, who would never be described as patient, said he was going looking for Carol. He left me guarding the back door and Ramirez and Rogers at the front in case Skeeter was in the crib and decided to make a break, or if Carol or Skeeter were to suddenly show up.

The old adrenaline kicked in again, as I was in a position where if something was to happen at my location it would be on me to respond. When you are a young cop, your mind races with the possibilities and mine certainly was no exception. Fortunately, Carol showed up a just a few minutes after Bachman left and then he pulled in right behind her. Dave took the lead talking to Carol, who was accompanied by her brother William. Dave got her permission to go in and search the apartment. She stated that "Skeet," as she called Williams, was her boyfriend. Dave was careful to clarify with her that it was her apartment and who stayed in which rooms. She told Dave that the bedroom was hers and that Skeet just stayed there with her from time to time. He did not live there nor did he pay rent.

All of this would be of critical importance based on what happened next. William reached into the bedroom closet and began pulling out all sorts of interesting stuff like the murder weapon, a .38 revolver, and a draw string bag with the two male victims' wallets in it. Once the initial shock wore off, Bachman stepped in and took control of the situation, but it was clear we had just hit the mother lode. Dave's questioning was critical because it established that Skeeter had no expectation of privacy under the Constitution, and so the search was legal and the evidence would be admissible in court.

Investigators found out later that Carol did not want to stop when she came back to her apartment and saw the police there. Fortunately for us, William persuaded her to stop and get things taken care of. He wanted his sister out from under the whole mess and saw cooperation as the best thing for her. He was of course right as Carol was an unwilling player in the whole scheme of events. Timmy and Skeeter had come to her apartment after the robbery and murder and dumped all this shit on her. She was lucky to have a brother who had the courage to act and to do it without hesitation.

Later testing would find Skeeter's fingerprints on the plastic photo carriers in both wallets and Timmy Mays' prints on the .38 revolver, which although not fired in the robbery matched perfectly the gun the victims reported seeing.

Unknown to the officers at Carol's apartment, Skeeter was enjoying his last minutes of freedom just three blocks to the east while this search was underway. Information came in that Skeeter was at a residence at the corner of Everhard and Morrell. Carol's place was near the corner of Maple and Morrell. I had jumped in a car with Carl

Roberts because Dave was still tied up dealing with all the evidence William had offered up. Carl and I drove to where Skeeter was reported to be. Detective Conant and "Stubby" from the Sheriff's Department also went there with us.

Skeeter was sitting on the porch eating a sandwich when we pulled up. All of us exited our vehicles with weapons drawn and I vividly recall Conant telling Williams to put his hands up. Skeeter was less than cooperative and Conant told him, "This ain't no bullshit Skeeter, get your hands up." Skeeter decided he'd rather finish his sandwich, at which time Conant grabbed him and took him to the ground with Carl and Stubby jumping on him for good measure. There was no room for my skinny carcass in the dog pile, plus I had a pump shotgun in my hands so I kept my eye on the bystanders who didn't seem too interested in jumping to Skeeter's defense. My theory on that was they knew what this was all about and figured, considering the level of force the cops were showing, now was not the time for demonstrating any kind of solidarity with that stupid motherfucker Skeeter. Considering what he had done, I suspect they were surprised he didn't get his sorry ass capped by the cops.

CHAPTER 31

I felt a real sense of pride to have been even a small part of these arrests. Those two had breached the peace and security of Jackson in the worst possible way and, as guardians of the peace; it was the responsibility of the Jackson Police Department to respond. I felt the Department had really stepped up and done a fast and professional job in getting these evil bastards locked up. I knew that I was little more than an observer and just got incredibly lucky to be involved in both arrests. I also felt good that while the blockade wasn't effective, I didn't turn it into a complete cluster. Even though I wasn't much of a factor, I still took pride in the Department's work done on the case. I considered myself a Jackson Police Officer and, like any team player, took pride in my team's success no matter what my role was.

The case against the two was solid but due to the amount of publicity surrounding it a change of venue was granted and, in a strange coincidence, the trial was moved to Saginaw County, my home county, that winter. That benefited Tom Lafferty, Sr., my hometown buddy's dad, who was a potential juror for the case. He wanted no part of being on that jury, so he was very happy to be able to say he knew me, that I had helped arrest the two accused, and so he had no doubt they were guilty. That got him excused without any problem, which pleased him greatly. He did say later he felt a little guilty lying since in truth he never did trust me or that goddamned kid of his either.

Even though convictions were pretty well expected, the trial wasn't without drama. At one point while Prosecuting Attorney Ed Grant was addressing the Court, the suspects suddenly raised a ruckus, causing the judge to hit the courtroom alarm, the court house to go into lockdown, and deputies to pounce on the defendants before, as they say, there was "Order in the Court" again. Once order was restored, Prosecuting Attorney Ed Grant would go down in Jackson Police lore when he calmly looked at the two defendants and said, "Nice try assholes." While that made him a hero to every cop who heard about it, it didn't win him points with the Judge. In fact later, when the two appealed their convictions, the Michigan Court of Appeals would call Grant's conduct reprehensible but would rule it was not cause for reversal. I bet those judges secretly pumped their fists at the thought that someone actually said what they all had thought about some scum ball killer at one time or another in their careers.

The bottom line is the two were convicted and sent to prison for life without parole and to be forgotten about fairly quickly by the majority of Jackson. They would, however, never be forgotten by the family they caused unfathomable grief, the men they terrorized, or the police officers who hunted them down and saw them held accountable for their evil deeds. Here it is 30 years later, and the harm they caused lives on. I'm not sure what that means; I just know it doesn't seem right.

·

CHAPTER 32

A week or so after our charges from the pursuit got dropped, a few of the boys were down at Evanoff's and Howard was ripping on the troopers for what they had done; I tried to cool him out a little but didn't have much luck. Howard was a great guy but once he decided something, his mind was not going to be changed. I learned that any form of disloyalty was something Howard could not tolerate. I didn't know if this came from the Marines or somewhere else, but if Howard thought you had stabbed someone in the back, you were dog shit on his heel for the rest of your life. I could certainly understand that attitude, but I just didn't see the troopers as being all that treacherous by telling what they believed to be the truth. I was smart enough, however, to not waste a lot of breath trying to convince Howard of the error in his thinking. Besides, I admired his loyalty and knew I could count on it too.

I was really starting to enjoy working with Dave and the month was flying by. I had definitely learned a great deal about getting things done from working with him and was gaining more and more confidence each day. Dave also introduced me to a non-approved method of target practice on Mansion Street near the City's Water Treatment plant.

The area was full of groundhogs and Dave loved to sneak up on them and shoot them with his service revolver using practice ammunition. Groundhogs, a.ka. woodchucks, weren't particularly bright, so if you scared them into their dens within 30 seconds to a minute they would pop back up to see if the coast was clear. That presented the perfect chance to take a shot at them, which we did on several occasions, knocking off enough that it helped keep the ground around the area from looking like Swiss cheese. I continued the practice after getting out on my own before deciding the trouble it would cause if I got caught wasn't worth the risk.

Bachman also gave me some fashion advice that I appreciated. He told me to get my uniform shirts tailored. Dave explained they will fit a lot better and you'll look more professional. I had to admit Dave was a handsome bastard and looked a lot better in uniform than I did, so I figured it was worth the shot. I had just enough conceit in me to want to look sharp. Besides, I still considered myself single and looking better for the ladies was important.

I had noticed an ad in the church bulletin for a lady who did tailoring and alterations out of her home, so I gave her a call and made an appointment to drop over to get the shirts done. Joan Larsen was a young married woman who lived on West Franklin just past West Avenue and was happy to help me out. The extra bucks she made doing this kind of work helped out a great deal, as she and her husband were raising a family on a single salary. Joan was a little taken aback by the Kevlar vest I put on so she could properly mark up my shirts, but I explained it was sort of like a seat belt. You wear it all time but probably will never need it. I joked that if I did get shot, I promised to hire her to sew up the holes. I'm not sure she really liked my humor at first, but over the years she became a good friend and always had a smile for me.

I was very happy with the results when I got the shirts back and promised to recommend Joan to any of my fellow officers needing work done. I also explained I was single, so I would likely be bringing over more than just my uniforms. Joan teased me that now that I was all spiffed up, I likely wouldn't be able to stay single much longer.

Chapter 33

I found out that in September I would be going to day shift. I didn't exactly welcome the news, as I envisioned days as quiet and sedate with lots of older laid back officers. Nice if you didn't like to work, but hell if you were all about chasing felons and having fun. I tried to sweet talk my sergeant, Dave Zomer, into keeping me on afternoons but Zomer told me the variety and change of pace would do me good. He also told me not to worry too much because I'd likely be back on afternoons sometime next year. The good thing about going to days was that I would probably start getting a chance to work on my own after I had been there for a few weeks.

Sergeant Dave Zomer was probably one of the nicest guys on the Department and I hit it off with him right away. Zomer had made Sergeant in just 4 years, the minimum necessary to be promoted, so naturally that pissed off a bunch of people in a department like JPD where seniority was king. Zomer was a Vietnam veteran who had gone to Michigan State and was a pretty good athlete. He also had a great sense of humor and loved to laugh. He had grown up in Kalamazoo and was Dutch like so many people on Michigan's west side. The standard line over that way was, "If you ain't Dutch, you ain't mutch."

Zomer had become a good Baptist but was still known to play poker with the boys or deal a little blackjack while knocking back a beer or two. I was never quite sure what Mrs. Zomer would think of all this, but I admired the Sarge for having the nads to take the risk. I later met Mrs. Zomer, and while she was a lovely and sweet woman, I could understand not wanting to incur her wrath.

Kevin M. Courtney

CHAPTER 34

Bachman was going to be off on his vacation for a week towards the end of the month and told me not to worry about it because I would be working with Jim Syrek. Dave told me "Jim is a good officer and a lot more patient than me; you'll learn a lot from him." Dave then told me, "Look I've shown you how I do police work and what is expected of a good police officer, but you've got to do things the way that fits you best. You can learn something from everyone you work with, even if it is how NOT to do something. I've got bad habits up the ass and so don't repeat those, but make sure no matter how you do things that you hustle and show people they can count on you."

I listened to what Dave said and realized he was right. I was my own man with my own ideas on how I should be doing police work, but at the same time I had so much to learn that at times it seemed an impossible task. I found myself wondering exactly what kind of cop I would be and whether I would ever come up the standards of guys like Roger, John, and Dave. I decided if I didn't it wouldn't be because I didn't give it my best shot.

I was told that Syrek's nickname was "The Viper" because he was silent but deadly. I wasn't sure about that since the guy seemed so laid back and quiet I figured there was no way he could be deadly in any sense of the word. Not that I would want to tangle with him. Jim was a solid, square-built guy who looked like he would make a fine football lineman with a little time in the weight room. He was a very competent and conscientious officer and a great person from whom to learn. He not only was very quiet, he also had the patience of Job. If Jim Syrek arrested you for disorderly conduct, you freaking well deserved it and must be a complete asshole, since he gave everyone two extra chances to move on and not get locked up.

I was a little unnerved at first working with Jim because he was so quiet and I liked to talk. After the first shift, the Viper relaxed a little and began to talk with me quiet a bit. He was married and was very proud of his family and mentioned them quite often in conversation. He emphasized to me that he saw the job as pretty easy as long as you kept your wits about you. His philosophy was that most times people just want someone to listen to their side of a dispute, so if you give them a chance to vent their frustration you likely will take care of the problem without taking anyone to jail or fighting with people. He pointed out that those fights, while they may sound cool, get police officers hurt a lot more often than they do suspect--a fact that the media ignores whenever they do any kind of investigative reporting on "police violence."

CHAPTER 35

Jim and I were sent on a call of trouble with a possible 10-13. The code 10-13 meant "mentally disturbed" and was one of the few "10" codes the Department still used. In the old days, every call had a "10" code but since they were a pain in the ass to remember, like most all Departments, JPD had switched to using plain English. I assumed in this case it was to keep everyone in scanner land from knowing who was nutting up. Jim and I drove to the call and made contact with one Thelma Hays, a black woman about 28 years old who was clearly having mental health issues. She was hearing voices and having real trouble staying tight with reality, although she did have lucid moments and could answer the usual basic questions.

The procedure for dealing with seriously mentally disturbed people at that time was to transport them to the emergency room at one of the two local hospitals where an M.D. would examine the person to determine if he or she came under the provisions of the Michigan Mental Health Code. The code basically allowed involuntary commitment of people if they were a danger to themselves or others, were unable to care for themselves, or were so disturbed they did not understand their need for treatment. If the M.D. found the person met this standard, the Doc signed paperwork to that effect and the officers transported the person to the Ypsilanti Regional Mental Hospital 45 miles east of Jackson. At Ypsi, as it was known, a psychiatrist would examine the person and if the head shrinker concurred with the ER Doc the person was involuntarily committed to the hospital for a minimum of 3 days. A hearing was held by the County Probate Judge, after the three day period, to determine what the course of treatment would be and if further confinement was necessary.

On the rare occasions Ypsi would not keep someone, the "patient" got a ride back to Jackson courtesy of JPD.

Jim and I managed to get Thelma into the car and up to the ER without much fuss, and once there she had little trouble convincing the Doc she was in need of treatment. Jim and I got the nod to take her east. Transports like this required two officers, so there was a "savings" to the Department when a rookie-assigned car handled a mental. I had never been to Ypsi so I was glad to have the chance to go on the transport. Jim's low key approach had a very obvious calming effect on Thelma and I was impressed. I also noted that Thelma readily called him Officer Syrek with obvious respect, so I guessed this wasn't her first contact with JPD.

The ride over to Ypsi was uneventful and went pretty quickly as the trip was expressway all the way. Pulling onto the grounds of the State Hospital, I was struck by the size of the complex and the number of buildings. It reminded me of a small college campus but, since I knew better, the place took on a depressing air. It obviously was not a welcoming place to Thelma as I could see the apprehension in her face as we drove up to the admissions building, which was a fair distance back from the main entrance. She might be crazy, but she knew what was waiting for her at a state mental hospital.

Jim and I made contact with the admissions staff and were told to wait for the Doctor. Thelma was obviously becoming very afraid of the whole place and process, and Jim was doing his best to calm her down. Thelma had tears in her eyes when she said, "Officer Syrek, I'm scared. I don't want to stay here." Jim told her that it hadn't been decided whether she would have stay but, if she did, he would walk her over to the ward himself. At this point I started getting scared and thought about crying myself.

I did not like the idea of "going over to the ward" at all. My mind was racing with images from "One Flew over the Cuckoo's Nest" and every other image of mental wards I had ever seen or read about. The size and foreboding nature of the place didn't help matters in the least. I actually started rooting for Thelma to get a return ticket to Jackson just so I didn't have to go with her to the ward.

The luck of the Irish apparently did not extend to lunatic asylums, so Thelma got admitted to the Hospital and Jim lived up to his word, the rotten bastard. The hospital employee assigned to take Thelma over to her designated building seemed mildly surprised at the fact the two officers would be accompanying him, but he wasn't the least bit put out. If anything, he appeared pleased that he had company. Once we arrived at the building Thelma would be staying in, Jim and I were advised we would have to lock up our guns if we went inside. I quickly said "No problem, this is as far as we're going," Jim on the other hand had a devilish smile and said, "We'd really like to go up to the ward if it's okay with you." The hospital guy was happy to comply and the next thing I knew we had locked our guns in a small security locker and I was walking into the middle of a mental ward completely unarmed. I was so scared all I could think about was how fast I might be able to get out of here. This time fear was definitely producing flight fuel, because my mind was screaming *"Run you stupid son of a bitch, RUN!"*

There were literally 40 people wandering around a large common room, jabbering, waving their arms, and doing nothing but sending my level of apprehension off the charts. Jim was getting quite a charge out of watching my reaction, but he still was truly there for Thelma and walked her over to the door that she had to pass through to reach her final destination. Jim was advised he couldn't go past that point, so he told Thelma she would be okay and to not worry.

Unfortunately for me during this time, I was approached by a wild-eyed man of about 30 who started talking to me with the speed of a machine gun. At first I just smiled and nodded at the guy, answering the few questions he fired off like: what's your name? why are you here? and where are you from? I got a little more attentive when the man asked me if I knew why he was locked up. I had a strong feeling that I really didn't want to know why this nut job was currently confined for the simple reason that it likely was not going to make me feel any better about being in a fucking mental institution.

I tried to slide by the whole issue by answering, "Because you want to get better, right?" Nice try but it had about as much chance of working as my former flamer of a fashion consultant had of joining the Hells Angels. No, the nice man pointed out to me, he was locked up at Ypsi for assaulting two police officers with a pool cue that was sort of like the ones over there on the wall. Yes, my fine Irish luck was that indeed there was a pool table and a fine selection of cues located in one corner of the common room. I figured with my current run of good luck, one of the other whackos, acting as this guy's bat boy, would bring him over his favorite cue when he decided to go to drumming on my skull.

At this juncture on the tour, I decided it was time to take matters into my own hands and jump out the window, my theory being a two story fall was better than the current situation. Fortunately, before I could act on this impulse, Jim showed back up and said "You ready to go?" like I was just hanging out chatting with the fellas instead of being surrounded by a bunch of freaking cue-swinging crazies. About then I wanted to grab a pool cue myself, and knock that shit-eatin' grin off the Viper's face.

Once outside, Jim asked me, "Now aren't you glad that we had the chance to see the inside of the place?" I said it was a great *one*-time experience and the only way I'd ever go back is unconscious or dead. Jim laughed and said, "OK, I promise not to make you do it again." I could see just how terrible Jim really felt and I proceeded to tell him what a low-crawling piece of white trash he was, which only made him laugh more and feel better about the whole night. The miserable prick.

I had to admit on the ride back that being inside the ward really made me understand what people with mental illness face, and it wasn't pretty. Thelma's fears were not groundless, and I began to wonder how she would get by inside. Maybe that is what that sneaky prick Syrek had in mind in the first place, and screwing with me in the process was just a lucky byproduct. Maybe that "Viper" shit had some truth to it after all.

CHAPTER 36

A few days later I would truly learn why Syrek's nickname was indeed appropriate. We were sent to a call on Teneyck Street, which is on the north side of C-23 district, for a family complaint. Seems one Paul Goodson was there and causing problems for his woman. Now Paul was a skinny black guy in his 20's who drank too much and rated pretty high on the stupid meter sober, so he was making a bad situation worse. On top of that, he could barely speak three intelligible words in a row without going into a mumble, and he always had an attitude with everyone but especially the police.

I could see Paul up on the porch of the house we had been sent to screaming and yelling at his girlfriend and waving his arms all over the place. The porch was about four or five feet above the yard so Jim and I had to climb a few steps to get up to Paul and the dispute. The back up unit pulled up, so Jim and I moved Paul away from the door where the other half was standing and left her for the other officers. Jim was using his normal, calm voice, saying things like "You need to settle down, Paul" and "Don't worry about what she's saying, just tell me your side of the story." Well Paul had enough booze in his veins and empty space in his head to decide he wanted a piece of that bitch's ass, and this quiet little mousy cop wasn't going to stop him. Paul's first move was to try and bull rush past Jim on the house side of the porch, but stout as he was Jim stopped that and said, "You need to calm down Paul" to which Paul replied, "Fuck you!" This time he shouldered into Jim with meaning as he tried to go past on the yard side of the porch.

Even though I was watching the whole situation unfold, I still couldn't explain what happened because it was over so fast. All I knew is that Paul was hanging upside down over the railing of the porch in the grasp of the The Viper. He was being told in the same calm voice, "I told you, you needed to calm down." All Paul could get out was, "Let me go you stupid Motherfucker," which is exactly what I would have done, letting his dumb ass hit the ground below. The Viper, however, calmly told Paul to put his hands behind his back and when Paul figured out that was his only way out of the situation, he complied and I cuffed him.

When I replayed the situation in my mind, I could see Jim grab Paul by the belt and collar and, with literally no more than a flick of his wrists, send one drunken idiot over the railing of the porch. There was no muss, no fuss, and no change in Jim's demeanor. It was just how a Viper strikes; silent and deadly. I could see without a doubt that Jim Syrek was no one to fuck with even if he wasn't the typical macho cop.

CHAPTER 37

The remainder of the month slid by and I found myself assigned to the day shift, which was run by Lieutenant Henley, a fine Irishman if ever there was one. The shift was very seniority-heavy. In fact, I was the only guy assigned to days with fewer than 8 years on the Department. I was just a little intimidated and also concerned, because afternoons had the reputation of being full of a bunch of wild-eyed young officers that the old timers wanted nothing to do with.

My first training officer on the day shift was Arnie Vasher. I hit if off with him right away because Arnie loved to hunt, fish, and talk. He was also a good cop and enjoyed having me along in the car. He had spent a fair amount of time working undercover in the multi-county drug unit and so had plenty of good stories for me, all of which I ate up. Not only were Arnie's tales fun to listen to, they also gave me a fair bit of information on how the dopers operated and what to look for on traffic stops. Arnie's brother owned a restaurant in Harrison, not too far from my family's summer cottage, so we had that in common too.

The two of us managed to stay out of any serious trouble, and after a few weeks Arnie suggested to the Lieutenant that he thought I could handle things on my own. Lieutenant Henley wasn't quite ready to turn me loose so assigned me to work a couple of days with Officer Glen Baremore, who worked one of the traffic cars.

Glen was a youthful-looking officer with a round face, a huge smile, and a quick, infectious laugh. His theory on traffic enforcement was if the violation was worth stopping a driver for, it was worth writing a ticket. He'd once written a single driver six tickets because the driver wasn't smart enough to shut his mouth. The driver kept talking and Glen kept writing. Most of the time, though, Glen's big smile and light hearted approach made people thank him after he gave them a ticket, whereas they'd be "motherfucking" any other cop who slipped them a biscuit, as tickets were commonly called by the cops who wrote them.

Glen and I hit it off pretty well, and I spent a couple of days running radar, watching intersections, and policing accidents. Glen told me I was ready to handle things myself and so he switched to the passenger seat and pretty much let me run the show on our last day together. He wasn't real happy when I let a couple of drivers off with warnings but said, "It's your call." Glen told the lieutenant at the end of the shift "the kid's ready" and Henley just nodded. I could start to smell the freedom of a one man car, but I also knew Henley wasn't convinced yet of my worthiness. Clearly, there was no ethnic brotherhood bonus involved in his decision.

The next day I was back working with Arnie, but Henley told me I would be assigned to the traffic car a few days here and there, starting in October. I told him thanks and tried to act cool about the whole thing when inside I was bursting with excitement at the thought of "being on my own." Those were the words that every rookie cop couldn't wait to hear because it meant you had measured up and were now trusted to work by yourself.

Chapter 38

The remainder of the month went by without a hitch, and I started off in October assigned to Dave McCollum, nicknamed "Big Mac." Dave was a rangy 6'4" and one heck of a basketball player even then in his mid 30's. He could shoot the lights out from 20 feet, was a solid rebounder and defensive player. He also lived up to the stereotype regarding white men: his feet had never been more than six inches off the ground in the last 10 years. He was therefore christened by Mike Brunk as having the greatest "no jump, jump shot" in the history of the game.

Big Mac was a good training officer for me because he emphasized staying out of the station and getting around and through as much of our section as possible each day. We were assigned to Baker 22, which was good because up to this point I had spent little time outside of Charlie 23 and David 24. I was learning the north side of the section had quite a nice residential area and it was a great place to work traffic. Folks just loved to speed down North Street and blow the lights the length of Cooper and Michigan Avenue. Coupled with the folks who had warrants on them along the southern edge of the section, an officer had no trouble staying busy working Baker 22 even on the day shift.

Dave did get a fair bit of mileage out of me over my wiping out one of the resident squirrels in Loomis Park while we were driving through. I swore I never hit the little limb rat, but Dave said the evidence was irrefutable and I was just try to duck having killed an innocent squirrel. I said I had been killing and eating the little rodents since I was old enough to go hunting, so guilt had nothing to do with it. I just wasn't going to take the rap for a crime I didn't commit. The dispute became standard banter between us and 30 years after the incident Big Mac still reminds me of my felonious driving.

The older officers on the shift enjoyed hearing the story and also got some mileage out of me over it. Not as much as they would get out of one of my fellow rookie officers who backed over an injured dog's head to put it out of its misery because he didn't think the Department policy allowed him to shoot it. Out of respect for my buddy, I just can't reveal his name, but he is known in JPD history. I just thank God it wasn't me.

The poor lieutenant that took that citizen call could hardly believe what he was being told. Of course the little old lady who watched the whole thing go down couldn't believe it either. She probably could have used some of my good Irish whiskey in her tea after seeing that little bit of police work unfold. That was the kind of shit that ended up on your police epitaph no matter WHAT else you did in your career, so I was more than happy to stick with my rap as a squirrel killer.

One of the favorite pastimes of the old timers on the shift was to talk about when I would be eligible to retire. Each of the senior guys could tell you down to the hour when they would have their time in, but for me it was not even a real date. The old timers loved to point out I wouldn't be able to retire until 2004. That was a different fucking century, they'd howl. I didn't understand what the big yuck was because I was in no hurry to go anywhere, but, hey if it made the old dogs happy, it was okay with me.

Big Mac invited me over to his house one evening to watch a World Series game, and so I brought along a 12-pack of beer figuring that would be plenty for the two of us. Wrong. Dave had the ability to consume beer at a rate that would make the best pint drinkers in Ireland stand and cheer. I had four out of the 12 and Dave the other 8 in the same amount of time, while showing no obvious change in demeanor or behavior. I would learn this was child's play for Dave and that he was capable of much greater intake while still showing no change in personality. This was a rare thing since most people who consume that amount of alcohol hit one of several stages, which include happy drunk, everyone's buddy, know it all, asshole, or unconscious. Big Mac skipped all that and just stayed Big Mac.

CHAPTER 39

A few shifts after the game, I got my big break. I would work T-30 on my own. I came into work grinning like an ape, and even the old timers got a kick out of seeing a rookie so charged up. They immediately started in on me during detail and suggested to the sergeant that the lieutenant must have lost his mind to let this dipstick out on his own. They then tossed in the friendly advice of "don't get things all fucked up and expect me to come save your ass." They were all smiling and so I knew that the abuse was good natured and intended to let me know they were happy for me and that I was one of them.

I went out to the car with a real spring in my step and did everything by the book. I checked the car thoroughly for any contraband that might have been left in it. I checked the shotgun to make sure the magazine was loaded and the chamber empty. I calibrated the radar unit, and I made sure the siren, loud speaker and all the lights on the car were in working order. Calling in service that day was a major charge when I only gave my badge number instead of mine and a training officer's, as I had done the previous four months. That said to everyone on main radio channel, "Hang on. Courtney is out here and ready to kick ass!" To the dispatcher it said, "Here's another one of these crazy new guys who's gonna be driving me nuts making traffic stops and running file checks all goddamned day."

The dispatcher was right because I wasn't out there 10 minutes when I made my first traffic stop for speeding on North Street. Suddenly I realized everything was my responsibility and I had no "partner" to bail me out. This made me even more alert as I approached the car. I always tried to be tactically sharp on traffic stops and while handling calls, but I realized when there was a training officer present, you could afford to make mistake here and there. Well the safety net was gone and I knew I had to step up not only for my safety but for the safety of every officer on duty at the time.

I was tempted to ask the driver to have a photo taken with me but figured that would be over the top, so I just wrote the ticket and sent him on his way so I could bag another one. I stayed busy the whole shift making traffic stops and handling accidents. All in all it was a good day, and I was pretty proud of myself when I came off duty. I ran into some of the second shift guys who were assigned early cars when I got off duty at 3:00 that afternoon, and I tried to act nonchalant about being on my own but it didn't work. They could see I was geeked and teased me about the city no longer being safe if I was out there without supervision.

I drove home that afternoon pleased with what I had accomplished, but I wasn't getting too far ahead of myself. I was assigned a "T" car again tomorrow, but then the next three days I was back in the car with McCollum working Baker 22. I thought of the things I had to do to become a good police officer. On the mundane side I was getting better at military time, which the Department used exclusively. It was basically just a case of numbering the hours 1 through 23, but for whatever reason 1700 and 1900 screwed me up. I figured the fact that 7:00 pm sounded like it should be 1700 and not 1900 was the reason for the confusion. On the more serious side was the habit of putting my hands in my pockets once things relaxed on a call--a big mistake since your hands are what will save your ass 99 times out of 100. Sgt. Larry Finton, who was on second shift when I started, used to get on my ass about it all the time and I had broken the habit by the time I started working with Bachman. Still, I was conscious of it, and didn't want it slipping back into my mannerisms.

This police work was serious business and I realized, not for the first time that, in the not too distant future, I would be responsible for all my decisions and actions as a Jackson Police Officer without the benefit of a "coach" looking over my shoulder. I didn't take the thought lightly, but, at the same time was confident enough in myself that I was looking forward to the challenge.

Chapter 40

Julie and I were dating regularly by now and I was quite happy about that. I sort of liked this steady dating thing and not having to try to impress anyone. Julie seemed pretty happy with me just as I was, with no desire to change me. That seemed to baffle my buddies on the Department, but I wasn't complaining.

Julie and I had begun hanging out quite a bit with John Stressman and his wife, Beth. We weren't much different in age, and Beth was just very spontaneous, and boisterous--the exact opposite of her tight assed husband.

Towards the middle of October, Gary and I decided we should have a little dinner party like normal people, as opposed to the all-out drunken displays of degeneracy we had been so happily involved in during our four years of college. Gary was dating a cute local girl named Lisa, and so the plan was to have her, Julie, and the Stressmans over for a spaghetti dinner on a Tuesday night, when we were all off duty. Although, Julie had to go into work that night at midnight, it wouldn't be a problem with a low-key event like a simple dinner.

Even though Gary and I didn't work the same shift much in our first couple of years on the Department, we did get the same lousy days off so we socialized quite a bit together. Gary was always a lot of fun to be around because he had a quick wit and had an off-beat sense of humor you just had to love.

I should have suspected the dinner party was not headed in the right direction while I was cooking the spaghetti sauce. Since I was Irish and not Italian, I had bought a couple of jars of Rago. Had I been a good dago, I would have known how to make sauce from scratch, but since I was Irish I only knew how to sing, drink, and fight. I did buy some extra goodies like good ground beef, mushrooms, and wine to add to the store-bought sauce to fix it up a bit. The wine is where the problems started.

My roommate Gary saw the vino jug get opened up and assumed he would be given a glass. I told him to back off; the wine was for my cooking and, besides, it was only 4:00 pm and too early for Gary to start hitting the booze. I pointed out dinner wasn't until 7, so Gary needed to show some self control. He was completely offended. He went so far as to put his hand on his hip like a swish and say to me, "You bitch. I'll get my own." I figured I better give him a glass of the wine to avoid getting slapped and if he was going to have one, I should too.

That was the beginning of a series of bad decisions. After a glass or two of wine, Gary reached up on top of the refrigerator and pulled down a bottle of Jim Beam and poured himself a healthy portion over a single ice cube. He then shook an empty glass in front of me so I said, "All right you cheap slut, I'll have one just to make you happy." Right. And Hugh Hefner is going to bang "just one" playmate.

Well, we managed to get rid of about half of the bottle of Cousin Jim by the time the guests arrived. Julie figured it out right away that we had been boozing, but Lisa wasn't quite onto our act yet. John needed no encouragement to have a taste of old JB before dinner, and of course Gary and I couldn't let the boy drink alone. Dinner was actually very good and my sauce surprisingly tasty after my modifications. John and Beth both like good wine so they brought a couple of bottles with them that promptly got consumed with dinner.

After dinner, the serious drinking started and, pretty quickly, our limited supply of booze was depleted. This called for a run to the liquor store around 9:00. It was decided that since Julie wasn't drinking, she should drive the other two ladies into town so provisions could be purchased. John, Gary, and I kicked back in the apartment and were swapping lies when the phone rang. I grabbed it and heard Beth ask for John. John took the phone, and quickly turned ghostly pale, and started making very short replies like "what" and "where are you" and "where's the car" that let Gary and me know something was definitely not right. The conversation went on for just a short time in the same manner until John said, "very funny" and hung up.

John had a look on his face somewhere between pissed,

embarrassed, and relieved when he said, "My wife just had me believing that she had been in a minor accident and had gotten locked up for drunk driving. You'll be pleased to know your girlfriends were laughing in the background when she finally coughed up that she was joking." I thought that was pretty funny; but clearly John wasn't nearly as impressed.

Gary and I at first were amused by the girls' ruse, but on further reflection decided it was just not right. We decided gender loyalty demanded that we help John get even and restore a little of his manhood. We had a fairly large supply of bottle rockets, and so we laid an ambush for the ladies in the parking lot next to the apartment building. It didn't take long for the girls to pull into the lot and starting walking across towards our apartment door. Our timing was good and the "rockets red glare" went streaking past the unsuspecting victims with the exact desired effect. All three screamed, and Lisa even dropped a bottle of Vodka in the parking lot causing it to shatter and spill its precious liquid all over the asphalt. We took an ass chewing for that, but after a little more shouting and screwing around we headed back into the apartment.

The ladies had brought back substantial provisions for serious liver damage even with the parking lot casualty. With all this good booze, we collectively decided that Julie needed to join in on the festivities. The problem was she was scheduled to report for work in 2 ½ hours. That problem was solved when all the drunks she was with convinced her to call in sick, pointing out with typical drunk logic she hadn't missed a day in five months of work and the dispatch center wouldn't miss her on a Tuesday night anyway. It turned out to be the only time in a fourteen-year career she would ever call in when she wasn't sick. It would also be the only time she ever listened to one of Gary's or my dumb ass ideas, but on this night she succumbed to peer pressure.

With the last restraint removed, the party really got rolling. Finally, at around 3:00 am, I figured out that I had to be in the station in three and a half hours, so I might better try getting some sleep and hopefully sober up a little. That broke up the party and the Stressmans headed for home. Sobering up and getting some sleep were both good ideas, but I was about four hours and a half gallon of wine, whiskey, and beer late. The alarm sounding at 6:00 am confirmed this.

Kevin M. Courtney

.

CHAPTER 41

I dragged myself across the hall to the shower and was hoping it would help my condition, but all it did was make me a clean victim of a full-fledged fatal hangover. My condition probably couldn't be completely classified as a hangover as I probably still had enough alcohol in my system to fuel a Bunsen burner. I felt bad enough to consider slitting my wrists, but my hands were shaking too hard to unwrap the razor blades. Shooting myself would be far too noisy with my current headache, so I dragged myself outside for the drive into work.

At the station it took my fellow officers all of about eight seconds to figure out what was ailing me, and they started right in on my sorry ass. That was bad enough, but I would have to face Sergeant DeWayne Kope, a rigid Baptist who was known to still lock people up for profanity in front of women and who saw alcohol as the devil's brew. This was not the man for a rookie officer to show up in front of shaking like a Michigan Avenue wino coming out of the DT's.

I did my best to get my shit together and make it through the 20-minute detail without ending up on the wrong end of a Baptist's righteous fury. Sergeant Kope, good man that he was, immediately saw I was not looking good and asked, "You all right Courtney?" I nodded and said, "Yeah Sarge, just a bit of flu but I'm feeling better." This caused all sorts of guffaws and remarks about the origins of this flu being self-inflicted, but fortunately that all seemed to go unnoticed by Kope. I was relieved but too shaky to even say the drunk's prayer of, "Just get me through this one Lord and I'll never drink again."

Fortunately for me, this was one of the days I was assigned to work a traffic car on my own so as soon as I got out of the station and into the car, I headed for a party store where I bought an orange soda. Previous experience told me slowly sipping this both "cooled the pipes" and put some of the sugar back in my system that the excessive alcohol had depleted. I then parked my car under a tree up on North Street and set the radar to automatically lock in on cars traveling over 42mph in the 25 mph zone, my fervent hope being no one would go by me that fast. I was lucky twice. First, no one wanted to speed this morning and, secondly, there were no accidents reported so I was left completely alone for the first two hours.

I was allowed to suck on my orange soda, curse the rotten bastards I was with last night who were still asleep, and gradually shake off the effects of my world-class hangover. I figured I owed the Department a little something for the two-hour sabbatical, so once I got past 9:00 a.m. and returned to relative human form, I spent the remainder of the shift humping pretty good, so that by the end of the shift I had written a fair number of tickets and handled a few calls for officers who were tied up with other calls in their districts.

.

CHAPTER 42

I was looking forward to a nice, quiet nap when I got back to the apartment, but that wasn't in the cards. I was met in the apartment by Gary, who asked me how the day had gone. I said it was rough the first few hours but I'd managed, and now I was going to take a nap. Gary said don't count on it. The manager says she's going to evict us unless you go up to her office and engage in some serious ass-kissing.

"What the fuck are you talking about?" I asked. "Well, according to her she had over ten complaints about our wild party last night and she had me out in the parking lot picking up broken glass and bottle rockets at 8:00 am," Gary replied.

"You gotta be shitting me." I said in disbelief.

Gary added, "That ain't the half of it, the old lady that lives above us started calling every 10 minutes beginning at 7 am to see how we liked to be woke up when we are trying to sleep. Seems the apartment manager thought it would be a good idea to give her our number when she called to bitch at her about the party."

I was having a hard time getting my arms around how a gathering of six people could cause so much upset. Jesus, I was at a college parties that had that many people in the bathroom let alone at the whole freaking party. Well, I figured the quicker I went up and tried charming the manager, the sooner I could get some freaking sleep. I decided these people must all be tight-asses to complain about a little dinner party.

I was, of course, overlooking two very salient facts. First, the party was on a weeknight when all the normal folks (non-cops) went to bed early because they had regular jobs. Second, drunks have another stage I had forgotten. It was called loud. Alcohol seemed to have the effect of magnifying the power of one's vocal chords and, of course, if one person is talking loudly, the next person has to talk louder to be heard. This didn't even take into account the bottle rockets, the result was the little incident in the parking lot was probably loud enough to piss people off in the complex half a mile down the road, let alone in Gary's and my building.

I went to the manager's office, which just happened to be conveniently located on the second floor of our building, and while I still had the remnants of a hangover and never really liked having my ass chewed, I figured I better play it low key. The manager apparently had just used Gary as a warm-up because she started right in taking a piece of my ass over the "outlandish drunken orgy" that she'd had over 20 calls on this morning. I was about to say if there was an orgy I was damn sorry I missed it but figured keeping my smart-assed Irish mouth shut was probably the best call at this point.

The manager then went on about the huge mess and hazard she found in the parking lot and how it just could not be allowed to happen and, if it happened again she would not hesitate to evict us. She tossed in she didn't care if we were cops or not. This rubbed me the wrong way and my bad temper started up, but I curbed it and managed to only say to the manager that where my room mate and I worked was none of her concern and I would appreciate it if she stopped giving out our *unlisted phone number* without our permission. That seemed to give the snarling old bat pause, and she calmed down a little. I saw my chance and said, "We're both sorry it got a little loud last night and you won't hear from us again." I then walked out and headed back to the apartment.

Gary was all ready sacked out and I did the same figuring all in all it was worth it. I woke up from my snooze about 6:30 that evening feeling like a new man and soon was headed off to get something to eat. I was thinking about December, it would be safe to toss another little social gathering--and maybe even invite the neighbors this time to see if that might not chill things out a little. Besides, Becky was a real looker even if she did bring her old man with her.

CHAPTER 43

The remainder of the month I spent working with Big Mac and getting a few more days in the traffic car. I was told I would be going to midnights the first of November and I wasn't really looking forward to that, except for the fact the plan was I would do a week with a training officer and then would be on my own permanently. That part I was anticipating quite happily.

Neither my anticipation nor happiness would last long. Just a couple days later, I got served with the papers saying Bachman and I were being sued for a million bucks over the state police pursuit fiasco. Now I wasn't sure if I would have a career long enough to work on my own. I was ready to stroke out and resign, but the captain said not to worry about it. It's the price of being a cop and the city will cover you anyway. I chilled a little, but I didn't like the idea of going to court as a defendant. Not one bit.

After calming down, I did recall my sister Cheryl telling me right after I got the job that with my temper she gave me six months tops before I was in federal court for brutality. Well, she was wrong. The suit was filed in state court. Shows how much she knew.

Thankfully the suit was settled out of court a year or so later for a relatively small amount of money and I kept my job. It also turned out to be the one and only time I was sued in my 27 year career. Thank God.

Kevin M. Courtney

CHAPTER 44

Night shift is a real bitch on cops for several reasons, not the least of which it is just not normal for human beings to be up from midnight to 8:00 a.m. Humans are diurnal animals and so staying awake when your body wants to sleep, combined with the lousy eating habits night shift encourages, are going to cause physical problems--not to mention most of the time you're about as pleasant to be around as a grizzly with hemorrhoids. There are also very few normal people out wandering around after midnight, and that means pretty much everyone you deal with is a drunk, a nut job, an asshole, or some combination of the three. That tends to give night shift cops a very skewed view of the world. You want to see burnouts and lousy attitudes? Go to the night shift of any urban police department--the hours and working conditions could make Mother Teresa a problem employee. Or as Brunk was fond of saying, "There once were two brothers. One went to sea and one went to nights. Neither one was ever seen again."

I saw one good thing about going to nights: Howard Noppe was on the shift, so I would not be the only rookie assigned among all those grizzled veterans. Nights was as seniority-heavy as day shift. The only difference is by and large most of the night shift officers had lousy attitudes. That included the lieutenant who had so much fun laughing at me my first night on duty when I needed some help getting back to Gary's parents house. One of the Sergeants assigned to the shift was Cliff Sampson a grizzled, profane, hard drinking old-timer who would rather be in the horse barns at a harness track than in a police uniform, but trotters and pacers didn't pay the bills and JPD paychecks did. The only good thing is that since he didn't give a shit, unless you really screwed the pooch he didn't much care what you did while you were on his shift.

The lieutenant was much the same, except if you screwed up he'd throw you under the bus in a heart beat if he thought it would keep his ass out of trouble. Fortunately, he had enough of his own problems with the brass that it kept him too busy to spend too much time screwing with the troops. I figured I wasn't going to be doing anything other than what I was supposed to do anyway, so his attitude was not really an issue for me to worry about. Besides, the lieutenant got the weekends off and I didn't, so we'd only see each other three days a week.

I came onto the night shift at the end of October. This was always a great time for me, as it was late fall and that meant the Michigan firearms deer season would open soon. I loved to hunt and I was figuring that working nights would let me hunt afternoons and evening on days I worked and all day on my days off. I lucked out in that Julie had an uncle who owned 300+ acres out past Parma, in the western part of the county and he had offered to let me hunt there except on opening day when there would be a lot of relatives on the place. I was just happy to have a place to hunt and, besides, I had to work opening day anyway.

CHAPTER 45

The first week on nights I was assigned to a couple different officers for sort of a "check out" flight, and when I came back from my days off I would be on my own. First up for me was Dean Schuette, better known as "Spot."

Schuette got his nickname from the fact he had numerous blue spots on his face around his eyes. These were the result of a firefight in Vietnam in which a North Vietnamese Army soldier's backpack full of explosives blew up, badly wounding Dean and permanently scarring his face with his distinctive blue spots. It didn't take a rocket scientist to figure out that the NVA were on the losing team that day and who fired the shots that caused the backpack to blow up. The fact that all of that was the source of a nickname was proof of what type of sick humor that was common place in a police station.

Spot was also known for having the most active mind of any member of the Department. He was a card carrying member of the BOAS and was always inventing ways to keep himself from being bored. That usually meant some form of practical joke or other juvenile behavior that everyone, besides the brass, thoroughly enjoyed. On top of all this, he was one fine police officer and a guy you wanted next to you in a tight spot.

The only thing I had heard previously heard about Spot was that he drove my fellow rookie, Karl Ankrom, just about nuts during the time they spent together. One of the ways Spot invented to keep himself occupied on the night shift was to see if he could pick up enough returnable bottles in a shift to pay for his lunch every night. The deposit on pop and beer cans and bottles in Michigan was 10 cents, so Spot needed about 30 a night to make his plan work. The first night he had Karl in the car, they were coming up Francis Street at about 1:00 a.m. when Spot pulled hard to the curb and yelled. "There's one."

Karl was so startled he didn't know whether to shoot, spit, or run for his life. He was looking for anything from an armed felon to invading Russians when he finally was able to croak out "What?" Spot said, "Right there. Don't you see'em? There's two empty Coke cans." Ankrom about went nuts. That crazy fucker had almost given him a heart attack for 20 cents worth of goddamned returnables. As a former Vietnam vet himself, and more mature and self confident than the normal rookie, he wasn't going to take that shit. He told Spot if he wanted the fucking cans, he could pick them up himself. Spot just laughed and got his cans. He didn't take Karl's insubordination personally and proceeded to kid him about it the remainder of their careers. Unfortunately, it got Karl a bit of reputation as hard to get along with, which he wasn't. The fact was he was a bit sensitive about how people viewed him, and unfortunately it took a little while for him to live down the reputation with some of the folks on the department. None of his fellow rookies had any problems with him, and I couldn't ask for a better friend, so the "can incident" didn't leave much of a scar.

By the time I started working with Spot, he had given up picking up empties so I avoided the whole issue. The truth was I was not above making some quick cash, and I probably would have fought Spot over the money when it came time to turn in the empties.

Along with a ridiculously active mind, Dean had a great sense of humor in the "Monty Python" style, so I considered myself lucky to be assigned to work with him. He and I were working C-23 and were coming down Michigan Avenue westbound when we stopped for the light at Milwaukee Street. Just a block north was Amanati's Party Store, and we both just naturally glanced towards it. Party stores don't have the nickname "stop and robs" for nothing, so cops always give them the once over when they pass by one. At JPD we were also expected to stop in and chat with the counter help of the stop-and-robs in our sections. It helped create some cooperation and made the workers, many of whom were young females, feel more secure. Dean continued to drive westbound onto Glick Highway when the light changed, and we were just approaching Mechanic Street when Dispatch called and advised us of an R/A in progress at Amanati's. "RA" meant Robbery/

Armed, and the mere words caused an immediate adrenalin dump to any officer hearing them.

Dean let go with an emphatic, "Shit!" and then stomped on the gas and cut left on Mechanic so he could circle back to the store. Due to the one way streets in that part of town it was not simply a matter of turning around and heading back to the store. Still, he had us approaching the store from the south in a matter of less than 60 seconds. I had the shotgun out as we approached and Dean stopped the car in the middle of the street about 25 yards south of the store.

I was experiencing the tunnel vision that often occurs in critical situations like this and was focusing on the front door and the area immediately in front of the store. I literally had to swivel my head to take in the whole scene. It was just two months ago that armed robbers had murdered an innocent young woman so I had no reason to not think people just as violent wouldn't be at this location. I certainly didn't want to shoot anyone, but I wasn't going to get hurt either by not being ready to deal with whatever some shithead wanted to throw at me.

Both of us had the doors of the car open and using them for cover when I saw the door of the store fly open and a man carrying a sawed off shotgun coming boiling out. The man was looking north of the store and away from us but I had started to take aim just in case he turned towards us. Just at that moment, Dean started hollering, "Don't shoot, that's the owner." About that time the owner looked south, and saw the patrol car and immediately put the shotgun down in the parking lot. He figured while he knew a lot of the cops, he didn't know enough to count on not getting his ass blown away running around with a sawed-off shotgun when they're all geeked up looking for an armed suspect.

The owner quickly made contact with us and advised us that we had just missed the robbers, who had fled on foot going north on Milwaukee Street. He gave us a description of the suspects who were wearing Halloween masks and were both armed. I got that information out on the radio as quickly as possible and other units flooded the area looking for the suspects.

It was an interesting phenomenon that even though they were supposed to work the areas outside of the city, both county and state units had a habit of coming into the area of a hot call that occurred in the city. They were no different than any other good cop. They liked the excitement of a major crime and lived for a chance to lock up serious bad asses like these two armed robbers.

Even with the help, the additional units searching did not locate the suspects, and so the case would be turned over to the detectives. Dean complimented me on my handling of both the situation and shotgun. He said he especially appreciated the fact I hadn't shot the store owner, even though the dumbass deserved it for running out in the street with a freaking sawed-off shotgun. I never really considered dumping the guy because of the lack of a direct threat, but I too was glad the guy put the gun down. I didn't want to hesitate if it was necessary to shoot, but I also didn't ever want to be trigger happy.

In an odd twist of fate, the robbery ultimately was hung on one Steven Mays, brother of the Tastee Freeze perp Timmy Mays.

CHAPTER 46

I remembered a conversation I had with my big brother Stan. Stan was 10 ½ years older than I and although as my big brother he was someone I looked up to, we really didn't get close until I was in high school. Stan did a lot of carpentry work when he was laid off from the Buick factory, which was pretty common in the mid '70's, and my brother-in-law, Steve, and I worked with him. Mostly we did siding, roofing, and concrete work but on occasion we built a garage. Just as importantly, Stan taught me how to drink, play poker, and hang out with his buddies. Even though it angered our mom to no end, these were key skills that I would continue to use throughout my adult life.

Stan had been in Vietnam and, while he rarely talked about it, I figured out he had seen his share of combat. We were b.s.-ing about police work at ma and dad's house back in August, after I'd been on the job a couple months, when suddenly Stan got serious and said to me, "Listen, I know how you think but don't be pulling any of that hero shit. Keep your stupid ass behind cover and don't hesitate to shoot if some asshole pulls a gun on you. Your job is to come home alive and don't fucking forget it. I ain't burying your ass, you understand?" I was almost speechless but finally came up with, "Don't worry big brother. I'll be careful," with a big grin on my face. Stan shook his head and said "Yeah right. Once again I'm wasting my wisdom on you." The truth was I had listened and Stan knew it. We both just hoped it was unnecessary advice.

After another, and uneventful, shift with Spot, I moved on to Ed Casad. Ed was a massive man about 6' and all of 300 pounds, with hands the size of hams. He was definitely fat but he had been quite a high school athlete. One of the guys who grew up with him told me that when Ed was in high school he went about 225 and could dunk a basketball with two hands. Ed liked to chew on a cigar and was just a big old softy, even though he had a gruff voice and was intimidating as hell. I remembered Ed's reaction the night of Paula Samuelson's murder and I still held him in high regard for it.

Ed's approach to work was "don't get too excited" and "don't arrest anyone unless they really ask for it." You had to do some serious asking to get Ed to lock your ass up. He took his calls and went about his business, but he wasn't going to set any new standards for self-initiated activity.

Ed was a huge sports fan and very easy to talk to, so he and I hit it off very well. All of our calls were pretty routine, and I came to appreciate Ed's easy way of talking to people. He showed the people he dealt with respect and never pushed them into corners, and as a result Ed got along with just about everyone he encountered. I was realizing that was a whole lot better than trying to fight everyone you dealt with, but still I figured you needed to be a little more aggressive about going out and doing your job. I still learned from Ed's approach, however, and always respected him.

The two of us were sent to a domestic on South Elm near Page, and I just knew that a family argument after midnight would involve at least one if not two drunks. That made for difficult negotiations, since getting a pissed off drunk to do anything reasonable was next to freaking impossible. Ed let me handle the call, and when we knocked a woman came to the door and said she and her husband had been arguing and that he had pushed her. I asked where he was and the woman said he ran upstairs when he saw you guys pull up.

I asked the most important question right away, which was, "Are there any guns up there?" and unfortunately the answer was, "I don't know." The next question was "how much has your husband had to drink?" which of course got a firm "a lot" for an answer. Great. I peered up the stairway and saw it curved around to a landing at the top and that it was dark. I didn't necessarily mind that because I could shine my flashlight up towards the top and temporarily blind anyone who stepped out into the beam. I was hoping no one would do that, but I knew enough about my luck to assume the crazy bastard up there probably had a flame thrower and getting him down wasn't going to be easy.

I started up the stairway, gun drawn and held at the low ready, with Ed behind me. A month ago our positions would have been reversed, but if I wanted to be out there on my own, I had to show I could take charge on a call. I was announcing our presence by yelling, "Police, come out where I can see you with your hands up," as we slowly climbed up the stairway. Each step up the stairs had my heart hammering louder when suddenly the male half of the complaint jumped from around the corner with one hand raised up over his head and something in it.

I immediately raised my gun screaming, "Drop it!" while trying to identify exactly what the idiot had in his hand. All of this was happening in milliseconds and what each of us decided to do at this precise moment could mean life or death. Lawyers, judges, and juries got to lean back in soft chairs and ponder and think. I had to see, evaluate, and act in less time than it took for a heart to beat once and then live with the consequences for the next 40 years.

I saw a flash of white and realized what the guy had in his hand was a clock-radio. This a split second before the idiot hurled it at my head and I needed to make a decision about whether to shoot him or not. I managed to duck the two pound missile, and I heard it smack against the wall behind me. Now I was pissed and had had enough of this asshole's game, so I charged up the stairway. I was not by nature an exceptionally courageous man, or even overly aggressive, but I had a true Irish temper and when I lost it I would do battle with anything or anyone. Such was the case right now.

I kept my gun drawn as I reached the top of the steps just in case the fool switched from clock-radios, to guns, but as I rounded the stairway I saw him standing in the middle of the room empty-handed. I ordered him to ground and at this point shit-for-brains apparently decided he'd pushed his luck far enough and complied. I held my gun on the guy long enough for Ed to make it into the room, and I then holstered my gun and cuffed the jerk. Ed told the guy he was lucky he didn't get shot doing stupid shit like jumping out in front of cops in the dark, but the drunk didn't seem to care. Bottom line was this was one domestic that wouldn't be a repeat customer tonight.

Once we got our prisoner booked, Ed and I wandered up to the front desk to shoot the bull with the desk sergeant. Ed made a point of telling the sarge how old Kevin didn't hesitate to draw down on the guy and then ducked the clock without even flinching. He said I was on the guy like stink on an ape before the moron knew what hit him. Praise like that coming from an old dog like Ed really would score some points for me and I knew it. I was even prouder when I heard Ed repeating the story in the locker room that morning as we went off duty. Ed and I stayed friends the remainder of my career and years later, when Ed passed away, I immediately thought of the flying clock call and how the murder of a young girl affected him so deeply. I'll not see the likes of him again and I'm a better man for knowing him.

CHAPTER 47

Sleeping the first week on nights was tough for me until I learned to make the room as dark as possible. I hung an oversized towel in the window that coupled with the drapes, made a big difference. It also helped that the apartment was halfway below ground so it didn't catch as much sunlight as would having windows at normal height.

I found out when I came on the shift that the old dogs had been on Howard's case pretty hard about damn near everything. Howard was a hard worker and wanted to get busy. The old timers didn't like that too well as it made them look less than productive. They apparently said as much to Howard in a polite fashion and he, in his typical blunt manner, told them to get fucked. Howard pointed that out he wasn't there to make them look good, a sentiment that went over about as well as a keg at an AA picnic, and the battle was on. No matter what Howard did he was criticized, and instead of trying to cool things out, he just fired right back at his critics.

Several veiled remarks were made to me about making sure I didn't act like Howard, or wasn't a hardass like Howard, and all I would say is, "Hey, Howard's a good cop and we get along fine." There was a fine line I had to walk between sticking up for my friend and pissing off the veterans on the shift to the point they started to jam me up. I did my best, but the bottom line was that I sure wasn't going to throw Howard under the bus just to get in good with the guys on the shift.

Besides, I really did like Howard. In fact, I jumped at his offer to head back up to Ferris for a night on our days off. Howard was dating an absolutely beautiful nursing student named Tammy who was going to Ferris. He met her while she was back home in Jackson for the summer, and he wanted to go up and visit her. Gary was up for a trip back to the old stomping grounds too, so the three of us headed north, as soon as our days off rolled around.

The plan was to get a room at a hotel and then head out for a little visiting, after which we would meet up at one of the college bars. Gary and I both still had friends at Ferris, and Howard was of course going to see his squeeze. Unbelievable as it was to Gary and me, Howard's new love interest was a very straight-laced, conservative Baptist girl who saw bars, alcohol, and cursing as bad things. Of course, former Marine Howard's life was pretty much made up of bars, alcohol, and cursing. How this relationship was going to work out was beyond the psychic capabilities of Gary and me to comprehend. Some might argue that going beyond our capabilities didn't really take a lot, but this situation did truly boggle the mind.

Once up in Big Rapids and checked in at a local motel, we all left the room with the agreement to meet at the Alibi bar around 10;00 which gave us hours to head off visiting. I had called a girl named Deb from Saginaw who I knew and went over to the house she and some friends were renting. Gary was off to parts unknown, and we figured Howard would be at his new squeeze's dorm room.

Deb's roommates were all home and studying, so she suggested we go somewhere else so as not to disturb them. I suggested we head back to my motel room since it was unoccupied and Deb agreed. I'd had no real "plans" up to this point, but I was thinking maybe I would have to revise my thinking. Deb and I were getting caught up on each other's lives as we walked into the motel and up to my room, and I was definitely pleased with the tenor of the conversation. I opened the door to let Deb in, and my mouth fell open when I saw Howard and Tammy sitting on the bed watching TV.

Howard of course looked at me with a sly smile and said, "Jeez, I didn't expect you back here. Come on in." I could not believe how quickly my luck had changed. I went from being alone with a beautiful girl in a motel room to watching TV with Howard and a Girl Scout. I could not get a break. Howard didn't make matters any better by constantly catching my eye and laughing at me or making comments that slipped past Miss Priss but hit me squarely below the belt.

I did my best to hurry Howard and Tammy out the door, but it was a blown opportunity. After the two finally did leave, Deb made it very clear to old Kevin that he couldn't just blow back into town after five months and have her throw herself at him. No, she made it clear she was definitely available but I would have to act like a gentleman and "court" her properly. I had to admit she was right and told her so. I said I would have to give it some real thought, so we sat around talking and then I gave her a ride back to her apartment. As I backed out of the driveway, I was thinking she was awfully sweet, but I decided I wasn't up to meeting her conditions.

I met the other two guys at the Alibi and thought Gary was going to hurt himself laughing as Howard recounted the motel scene. I had to admit Howard did not kill the story in the telling, and it was pretty funny to hear him recount the look on my face. I wanted to know what the hell Howard had in mind bringing a good Christian girl back to a motel room, and what the hell she was doing there with a scum ball like him. Howard took on a very pious look and said, "She trusts me because I'm a gentleman." This got a "You gotta be shittin' me," from both Gary and me but Howard just smiled adding "I can't help it you fuckers are jealous but it's the truth." With that, the three of us gentleman called for another round and spent a nice night drinking, laughing, and checking out the college girls.

Kevin M. Courtney

.

Gary had been getting terrible sore throats in October and November and had run out of sick time, which was pretty easy to do considering officers only earned one sick day a month. Gary was finally told by his Doctor that he needed to have his tonsils out. He got it set up as quickly as he could and scheduled it to try and miss as little work as possible. The operation was done at Foote West Hospital, and that night after his surgery I decided my roomie could use a little cheering up.

Gary's girlfriend, Lisa, couldn't get to the hospital to visit until 11:00 pm, which was way past normal visiting hours, so it didn't look like she'd make it up to see Gary at all. I came to the rescue and told her to meet me at the rear of the hospital at 11:15 after I came on duty and I'd take care of the rest. Lisa showed up as directed, and I said just look straight ahead and don't say anything. I then took her by the arm and walked her into the hospital and straight to the elevators. I had my best "serious cop look" on and no one bothered to ask me why I was walking this woman through the hospital. The same thing worked once we got on Gary's floor and I just walked Lisa right into the room. I said a quick hello and goodbye to my roomie and left Lisa there to visit with the boy. I felt a bit like a pimp as I drove away from the hospital and thought maybe that would be a good fall back career if the cop thing didn't work out.

I ran into my first "bump" on nights in the middle of the third week that I was on the shift. I was sent as a backup on a man-with-a-gun call in the 200 block of E. Franklin, and so using the good tactics I had been taught, I pulled up several houses short of the address where the gunman was supposed to be. I grabbed the 12-gauge pump shotgun from the rack and started moving towards the house. The other officer assigned was Chuck "Willie" Willinski, who pulled up in front of the address in question, walked up, and knocked on the door while I was sneaking and peaking my way forward so as not to get surprised by some gun wielding scum ball. My approach apparently was not standard procedure on the night shift.

Willie got no answer at the door and turned and swept the area with his flashlight. He gave me a strange look and mumbled, "Guess its GOA" and drove off--GOA being shorthand for "gone on arrival." I got the distinct feeling Willie thought there was something wrong with my response to the call, but I KNEW that Willie's response was freaking nuts. All a guy with a gun had to do was step out the front door of the house or out from behind the house and he could have shot Willie 40 times before Willie ever cleared his holster. That kind of approach to danger could get someone killed but not me if I could help it. I didn't give a shit what these old timers thought. They could do things their way if that's what they thought was best but that didn't mean I had to follow suit.

Chuck Willinski was different than most of the other officers. He pretty much came to work, did his 8 hours, and went home. He was married, had kids, and lived in a nice neighborhood just outside the city in Summit Township, but that was about all anyone knew about him. He wasn't hanging out at Evanoff's or playing poker with the boys. He was however as honest as the day is long and took care of his section. The thing that made him unique was he had a savant-like memory for cars and license plates. On numerous occasions officers gave dispatch a plate number over the radio only to have Willie call them and tell them the type of car it is on, where it was usually parked, and who owned it. No one had ever known him to be wrong. The joke was you could run LEIN but a "Willie" was quicker.

That morning after the shift was over I was standing at my locker putting away my gun belt and Kevlar vest when Willie approached and said, "You don't want to be like Noppe, running around pulling your gun all the time. You can't do this job if you're a coward." My first reaction was to tell Willie to go fuck himself, but I figured since I had to work with the guy that likely wasn't a good option. I instead just continued to put my stuff away and in an even voice said, "Look, they put a shotgun in the car for a reason. I figure that reason is to protect the officer in the car, so until they take it out of the car, I'll use it whenever I think I need it. If you don't want to use it, that's your business and I'll respect your choice, but I'm not going to get killed just to make you or anyone else feel better about the way they handle calls." With that, I closed my locker up and left the station.

As I walked to the car I figured that unless Willie was a completely clueless he would figure out I had more or less told him to "go fuck himself" only in more polite language. I wasn't sure what the fallout would be, but I was serious about not getting killed by being as nonchalant as Willie was. Besides I couldn't very well ignore the wisdom of my big brother, now could I? After all, he had so little wisdom to offer it would be a shame to waste it.

Kevin M. Courtney

.

CHAPTER 49

The next time I stepped on the toes of the "establishment" on the night shift left me more pissed off than the first. It was just a few weeks later and I was on routine patrol headed westbound on Glick Highway towards Wildwood when I saw the vehicle in front of me start to do the unmistakable weave of a drunk driver. I got excited thinking I was going to get my first DUIL (Driving Under the Influence of Intoxicating Liquor) arrest on my own, but I knew I had to calm down and do it right. I would have to be ready to testify in court as to the probable cause for my traffic stop, so I immediately began making mental notes of the fact that the car was crossing the lane markers and moving in and out of two well--marked lanes.

I took note of the fact that the car turned onto Wildwood from the center lane and did so without signaling. All of this gave me the facts I needed to initiate a traffic stop on the suspected drunk driver and which would support my decision in court if it came to that. All of this would become moot in 20 years or so when patrol cars would be equipped with on-board cameras that recorded all of what I was trying so hard not to miss.

I walked up on the car with my flashlight in my left hand, keeping my gun hand free. I am a total left-hander except when it comes to shooting firearms of any kind so it was easy for me to handle things like flashlights and nightsticks in my non-gun (left) hand. I kept close to the side of the car so it would be hard for an armed suspect to exit the car and acquire me as a target before I could see the threat and react. Plus, the bright, four-cell flashlight gave me an additional tactical advantage.

As I got up to the driver's door, one look at the driver told me I had hit pay dirt. The guy's eyes were bloodshot and he was already fumbling in his pockets trying to get his wallet out. I shined the flashlight on the driver and told him to roll down his window. The driver did and I thought I was walking past the brewery in Frankenmuth where my buddy Tom worked. The driver of course asked, "What's the problem?" and I said "You were weaving and made an improper turn."

I then requested his driver's license, registration, and proof of insurance. The driver gave a sort of whipped dog nod that said, "I'm screwed," and began fumbling again for his paper work. He managed to get his driver's license out of his wallet after going past it twice, but registration and proof of insurance were too much. He finally handed me a wad of paper from the glove box which included receipts, notes, expired registrations and proofs of insurance, which I sorted through to actually find the correct documents.

Once I got the proper documents, I ran a file check on the driver so that if the idiot was wanted for a mass killing in East Stinkweed, Arkansas, I would find out sooner than later. At this point, I asked the driver to get out of the car and escorted him around to the rear of the car and onto the sidewalk for our safety. The first test I requested was for the driver to recite the alphabet. I liked this test because it was a simple one and not affected by bad knees, bad backs, slippery surfaces, and every other lame freaking excuse drunks could come up with for why they were staggering all over the place when the cops tested them. I found it amusing that people all talked about how the cops made them recite the alphabet backwards, which was bullshit.

My man made it is as far as "O" before he hesitated and started over. The second attempt stopped in a mumble at around W. I then ran the guy through a couple of balance tests which he couldn't handle, and so I was confident I had one for the backseat. This was in the days prior to portable breath-testing equipment which could be used on the road side, so balance and dexterity tests were doubly important. The driver gave me no trouble when told he was under arrest, and once I got him cuffed and stuffed, I called dispatch for a tow truck to impound the car and requested an incident number for a DUIL arrest with more than just a little pride in my voice. I thought about posing for a photo with him like I would after bagging a trophy deer but decided that was a tad unprofessional.

I needed the number for the impound report along with my arrest report and so it was a free chance to announce to the world that yes, I, Kevin M. Courtney, was out here making the roads safe for the citizens of Jackson. Of course most of the citizens of Jackson were home safe in bed and didn't give a shit what Kevin M. Courtney was up to, but that didn't bother me or take anything away from my moment.

The wrecker arrived, as did a second officer who offered to write up the impound report for me and do the inventory search so I could head to the station with my arrest. This was pretty typical for officers to do for each other and it kept things moving a little more smoothly. On my way in I called the station on the admin channel to advise that I was enroute with one for DUIL. This was done so the lieutenant or sergeant on desk could call in a breathalyzer operator from the road if they weren't certified themselves. The old breathalyzer machines were quite complex and it took some fairly extensive training to be certified as an operator. The result was there were only about 10 people on the whole Department certified to run them. Conversely, today's new infrared machines are almost idiot proof and don't require that level of training, so almost every officer is trained in their use.

Officer Galen Terry was called in to run my drunk, and by the time I was done filling out the arrest report and taking the guy's property, Terry was ready to administer the test. The drunk was cooperative and gave a "good blow," meaning he emptied his lungs as he blew into the tube attached to the breathalyzer to collect the sample of lung air needed to determine an individual's Blood Alcohol Content of the driver (BAC). The best air for sampling was at the bottom of the lungs, so the longer the blow the better the sample. Two tests were given just for verification purposes and to give the drunk an extra chance to screw himself by providing even better evidence.

The test results for my boy came back .14 and .14. The legal limit for DUIL in Michigan at the time was .10, so I had a keeper by almost 1/2. I was relieved when I saw the numbers because the last thing I wanted was to have my first DUIL arrest have a BAC below the legal limit. I finished up fingerprinting and photographing the drunk, and the sergeant put him in the large holding cell in the booking area.

JPD had a large tank-type cell that could hold up to 16 prisoners, with a small isolation cell attached to it affectionately known as the "squirrel cage," and a one person cell separate from the tank. Only male prisoners were housed at JPD. Female prisoners were all housed in the County Jail. Our cells were generally only used to hold prisoners until the next arraignment at either 9:00 a.m. or 1:30 p.m., so usually the longest anyone stayed in there was overnight. Once in a while a prisoner was there over a weekend, but that was rare. Usually they would get bonded out or transferred to the county jail if the deputies weren't being pricks and would take a city ordinance misdemeanor arrest. By law, the county only had to take felony arrests and state statute misdemeanors prior to arraignment, but most times they would take an ordinance misdemeanor in special circumstances, such as when the poor bastard was going to be stuck in a cell with no shower or regular food for a weekend. JPD's idea of a meal was a hamburger from the Coney and a cup of coffee from the machine, so no one really saw a weekend at the city as a good thing. After I became Sergeant and was responsible for getting prisoners fed, I actually felt guilty enough about the lousy food to spring for an order of fries and a shake from Burger King out of my own money once in a while.

I was pretty happy with my arrest and the way I handled it as I headed back onto the street. I would tape record the report so there was no need to stay in the station. I spent the rest of the night doing the typical night shift work of checking commercial properties for break-ins and making a few more traffic stops for mostly equipment violations. These were good stops because drivers got no points or fines if they fixed the defect, and it gave officers a chance to file check the driver for warrants and see what the person was up to at 4 o'clock in the morning. Many a felon ended up in a jam because of a burned out headlight.

I was still feeling pretty good about things as I walked into the basement, headed for the locker room, when I was approached by Officer Galen Terry. Galen was a good sized guy with a constant grin on his face. He was known for the fact he would walk into detail most nights one minute after it started. That was mostly because he didn't pull into the station parking lot until two minutes before starting time. He did this so regularly the brass let him get away with it. It was known as being on "Terry time."

Galen put his arm on my shoulder and said, "You know you

don't want to get the reputation of being a dick out there." I couldn't figure out what the hell he was talking about and said as much. Galen said, "Well tonight's arrest was a little shaky and you don't want that reputation." I went straight to pissed off and said, "What the fuck do mean shaky. That was a good DUIL!" Galen gave me a big smile and said "Now don't get all riled up. I just mean .14 isn't that bad and maybe you could have just let the guy drive home. There's plenty of work to do without pulling in the borderline stuff." I was really hot now and simply said, "That was a good arrest and I'm not sorry I made it." Galen just shrugged and said "okay" and dropped the subject.

I wasted no time in getting out of the station and was smoking hot. It had taken all of about 30 seconds for Galen to ruin my positive mood. It wasn't until I was almost home that I figured out what the deal was. A lot of the old timers on nights at that time wouldn't lock up a drunk unless he ran over them or parked his car on the front steps of the station. If some snot-nosed rookie started bagging a few every week or so, the brass was likely to ask "Why the hell aren't you guys finding any of these?" I wasn't looking to make trouble for anyone, but I wasn't going to spend eight hours a night waiting to be sent to some bullshit call. Galen was a great guy and in his mind he probably did think he was doing me a favor but I sure didn't see it that way. The good thing was Galen and I got along fine during my career and we hunted together several times over the years.

Part of this was the attitude towards drunken driving. This was before Mothers Against Drunk Driving and all of the laws we have today. It just wasn't seen as the plague it is now and attitudes were much more lenient.

Still, that situation more than anything made it clear to me my place was on second shift, where you didn't have to explain doing more than the minimum. It also illustrated how you can literally have three different Departments in a single agency like the Jackson Police Department.

After working my way up through the ranks, I softened my view a little and realized you can't expect 20-year veterans to have the same hard charging attitude as new officers. The old dogs still need to pull their weight, but they will likely do it a little differently than the young pups, while offering some real stability to the agency. I also came to realize that the problem was seniority shift assignment.

Letting senior officers go to nights and stay there just breeds problems like what I experienced. A good department needs a mix of experience and fresh faces on every shift and some kind of rotation system that forces people to see a daylight shift at least once every year or two.

CHAPTER 50

Most cops early in their careers experience a situation where they get a little "badge heavy." Another name for this is the "John Wayne syndrome," where you think you can kick everyone's ass because you wear a badge. What happens to a lot of young officers is the authority of being a police officer goes to their heads and they behave in a manner that they later regret or which causes their fellow officers to wonder what the hell is wrong with them. Most of the time these officers recognize their mistake and straighten their ass up, or they are lucky enough to have a senior officer take them aside and politely tell them to knock that shit off. The final way they get an education is with an ass whipping from someone who isn't particularly impressed with the badge, the uniform, or the person wearing it. That's how I got my education.

I was sent to a fight in progress at the Tiger's Tap bar on Cooper Street and upon arriving found two guys who were brothers and one of their wives standing in the parking lot. It was obvious by their demeanor that there had been a scuffle of some type, but when questioned they simply told me everything was fine. Usually on calls like this, once officers see there is nothing wrong and that the situation was likely mutual combat, they send the nitwits on their way and report to dispatch the call was either gone on arrival or that it was a "citizen assist," meaning no report will be written.

It was drilled into my head during training on second shift to at least run file checks on the people at calls like this because you never know when you might get a warrant hit, and you also then had the people's names and information should something more serious be discovered after you have sent them on their way — say, for instance, the body of the guy they just beat to death. Most times, the folks you were dealing with handed over their ID and let you do your job so they could cruise on out of there as soon as possible. They understood the more they cooperated the less likely the cops would be looking for a reason to lock them up.

This was not the case with my folks in the parking lot. I asked for ID and they more or less told me that wasn't happening. They kept saying there was no trouble, they didn't need the cops, and I should just leave them alone. I took the bait and saw this as a challenge to my authority and since I had senior officers there for back up, I felt I couldn't back down. I told the three if they didn't fork over some ID they would be headed to jail. Not the best choice, but not completely unexpected for a young officer.

Of course the three told me to get fucked and when I reached out to make the first arrest the fight was on. This was no lightweight, typical cop wrestling match, this was a down and dirty brawl with wild punches and God knows what else. Fortunately, I've got a hard head so the one punch I took had no real effect. At one point, one of the men was choking me from behind and I ended up down on all fours. I was giving serious consideration to pulling my gun and shooting his ass when one of my fellow officers knocked him off me. We finally got the upper hand and got everyone arrested, but there was no way I would claim "victory." All of us had been knocked around pretty good and the idiots we arrested were not much worse for the wear. They did end up in jail as promised, but I'm not sure the effort it took to get them there was worth it. I ended up charging them with the most serious Assaulting a Police Officer charge, and eventually plea deals were worked out and the case was closed.

I learned two very valuable lessons that night. The first was being a police officer was not protection from getting beat on if you met up with the wrong suspect, and secondly don't let your ego make decisions for you. I was not necessarily wrong for wanting to get ID from these goofs, and if fact court decisions supported that the police had the right to detain and identify people involved in criminal activity. The problem was I let my ego talk me into demanding ID and not the facts of the incident in question.

It is important that as a police officer you never let people you deal with think you backed down from their challenge. That just leads to more problems down the road. The key is to not put yourself in a "do this or else" situation until you are sure you want to do the "or else." Looking back, had I kept the initial contact a little more low key and confirmed those involved had just been beating on each other, it would have been easier to send them on their way. I also could have done some quick file checks on the license plates of the cars in the lot and had names for future reference should something have come up requiring me to identify those involved.

The other thing it was important for me to remember as an officer was that the idiots we dealt with were usually frequent flyers, and so if you had to let them slide today you could pretty safely assume you would see them again and have the chance to balance the books then. More than one person has been told by a cop, "Don't' worry. I'll remember you." That sort of takes the enjoyment out of whatever they think they got away with. That likely would have been the better course of action at Tiger's Tap, but I'd taken the hard road to learning most of my life so this situation was no different.

The key is that I did learn and I can honestly say that I didn't repeat that mistake again. I still ended up having to back up what I told some low life would happen if he didn't comply with my orders, but I just learned to make sure that I didn't get to "or else" any faster than necessary.

Kevin M. Courtney

CHAPTER 51

Things moved along towards Thanksgiving and as I had to work it would be the first time in 23 years that I had not been with my family for the big feast. My family was not the huggy, kissy kind of close, but gatherings like Thanksgiving and Christmas were important and maintained the ties between us. My mom was philosophical about my not coming home, but I could tell it bothered my dad more. I had always been close with my dad and I knew that as the youngest in the family I had a special place in the old man's heart.

I suspected it was hard on my dad to see the youngest of his five kids become more and more independent and not be around the house any more. My mom told me that dad had said, "I'm an old man," after dropping off me at school for the start of my freshman year of college. Mom asked what he was talking about and dad said, "I don't have any kids to raise anymore; I'm an old man." I realized my Mother and Dad had children in the house for 30 years, from the time my oldest sister was born until I left for college, so I could understand how the old man must have felt. I would understand it a whole lot better 30 years later when I found myself in an empty house.

I made a point of calling my parents in the afternoon when I got up, and I explained that the Dispatchers would be fixing a full turkey dinner on the afternoon shift so there would be leftovers available for me when I got into work. The truth was I did miss the family dinner and all that went with it. Sitting around an apartment on your own just waiting to go to work was not my idea of a good time on Thanksgiving.

Julie had invited me over to her family's house, but I passed because I wanted to get a full day's sleep. Plus, my first meeting with her family during the summer hadn't gone all that well. Her mother had started in on a "what a stupid cop did" story and no matter how I tried to move away from the topic she stayed on it. I finally got pissed and stayed that way until I left. Julie's mother was actually a very nice person, but once she got on something she wouldn't let it go. For example, she is now totally convinced cougars roam the woods around Springport where Julie grew up even though no one has a photo of one or any other physical evidence of one. Julie's dad was very quiet and I figured he, like all fathers, had little use for the walking hormone chasing after his daughter. I could understand and respect that.

I did decide as I sat around on Thanksgiving that maybe now was the time to stick my neck out and make a commitment. I had six months on the Department and a few bucks saved up, even though it was tough to get ahead the first few months with all the unexpected expenses that come with moving into a new apartment. Still, I was making $15,000 a year and decided it was time to act. Yup, tomorrow when I got up I would head over to Knapp's department store in the Westwood Mall and check out their new color televisions. After all, the bowl games would be on in little over a month and the TV I'd dragged down to Jackson was pretty beat up.

I found a nice MGA for about $400 bucks and so I bought it with little fooling around. I was a salesperson's dream in that regard; and Knapp's was cool for a young guy just starting out because they offered 90 days same as cash as long as you paid 50% down and half the remaining balance each month with the final pay off in the third month. I decided I would pay it off just before Christmas so that I'd have the TV in time for the bowl games. This would also help me start to build a credit record. I graduated from college with no student loans and did not have a credit card so I figured I needed to start building some kind of credit rating for big purchases like a new car or house.

I wandered around the mall for a while, primarily scoping out the women but I also grabbed a soft pretzel at the stand inside the mall. That held me over until I could pickup a bag of grease to go from one of the fast food places on West Avenue on my way home. Night shift was really tough on eating habits. I usually ate a bowl of cereal when I woke up, fixed a sandwich in the apartment or maybe went out for some fast food around 7 or so and then was really hungry around 3:00 or 4:00 a.m. That sucked, since there weren't exactly a lot of restaurants open in Jackson after 2:00 a.m.

The Coney Island on Michigan Ave was open and Ed's Café down on Page Avenue across from the Conrail Yard opened at 4:00 a.m. Neither of these fine establishments was going to make any "Healthy Eating" list. The fact was if you found anything green on your plate, you'd better send the food back because it sure the hell wasn't a vegetable.

I didn't mind the Coney but it was usually full of drunks after 2:00 a.m., so it was the last place a cop wanted to sit down and eat. I did get take out from time to time, but you could only eat so many "sliders," as the Coney dogs were called, before your stomach rebelled.

"Greasy Ed's" wasn't much better for the stomach, but at least it wasn't full of drunks. Ed was an old Polish guy from the southeast side of town who had a deep gravely voice. He set up his restaurant across the from the rail yard to serve the train crews and yard workers, and when the yard was going full tilt Ed did okay. By the time I came to Jackson, traffic at the yard had slowed down and so had Ed's business.

A unique aspect to Ed was that he only charged cops 99 cents no matter what they ordered. You could have a steak and Ed would just growl "Ninety-nine" when it came time to pay. He was old school and figured the cops deserved a little respect. This was also a time before people had a fit over a cop getting a free cup of coffee, so no one got real worked up over the "discount" Ed offered. Plus, unless you were a completely shameless leech, you tried not to go in the place more than once a week. There were always a few cheap bastards that would hit a place like Ed's 4 or 5 times a week and think nothing of it. I thought if you're that hard up, bring a sack lunch.

Kevin M. Courtney

.

CHAPTER 52

The Michigan winter hit with full force in early December and things on nights slowed right down. No one is going to be outside acting the fool when it is five below zero with a wind chill of -20. The old timers liked the quiet nights but it drove me nuts. Not only did I hate being bored, but trying to stay awake until the shift ended at 8:00 a.m. was damn near impossible when you had nothing to do. The worse hours of night shift were the last 2 of the shift. The human body is chemically at its lowest ebb around 5:00 a.m. and that coupled with nothing to do made you virtually suicidal from 6:00 to 8:00 a.m. from just wanting to get home and into bed.

On most of these cold winter nights there wasn't even anyone out driving around to stop. In the rare instance that someone did make a traffic stop, every other officer on duty would drive by just for something to do. The poor bastard who got stopped was totally paranoid by the time three patrol cars rolled by him looking him over like he was John Dillinger. I remember one guy with a tail light out getting stopped twice while driving across the city on Michigan Avenue.

I made it back to my parents' house for Christmas and it was really nice to be home. I lucked out in that my days off happened to be Christmas Eve and Christmas Day. Julie came up for the traditional Courtney family Christmas on Christmas Eve and then drove back to Jackson around 10:00 pm. She was more than just a little overwhelmed by how loud and full of ourselves we all were. My brother-in-law, Steve, who was married to my oldest sister, Marcia, sat next to Julie and said, "You might as well sit here with me because you'll never get a word in with all those Courtneys anyway."

I was obviously getting pretty serious about Julie since she was the only female I had ever brought home to meet the family. They were all very impressed by her, but my dad probably said what they were all thinking when he remarked to my mom, "that Julie seemed awful sweet and quiet to be going out with Kevin." Apparently the old man more expected me to show up with a loudmouthed exotic dancer than a sweet girl like Julie. I figured he assumed if I wasn't bringing girls home, the ones I was running around with must not be fit to be around my mother, and so Julie clearly screwed up his theory.

I almost made my dad a prophet just seven days later when I came back home for New Year's Eve, which like Christmas Eve fell on my days off. Julie had to work that night, so we decided we would have dinner together on New Year's day and that I would cook. Julie liked that and seemed glad I would get a chance to go home and hang out with my buddies. That would all change.

My pal Dick Belill was renting his grandfather's old house in Birch Run and decided to throw a New Year's Eve party. He was happy to hear I was going to be able to make it back, and it turned out a lot of our buddies from town were going to be there, too, along with a few of Dick's family. I knew and liked all of the Belills, so I was thinking this was going to be a good night.

I was wrong. It wasn't a good night--it was a GREAT night. The booze flowed, the music played, and I had a great time being around the people I had known all my life. Jackson was great and my new friends there were wonderful, but I had only known them for nine months. These people had known me for as long as I could remember. That added a depth to our friendship that only time could instill. All of them knew being a cop was my lifelong goal, and they liked the fact that I made it. They all ragged on Dick about inviting a "fucking cop" to the party and busted on me about my profession, but it was the type of harassment that let you know you were among people who cared about you and respected you.

The only drawback to this was that I had such a good time I thought I should stop back by on my way out of town the next day. I left mom and dad's house around noon and since I didn't have to be back in Jackson until four o'clock that afternoon, and it was only a two hour drive, I had plenty of time to stop by Dick's house to pay my respects and thank him for the awesome party.

It seemed several of the other party goers from the night before had the same idea and had showed up at Dick's house too. A couple of them apparently never left, and so everyone was sort of flopped out around the living room watching an early bowl game. Being a good host, Dick passed out beers to everyone and we just sat around bullshitting and watching the game. Along about 1:30 I was thinking I needed to get my ass on the road, but the 3 or 4 beers I had drunk and all my buddies sitting around watching football told me maybe I needed to stay longer.

The boys were on me hard about growing a pair and staying instead of running home to Mama. Not only that, they had just ordered a bunch of pizza and the better games were about to come on. It was too much pressure for one man, and I cracked. I asked Dick where the phone was and a collective cheer went up from the crowd. I told them to quiet the hell down; I had some serious lying to do.

I got Julie on the phone and in my best and most sincere voice I explained that a guy I hadn't seen for a long time had surprised everyone by showing up at Dick's house, and that if she was okay with it I would really like to stay and catch up with my buddy. Figuring I needed to lay it on a little thicker, I pointed out my lousy shifts and days off normally would prevent something like this from happening. Julie was very understanding and I had just about sealed the deal when Dick picked up the other extension and shouted, "He's lying. The fucker's drunk and can't drive back!"

I heard all sorts of warning claxons and alarms going off because my ship of love just took a torpedo below the water line and was sinking fast. Before I could utter a word, Julie said with a voice that made a January day in Michigan seem tropical, "Tell your friend I don't appreciate his language and then you go right ahead with what you're doing." The next sound I heard was the receiver being hung up in my ear.

I walked out into the living room, looked at Dick and said, "Thanks a lot asshole." This of course caused the rest of the boys to erupt in laughter and I said, "Oh well, she knows I'm blowing off our date to get drunk and watch football with my sleazy buddies, so I guess there is no reason not to." I figured I'd weasel my way back into her good graces when I got back to Jackson. Besides, unless Julie booted me completely to the curb, it was worth a little pain to hang out with these guys drinking and watching football. It would take a few days to get back in Julie's good graces, but I pulled it off. Dick however stayed on her shit list for about the next five years. She still busts his chops over that incident 30 years later.

CHAPTER 53

All winter long I had been playing basketball at the Y and on the Department's city league team. I really loved to play and it was fun to be on the Department team because it let me get to know guys better and fit in more. Plus the team was pretty good, mostly because we had some real gorillas on the front line and driving to the basket against the JPD team put new meaning to the words "police brutality."

Along with Big Mac, we had Karl Ankrom who was 6' 7," and Steve Leider who was 6'2" and about 265. Steve's nickname was "Fozzie" after the bear he so closely resembled. We also had Bill Kennedy and Mike Brunk from the Department, both over 6'2." Along with these apes we had a local attorney who, like Ankrom, was about 6'7," and we had Kennedy's little brother, David, known as Harmon, who was 6'4" and 250. Needless to say, the lane was not a safe place to park with those boys around. We didn't give a shit about how many team fouls we accumulated because most guys in this league only shot about 50% from the free throw line. Besides, it became hard to shoot when your arms ached from getting pounded on.

I was 6'2" and only weighed 155, but I made up for my lack of weight with my aggressiveness, the code word for dirty play. My theory was you got five fouls a game. Finishing with a game with any fewer than that meant you wasted an opportunity to whack your opponent.

The backcourt was made up of Harvey and Ralph Locke Jr. Harvey was the cousin of Lieutenant Dave Locke, who had me over the coals, and Ralph was Dave's little brother. They were both tremendous players but likely the only way you'd get either one to pass you the ball is if they had to inbound it. The truth was that Harvey had one of the most perfect jump shots I had ever seen, and several times he scored over 40 points in a game. Beer league or not, that was some serious hoopin'. Ralph was cat-quick and a great ball handler and defender. I managed to score a few points here and there and did what I could, which was run hard, play some defense, and pick up a few garbage points off rebounds. There's only one basketball used in a game, so if your teammates ain't passing it to you, you gotta find other ways to get your hands on it.

There were two occasions when Ralph and Harvey both missed the game and I knocked in over 20 points each time, but that didn't last when they got back. Brunk pointed out that had I continued to score like that I would not have been allowed to sit by him on the bench or gain membership in the BOAS.

Mike Tash was a veteran officer who was the backup guard and player/coach. His current status with JPD was fired, but he was awaiting an arbitrator's decision on his appeal of the firing. He was a pretty likeable guy so I stayed away from the controversy that was swirling around his firing. Tash had gotten the ax over what the Department felt was his incompetent handling of a call, and they managed to get a couple of officers to testify in the arbitration hearing that Tash had not done what he should have. That didn't go over well with some of Tash's pals on the Department, so I stayed clear of the whole drama. Basically I pulled a Switzerland and remained neutral.

CHAPTER 54

The month of January was cold and miserable and so night shift truly was a graveyard shift. Dead was the only way to describe it. I was looking forward to shift change at the end of the month as this living like a vampire just wasn't making it for me. There were a lot of days in the dead of winter when I worked an early car that I got home before it was completely light out, and I didn't wake up until after it was starting to get dark again. I found myself turning away from the bright sunlight when I would see it on my days off or when I had to appear in court. That along with the boredom of nights told me I needed to get back on second shift.

I was checking out Paka Plaza one night in January at about 1:30 a.m. after its burglar alarm went off. Things had been so freaking quiet I was glad to have any kind of a call to go on. Paka Plaza was a long strip mall on West Avenue near the city's northern limit. There was also a big Sears store located across the parking lot from the main plaza complex. While I was checking the building out, the station called and told me to return to HQ. The building had checked out and there were no open doors, so I advised the other unit I had been called back to the station. I figured it must be something important for them to call me off an alarm, so I left the call and headed back downtown.

I arrived to find Sgt. Sampson on the desk laughing. He told me, "I didn't mean you had to come back right this minute. You could have finished up on the alarm." The other unit on the call was Galen Terry so he yucked it up even more when he came in. Surprisingly, he and I got along fine after the DUIL arrest and Galen never said another word about how I went about my business. In fact we had gone deer hunting together out on Julie's uncle's place in Parma and he always treated me well.

I was wondering what was up since the whole shift was now back in the station. Sgt. Sampson said, "We got some training films in the Historical Room." The Historical Room was a small conference room with glass display cases full of JPD memorabilia along the walls. It was actually pretty cool and told the history of the Department. Once we got in the room I saw an 8mm movie projector was set up and the movies being shown were low grade porn. I was never big on dirty movies but figured it was better than freezing my ass off outside.

There were never any encore performances while I was on nights, and I was fine with that. A little goof off time now and then when things are slow is to be expected, but I really didn't see watching x-rated flicks in the police station as a good thing. The fact is it was just the kind of thing that would get blown up all over the front page if some reporter ever found out. Was it scandalous? Not really. But in a town like Jackson it would have been.

The problem was deep down a guy like me knew the movies were wrong, and not because I was any kind of prude. Porn movies just didn't belong in a police station. I would in the future learn to just walk away from this kind of stuff but in truth I should have had the balls to put an end to them. The question always seemed to be, "Who are they hurting?" In this case, the answer to that was the department's reputation and standing in the community if the "film review" ever became public knowledge. Still, I took the typical—and cowardly--approach of steering clear of the mess and leaving those involved to deal with the risk of getting caught. I reasoned, or rationalized, that if the behavior was drinking on duty or stealing, I'd be in the Captain's office in a heart beat, but fortunately I never saw anything like that.

Nowadays the problem is officers spending too much time on duty checking out Facebook, ESPN.com, and God-knows-what-else on the computer.

I would develop the reputation later in my career as an administrator who didn't put up with inappropriate behavior and in part it was because I figured my officers were in the same dilemma I had been. I understood it was in effect the responsibility of the administration to be alert for this kind of thing and put and end to it. Or, more importantly, to create an air about the place where people wouldn't think of pulling some crap like that so officers didn't have to decide between looking the other way and ratting someone out. Still, no matter what is done, somebody is always going to spend more time avoiding work than doing it.

Kevin M. Courtney

.

CHAPTER 55

I went back to second shift when the shifts changed at the end of January. The Department developed a system that guaranteed 50% of the positions on a shift would be filled by officers using seniority and the other 50% with a modified draft system. The draft system allowed the lieutenant from each shift to pick the officers he wanted on their shift after the first slots were filled by seniority. I got picked for the afternoon shift and felt pretty good when Lieutenant Johnson told me he wanted hard charging officers on the shift and knew I wouldn't let him down.

I was glad to be back on the afternoon shift; it fit my lifestyle perfectly. I wasn't big on getting up in the mornings and I liked to have a few after work, so, working afternoons was perfect. Plus, I had a girlfriend who worked the same kind of hours and had the same lousy days off, so it didn't even cramp my social life at all. The fact was that the majority of my social life was somehow connected back to the Department anyway.

Younger cops tended to be pretty clannish in those days and usually only hung out with other cops. This was caused by several factors. First there was the work hours and days off situation. Regular civilian-type people weren't usually able to party all night on a Tuesday or head to the bar for a couple of beers at 7:00 a.m. on Monday. At the same time, most young cops weren't available to go to a party at 3 on Saturday afternoon because they had to work. The other reason the young cops figured out pretty quickly was when they were at a party that was made up of primarily non-cops they could become the center of attention in a hurry.

Being the center of attention is okay when you're surrounded by good looking women, but, it sucks when it is all about bitching about what this cop or that cop did when they wrote some asshole a ticket, or when you're getting grilled about some shit you had nothing to do with. That gets old in a hurry and is why most young cops prefer the company of other cops. As they get older, cops tend work more normal shifts, and they have kids in school, so they mingle more with the average citizen. Still, they never lose their wariness about becoming the center of attention and usually enjoy being around their boys telling war stories more than being at the local PTA tea.

Most of my fellow rookie's and I ended up back on afternoons, and I was very excited by the prospects for working with my "boys" on our own. I genuinely liked those guys and it was fun to head over to Evanoff's for a couple of beers two or three times a week after work. If I worked an early car I could relax and have a couple and still be home by 12:30 a.m. That gave me plenty of time to get a good night's sleep so I could get up and head down to the Y for an hour or two in the morning. I could also stay in the bar until closing time and sleep in until noon if I wanted, which was my method of operation the first 3 months I was on the Department. This time around, I really tried to avoid that.

The other good thing that happened during that winter was that John Stressman and his wife invited Julie and I up to his in-law's place on Burt Lake in Northern Michigan for a couple of days. We had similar days off and, by using a little comp time, we were able to get away together. Comp time was hours that officers could accumulate instead of getting paid for the overtime they worked. Most young guys took more comp than cash because they were more likely to need a day off than a few extra bucks. Plus, Uncle Sam took most of your OT anyway when you were a single guy with no deductions.

Even though it was the winter we had a good time drinking and just relaxing. There was a real good little pizza place in town and we hit it one night for dinner. The cottage also had a snowmobile we could run around on a little, and it was just a good time being up there.

Julie and I really had become good friends with John and his wife, and the four of us went out quite often. It happened that Julie lived in the same townhouse complex behind Paka Plaza as the Stressmans, so it was pretty convenient to get together. We all liked good food and road trips to Ann Arbor, Marshall, and Lansing for dinner became pretty common.

John was fairly reserved until he got a couple of beers in him, but his wife Beth was anything but. On one occasion when John was being a little surly at a party, Beth yelled out for everyone to hear, "What's the matter John, your hemorrhoids acting up?" No quiet she wasn't, but she was an absolutely gorgeous girl with a heart of gold, and Julie and I both thought the world of her.

Kevin M. Courtney

.

CHAPTER 56

I was working B-22 one evening and things had been relatively quiet for most of the night when Tom Bernardon and I got sent to a "trouble with subject" call on N. Milwaukee Street. Seems a young lady had traded boyfriends and was at the new man's house when the old flame showed up demanding satisfaction. I laughed to myself that some of the stuff I dealt with was better than what I saw on the *Young and the Restless,* my soap of choice. I'd had got hooked on Y&R in college as a way to kill time between classes and working afternoons made it easy to continue the habit. Fortunately, several of my fellow officers also had the habit so I didn't feel quite so light in the loafers for watching what was clearly trash TV.

Tom and I arrived out in front of the house at about the same time and observed the jilted lover standing on the sidewalk that led up to the porch. I left Tom to talk to the goof and went up and knocked on the door. At first the male resident wouldn't open the door but talked through it and denied there was anyone else inside with him. I was getting a little pissed off and told the yo-yo to either open the door and talk to me, or we were leaving and he could deal with dipshit #2 on his own.

The fool finally opened the door and said he just wanted the other guy gone from his house and nothing else. I told him to cough up some ID and I then asked to speak to the girl. This got a "What girl?" response. I had had enough and said, "Look I don't give a fat rat's ass if you got an aardvark dressed in drag in there, but you called me up here so I'm going to talk to everyone involved. Now quit wasting my time and get your girlfriend out here." That seemed to register and the girlfriend came to the door and gave me the low down that the guy out front was her ex and she was indeed at this location doing the dirty deed with her new man. She didn't want the ex locked up but did agree he needed to be gone.

I walked down to where Tom was standing to get the jilted lover's side of the story, while Tom went up and stood with the guy on his porch. Loverboy was a little more cooperative and explained to me his ex-squeeze had lied to him about hopping in the sack with the guy in the house so he tracked her here and just wanted to find out why she lied. He stated he didn't want any trouble because he was recovering from a broken jaw. I told him he would have to leave and, if he came back, I would lock him up. I then told everyone involved that once dispatch advised that none of them were wanted, I would let them go back about their business and Tom and I would split.

Bernardon had wandered back down and was standing on one side of the jilted lover and I was on the other as we waited to get our LEIN checks back. About the time the checks came back with no warrants, "jilted" decided it was a good time to point out to the new boyfriend that he was a punk for hiding behind the door and a woman. He also told his ex-girlfriend she knew where he was at when she got tired of that pansy she was with. I told him to pipe down or the offer of leaving was going to be exchanged for cuffs. I thought everything was fine when suddenly the new man decided it was time to show he wasn't a punk or a pansy. He took a run across the porch and launched himself at the ex-boyfriend in a move that was only missing a cape to make it perfect.

The guy had great aim, too, as he landed directly on his rival and the two started pounding on each other. I recovered from my shock and grabbed Batman while Tom got a hold of the other half in a great headlock. I could hear the guy screaming and remembered the broken jaw, so I quickly shoved Batman back towards the porch and told him to stay there or he was going to jail.

I grabbed Tom and said "Let him go, let him go." Tom wondered what the hell this was all about but he let the guy go. I said "Keep an eye on him" pointing at the Flying Wallenda, while my mind was racing. I didn't need this shit as one trip to the second floor for brutality was enough. I wasn't going to have Lieutenant Locke playing "pin the charge on the Courtney" again. The guy was holding his jaw and hollering about how much it hurt, and so I figured now was a good time for me to use every bit of Irish blarney I could muster.

I told broken jaw it was time for him to haul his ass on down the road, as he had caused enough problems for one night. The guy looked up and cried, "I'm the one that got jumped and damn near had his head torn off by that big ape cop. How come you're treating me like shit?" I quickly answered, "Hey, I'm trying to cut you some slack, but if you want I can take you both to jail for fighting in public. Remember you started this whole mess by coming over to this guy's house looking for trouble." To add a little drama, I pulled my handcuffs out and said, "Well what it's gonna be? You hauling ass or am I dragging you both in? Make it quick because I'm done standing around."

My bluff worked and lover-boy hit the road figuring this was one lousy freaking night. First his old lady is getting drilled more often than the Alaskan tundra by another guy, then some goddamned corn fed cop liked to have pulled his head right off. Like so many nitwits before him and yet to come, he asked the heavens the million dollar question: "Why's this shit always happen to me?"

I turned on Batman and explained very bluntly that the next time he pulled a stunt like that he wouldn't be conscious by the time he hit the ground. I advised him to get his ass in the house and consider himself lucky he met such reasonable cops. I made it clear if I came back in the next 20 years I was taking everyone to jail, including the woman that was the cause of all this bullshit. I might have been a chauvinistic pig to say that, but that doesn't mean I was wrong.

All the while this was going on, Tom was standing off to the side looking bewildered. He couldn't for the life of him figure out what the hell that crazy bastard Courtney was up to since I was not normally one to pass up a couple of good disorderly conduct arrests. That was until I filled him in about the broken jaw. Tom gave a surprised "No shit?" and then started to smile an embarrassed smile. Pretty soon the two of us were cracking up laughing about the whole thing and I was saying, "You looked like you were wrestling a steer and all I could hear was the little weasel screaming to beat the band. I just knew you had re-broke the dumbass's jaw." We were both still laughing when we got in our cars and called back in service.

I wrote the report up "gospel" figuring if the guy's jaw was messed up we were covered as the force was reasonable--if somewhat bad luck for lover-boy. I was hoping the jaw would be fine and that the guy would be happy he wasn't in jail and would take his ass whipping like a man, weasel eyed little fucker though he was.

CHAPTER 57

My fellow rookies and I loved being in on every "good call." These were defined as anything involving a gun, drugs, fight, pursuit, barricaded suspect, robbery or damn-near any felony in progress. As a result, we were constantly volunteering to respond on such calls regardless of where it was or what section we were working. Even if we weren't sent on the call, we would do our best to get close just in case the shit hit the fan and other units were needed.

You had to be careful doing this, though, as you were expected to stay in your section unless sent out of it. You even had to ask permission to leave it to go to lunch. You could get away with staying a block or two out of your area, but if you were working C-23 in the southeast corner of the city, it was pretty hard to explain why you were up in A-21 in the northwest part of the City. The risk of getting caught came from both the street sergeant, Unit Sam 11, and from the dispatcher checking your location while you were somewhere you shouldn't be. Lying about where you were could bite you in the ass if you picked a spot that just happened to be where the call was.

Even so, we young bulls did everything we could to be where the action was. It was just this attitude that got us our nickname one night at Evanoff's. Most of the second shift was in there seated around the big round table in the corner. John Stressman had just taken a long pull of his bottle of Michelob Light when he looked at Dave Bachman and said, "I don't know why I bother to go on the fucking street. I swear to God Bachman, you don't have a chance to take a call with these crazy fucking rookies running around. Once dispatch gives out a hot call, they all start chiming in to take it. They're like a bunch of little kids jumping up and down saying, "Pick me! Pick me! Pick me!" Those of us at the table who were the target of John's remarks really liked that handle and immediately started referring to ourselves as the "Pick Me Brothers." To us it was a badge of honor, and Stressman was left to just shake his head and smile and say "See?" How do you deal people like that?"

I knew John was proud of the "Pick me Brothers," as were the other senior officers on the shift. John, Dave, Roger, and Ric Cedillo trained us to do the job the way they did, and by and large it happened. I realized I was more and more a part of JPD in a way I had never belonged to any other group besides my family. I had my own trinity now, I was Irish, a Catholic, and a Cop--and the three became one. It would be that way for the remainder of my life.

CHAPTER 58

I learned a real truth of policing in a northern climate. Once you start getting warm weather in the spring, alcohol consumption goes up during the day and so does the work load of second shift. You didn't have to have an IQ of 145 to know things were going to be jumping when every porch on your beat had people sitting on it drinking. It was that way as April faded into May. The days not only were getting warmer but it was staying lighter longer, providing even more "porch time."

The truth was as a young hard charger, I looked forward to the "warm up" because it meant more action and excitement. It also meant a lot more good-looking women running around not looking like freaking Eskimos. It was a real bitch during a Michigan winter to judge a woman's figure since she had 5 layers of clothes on most of the damn time. Summer cured that and, while I was dating Julie pretty seriously I had not gouged my eyes out as part of the relationship.

Family fights, noise complaints, disorderly conduct calls, and other booze propelled business increased as the weather got nicer. I didn't mind, as it made the shift go by faster and it also resulted in more people out on the street available for a little friendly conversation. I always enjoyed talking to people, and I could tell some of the black folks weren't sure what to make of a white police officer who seemed friendly. Still, most people in Jackson were at heart Midwesterners, and as such were pretty open friendly people regardless of the color of their skin. That didn't mean race relations in Jackson were perfect because they weren't. I, however, figured that was a global view; my only worry was getting along with people on a one-on-one basis and generally I managed to do that.

Kevin M. Courtney

CHAPTER 59

Gary and I had decided it was time to give the apartment the 86 for something better. We hadn't had any more run-ins with the manager or neighbors but neither of us really liked the setup although I was the moving force to try something different. I suggested we find a house and Gary was okay with the idea. I happened to mentioned the plan to John Stressman and he said his younger brother, Rick, was looking for a place to live and would probably be willing to move in with us. Rick worked at a body shop in town owned by a JPD officer named Mose Lewis who ran it as a second job. Gary and I were cool with Rick as a roomie, and he was happy to move in with us, so I started looking around in earnest for a house.

I had found a place listed in the 700 block of Westwood Street, just a short distance outside the city on the west side and the owner agreed to show it to me. Gary and I showed up at the house and were met by a lady in her early 40's who introduced herself as Jan Matzen. The house was originally a two bedroom cement block house built on a concrete slab, and an addition had been put on the back with a second bathroom and an additional bedroom. Gary and I walked through and thought the place looked pretty good.

Jan said she and her husband had just bought the place and it was available immediately with the rent being $360 per month plus utilities. Gary and I were paying 300 a month for our apartment, so by the time we split this cost three ways we'd be saving money. When we told Jan we'd take it, she hesitated a little and said she'd have to check with her husband. I couldn't figure out what the hold up was but thought well, maybe the old boy runs the household and she can't do anything without his okay.

The truth was Jan's husband had told her that, no matter what, they weren't going to rent to single men because they'd tear the place up for sure and there would be wild parties every weekend driving the neighbors apeshit. Jan didn't realize I was a single man with two roommates when I called, and she didn't have the heart to tell me no dice when I showed up. Finding out that two of the three of us were cops made her think maybe there should be an exception to the "no single men" rule.

Mr. Matzen didn't react well to his wife's suggestion that two cops would be pretty safe bets as tenants. He guessed single cops would be testosterone-fueled skirt chasers and would tear his place up twice as fast as anyone else would. Plus, evicting cops didn't sound all that appealing to him. He finally agreed to rent the place to us after I laid on the Irish charm and provided references. As a result, I was subjected to my second background check in a year, but I got a new place to live starting June 1st. Gary, Rick, and I were all looking forward to the new place and liked the fact that it was in a quiet neighborhood and had a big driveway with room for all three of our cars. Anything would be better than the apartment complex.

The move from the apartment to the house was pretty easy since our buddies from the Department helped us, providing both pickup trucks and manual labor. The result was that for a few 12-packs of beer and some pizza, we got all our stuff moved over to the new place in record time. I liked the fact I was in a house with decent-sized rooms and was living like a regular citizen. Even if most regular citizens would not want me, or my roommates, anywhere near them.

Rick was a lot like his brother but a slightly smaller version. He had spent six years in the Air Force and was a very likeable guy. Rick worked straight days and had most weekends off, while Gary and I worked shifts with lousy days off. I figured it would be pretty easy for us to get along since we might only see each other once every three or four days. Rick wasn't making a lot of money, so Gary and I took the best bedrooms and agreed to each pay an extra 5 bucks a month rent saving Rick $10.

It turned out Rick was quite a ladies' man and didn't lack for company. His tastes were pretty wide-ranging, and one little princess he rolled in with on an evening I was home didn't seem to be too excited about there being a cop in the house. Based on her tattoos and general attitude, I warned Rick that the bitch had probably murdered her last three boyfriends so he better be careful. I pointed out I wasn't cleaning up the blood if he ended up on the floor gutted like a fish, and I sure the hell wasn't paying to have it done. Rick said not to worry; he'd keep the freak away from the steak knives.

Kevin M. Courtney

.

CHAPTER 60

The Department received a grant in 1980 to start a five person traffic unit and so it needed to hire additional officers to replace those who would get assigned to the new unit and also to replace a couple of retirements. The result was eight more new officers were hired in the spring of 1980, so right away the rest of the class of '79 and I moved up the seniority ladder a couple of notches. One of the officers hired was Elaine Mason, who was a year behind Gary and me at Ferris, and we both thought she was okay. Other officers hired at that time included current department cadets, Bill Kennedy and Mary Jo Crance. The other 5 people were new to the Department. All of them had at least two years of college and most had four year degrees. At a time when police departments in Michigan were just starting to consider hiring only college-educated cops, the majority of JPD's hires in the last few years had earned Bachelor degrees.

That was a good thing from the standpoint of professionalism but hurt the Department somewhat in recruiting minorities, the simple reason being that most minorities who made it through college had their sights set higher than being a cop. It was still not exactly a preferred profession among blacks, nor were there a lot of role models in the black community who were cops. That was one of the reasons the Department had the cadet program. It could bring in black kids right out of high school, give them two years of college, and create a pool of officer candidates that would not have otherwise existed.

The other bit of good news at this time was my old training officer, Roger, had been promoted to Sergeant. I was really happy for him and looked forward to having him as a supervisor. You couldn't ask for a better boss than a guy who had his work ethic and understood what being a good street cop was all about.

The Pick Me Brothers were too new to be involved in the training of the new officers--beyond giving them tips about what to expect from the officers that would train them and also what would get them a good and bad reputation with their fellow JPD officers. The new officers seemed to genuinely appreciate the tips, and I went out of my way to be nice to Elaine. We had gotten along well at Ferris and I figured I owed her the old alumni loyalty. Besides, she was a good person and clearly wanted to do a good job.

The new officers who got hired in seemed like a pretty good bunch. I was getting to know several of them, and overall I was pretty impressed. One of the new hires did drive a lot of the older officer nuts just by showing up, however. Ken Magee was a well-built handsome young man who just leaked arrogance. He was about 5'10," wore excellent clothes and fancy boots, was fastidious about his grooming, and drove a hot looking Firebird. The truth was that while he was a bit arrogant, he was actually a pretty nice guy and always willing to help someone out. He was also a good cop with good instincts, and I liked him. I distinctly remember how much I appreciated him taking the time to send me a card when my dad passed away in 1984. Ken left JPD after a few years and went on to a very successful career in the Drug Enforcement Administration.

Tom Eagle was one of the new hires and his ethnic background led to some completely non-politically correct nicknames. Tom had both native American and Japanese heritage and so immediately picked up the moniker, "Running Rickshaw." That wasn't as bad "Gook-a-roo," the handle Howard Noppe laid on him. Howard and Tom became fast friends and Tom never batted an eye at the name. Today, an officer using a nickname like that would get suspended and a whole ethnic sensitivity training program would be implemented for the Department under Federal Court decree.

CHAPTER 61

I put my name in for the traffic unit but didn't get the assignment. I wasn't really heartbroken over the rejection, having put in for the unit primarily to keep my name in front of the brass. One of the senior officers had told me to make sure I showed interest in learning more and becoming a better officer whenever the chance came up, and putting my name in for special assignments was one way to do that. Two of my fellow Pick Me's, Tom Bernardon and Scott Rogers, got assigned. They were both good at working traffic and Rogers had prior police experience. They also had motorcycle endorsements, and the word was the unit was going to get bikes.

One of the interesting facts about the traffic unit was that the guy chosen to be its sergeant was a long time detective named Ray Rhodes. Most people who got promoted to detective never left the rank because the Dicks worked from 8 to 5, Monday through Friday, got all the holidays off, and made just five percent less than a sergeant. They could easily make up the difference with overtime, and so there was little reason to want to promote out of the Detective Bureau and go back to working afternoons with Tuesdays and Wednesdays off. Rhodes was different. He had decided it was time for a change. It didn't hurt that the traffic unit sergeant would work days and have weekends off. Still, I admired his attitude.

Along with a couple of my fellow Pick Me's, I had decided that the end of our first year on the Department should not go by unnoticed. A new officer's probation period with the Jackson Police Department, as with most others, was one year in length. During that year, an officer could be fired for any reason and had no Union protection. They were not covered by any of the labor contracts provisions for appealing a disciplinary action, and that created more than just a little concern for new hires. It was a large part of the reason I was sweating so bad when I'd got dragged into the administrative lieutenant's office back in August.

The plan was to throw a bash at the FOP Hall right around the first of June, when the last of us passed our first anniversary on the Department. I managed to find a day that we were all either off duty or could get the day off, and I really threw myself into making this a memorable event. The rest of the rookies and I lined up food, got a couple of kegs, and passed the word around to all the area police agencies, dispatchers, and the emergency room nurses--all the usual attendees at a JPD event.

The day of the party was beautiful, sunny and warm, and the turnout was great. There were even a few of the brass who showed up to pay their respects to the eight new full fledged members of JPD. The party got rolling early in the evening and kept right on into the night, so that the second shift folks could come over when their shifts ended. Julie was there, and I took a little ribbing from people about my stringing her along. The point was made that now that I didn't have to worry about losing my job maybe I should start shopping for engagement rings. I laughed and said "sure" when in truth that thought scared the bejesus out of me. Married? No way. That was serious stuff and I was just getting my feet under me. No, that kind of thing was a long way off.

I looked around during the party and was pretty pleased with how it turned out. I looked at the faces of my fellow Pick Me Brothers and realized that, no matter what happened in my career I would be forever linked with those seven men. I was proud of that fact because I knew that every one of those guys would have my back when the shit hit the fan. I had all ready been in a couple of tight spots with them and knew I could count on them and, just as importantly, knew they believed they could count on me, too.

CHAPTER 62

My other big move when I got my first year in was to go car shopping. I really liked the Buick Regal and so, after doing a little dickering back and forth between my hometown dealer and Jim Winter Buick in Jackson, I settled on buying the one at Jim Winter. I had $2,500 to put down on the $6,700 car so I figured financing would be no problem when I headed into the National Bank of Jackson where I had my savings and checking accounts.

I was pretty relaxed when I met with the loan officer, and figured everything at this point was just a formality since I had dropped off the loan application a few days earlier. Wrong. The loan officer said, "I don't see a problem with your loan, Mr. Courtney, as long as you can get a co-signer." I handled that about as well as if the guy told me I'd have to start flying the British Flag and singing "God Save the Queen" every day. I glared at the loan officer and said, "What kind of bullshit is that? I've got more than 33% to put down on the car, I don't have any other debts, and I'm making over 16 grand a year." The loan officer was clearly taken aback and said, "Well, you have only been at your job for a year so no bank is going to take that kind of risk on you."

Now I was really getting pissed and I wasn't particularly concerned about controlling my temper. "Let me ask you something. If you hit the freaking robbery alarm because some asshole has a sawed-off shotgun half way up your nose and I'm just down the street, do you want me to come and try to save your ass right then, or would you prefer I wait for a co-signer?" Then I really got rolling. "You rotten, suit wearing bastards don't have a problem with me risking my fucking life for your stinking bank's money, but you wouldn't dare risk a couple of bucks on me." I added, "Why am I not surprised?" and stomped out of the bank, vowing I would never ask these assholes for another dime. And I didn't. Ever.

While I felt better about having told the bank employee what I thought, I was no closer to getting the new car. When I had talked with my dad about buying the new ride, he had said he wanted to buy my current car back and also mentioned he would loan me the money for the new one at an interest rate better than the banks would charge, which was still more than he was making on his savings account. I figured that was reasonable, but at that time I wanted the independence of not having my finances tied to the old man. Well, screw the independence, I'd borrow the money from dear old dad and the banks could go hump themselves.

I learned a valuable lesson when I called my dad up to borrow the money. He was more than happy to cut me the check, but he drew up a loan agreement and provided me with a payment book with all 36 months written in. I got the message loud and clear: When it comes to money and property, put things in writing no matter who it is. I took no offense to this because I knew the old man was making a record for both our sakes. This way, no one could ever claim I scammed the money or never repaid it, and dad had a record of his "investment" and interest for the IRS. Larry Courtney was an honest man, and he would claim the interest on his taxes just like he had claimed every dollar he'd made on the side, building garages and pouring cement, when his family was younger.

I took both these lessons to heart and "getting things in writing" has saved me a lot of grief over the years. Well, I signed the papers and got the cash needed for the car, and I drove away from Jim Winter Buick in a slick looking, two door, burgundy-colored Buick Regal with a landau roof. I celebrated my new ride with Julie and the Stressmans by going out for a drive and stopping for a bite to eat along the way. That car was the first real thing of value I had ever owned, and I was very proud of it. The status to me wasn't in the fact it was a new car; it was the fact that I earned the money to make the down payment and would pay every dime I owed on it on time.

CHAPTER 63

It wasn't just the cops who liked to party on a nice day. Karl Ankrom and I were sent to a party on Mason Street just off Francis one warm Saturday evening. An impromptu block party had broken out and folks were standing around in the yards, drinking and listening to music--which apparently yanked the chain of some of the less socially-inclined neighbors, who decided to call the police.

The party was centered around one Wendel Mills' residence. Wendel wasn't always on the best of terms with the police and, in fact, he'd had a few go rounds with the cops in the past. To make matters worse, he had been drinking all day before Karl and I showed up, which wasn't a good thing. It was Karl's call and I was his back-up, so it was up to Karl to run the show. He and I parked and were walking up towards the main crowd when Wendel stepped out and in a challenging voice asked, "What do you want?" Karl gave him a classic cop once over and said, "Are you in charge?"

Wendel stepped towards Karl and said very clearly, "Yeah I am," and the two were locked in stare down as Karl told him, "Well, we got a complaint about the noise." While Karl was 6'7" he didn't look that much bigger than Wendel's 6'3" and 200 plus pounds. Additionally, Wendel was doing one hell of a job of putting the angry into "angry black man." I was shoulder-to-shoulder with Karl and starting to think it was going to be "Frazier vs. Ali" in just a minute or so. I was scanning the crowd for who would likely jump my sorry ass once the battle started and trying to decide if now wasn't a good time to discreetly call in the National Guard. About this time we got the most unlikely of angels to help us out.

Just when I figured things couldn't get much worse, I heard a loud female voice shouting, "these white motherfuckers always got to be messing with us niggers." I looked up and saw it was that crazy bitch Thelma Hays, whom the Viper and I had taken to Ypsilanti. I knew for sure at this point the call was headed downhill like a rhino on roller skates. My only hope was that I would be able to yell "Help!" into the radio before the ass-whuppin' I fully expected to take was delivered. Except the most amazing thing happened: Wendel turned on Thelma and snapped, "Shut the fuck up bitch. This ain't got nothin' to do with that. We dealin' man to man." The crowd took their lead from Wendel and one woman stepped in front of Thelma and said "Get yo' crazy ass outta here," and Thelma faded back into the crowd.

The tension level dropped off and Wendel became Mr. Cooperation. He even apologized for the insulting behavior of Thelma. Fortunately, as a Catholic, I was familiar with miracles; I just had never seen one personally until then. Karl and I commiserated with Wendel and the rest of the folks about it being a nice day and people being all tight assed about a little music, beer, and dancing, but that's how it is. An agreement was struck for everyone to stay inside the sidewalks and on the lawns and for the music to get turned down a little. In return, Karl and I would consider the matter closed. That made everyone happy, and Karl and I even got offered a couple of cold beers. I said it hurt me to say no but we were on duty. I knew it damn near killed an ex-sailor like Karl to refuse free beer. One woman about 40 years old said, "Well, what time you get off duty baby, 'cause I'll wait for a good looking young boy like you." That cracked everyone up, including Karl and I. All I could do was shake my head and walk away red faced and laughing. That just made the crowd laugh even more.

Karl and I talked it over afterwards and the only thing we could figure was, since Karl kept his cool and didn't overreact to Wendel's provocation Wendel must have decided Karl was okay. We were both still amazed at how quickly Wendel turned on Thelma for trying to make it a racial incident. Nevertheless, we were both seriously grateful that Thelma's crazy ass showed up when she did.

There was a real advantage to going on calls with a cop the size of Karl because, if shit hit the fan, he could do business with just about anyone. The drawback was half the drunken nitwits saw a cop as big as Karl and decided they needed to give him a try. It was like they were a bunch of freaking sherpas looking at Mt. Everest; they just had to try climbing it.

CHAPTER 64

The new house was working out pretty well. I made a point of introducing myself to all the neighbors, and they were polite enough but really didn't go out of their way to be friendly. I figured since they were all middle aged they had nothing in common with me, so I didn't get worked up about it. They always waved when they were in the yard and I figured that was good enough. Besides, Gary and I worked such odd hours they saw Rick around the place a lot more.

Rick turned out to be a very good roommate; even with habits that I found to be very objectionable. For example, because of his military service he kept his room and bathroom spotless. He even made his bed every day. That really freaked out Gary and me since we might make a bed once every few weeks when we changed the bedding. Not only that, but Rick hung everything up. I usually had more clothes on the floor of my room than on hangers. I kept a pile of workout stuff in a corner of the room, and only washed it when the smell got to the point that I couldn't get close enough to pull something off the festering heap. Yeah, old Rick had some weird ideas.

He also liked tea. Now what kind of guy drinks tea? Gary and I were wondering if there might be some orientation issues involved, but since Rick had a freak-of-the-week club, we were pretty certain he was playing for the same team we were. Apparently, all the time Rick had spent in jolly old England while in the Air Force turned him into a tea drinker. I said I could tolerate that, but if I found any Union Jacks in the house I'd cut his throat. Little did I know at that time that the Irish consume more tea per capita than anywhere in the world and that after my trips there and to England I'd turn into a tea drinker, too.

The final thing about Rick was that watching him eat was just plain weird. It wasn't the quantity of food he consumed; no, that was normal. It was the stuff he ate. I walked into the kitchen one day at lunch time to find him waiting for soup to warm up on the stove. That was no big deal except that while he was waiting, Rick was alternating dipping a big hunk of onion and a big hunk of hot pepper cheese in a jar of English brown mustard. I told him his stomach must be like a sewer lagoon and left the room with Rick munching away happily.

CHAPTER 65

My move to the west side had me changing parishes. I had no problem with St. John's, but Queen of the Miraculous Medal parish was just 10 blocks away. "Queens," as it was known, was the City's largest and most affluent parish, with over 1,200 families. Many of the parishioners at Queens lived in the best neighborhoods in Jackson. I didn't really care who was next to me in a pew anyway, as I figured I had enough to worry about taking care of my own soul. The parish was served by Vincentian priests from the East Coast, and at least a couple of them were good Irishmen so I felt right at home. I also liked the fact that the 11:00 am Mass featured guitar music because I loved to sing. I knew my singing fell in the "joyful noise" category, but I didn't care. I let it rip.

I struck up a particular friendship with one of the priests, Father Mullen, who had grown up in a pretty tough neighborhood in Philadelphia. He was an Irishman's Irishman with a big laugh, down to earth manner, and a faith that was as solid as the Cliffs of Moher. He also loved Irish music and a good joke, so he and I got along right off the bat.

Father Mullen always had a kind word for me and reminded me often I was doing the Lord's work. That was important to me because I did wonder sometimes if I was making a difference. He also encouraged me to become a lector at Mass and said it would be a shame for me to waste such a fine Irish voice. I readily agree to do readings, having served in that ministry back in my home parish and at college. I saw a parallel between being a good cop and a good Catholic: They both required that you work at it. Sit on your butt and do nothing and pretty soon you'd be lost. Well, I didn't plan on wasting any of the gifts the good Lord had given me, and I considered both my faith and being a cop to be gifts, indeed.

I wasn't exactly broadcasting all of this to my fellow officers since there weren't too many practicing Catholics on the force at that time. I wasn't ashamed of my faith or embarrassed by it, but I just figured it was something people had to sort out for themselves, and I sure as heck wasn't anyone to be giving religious advice. My falls from grace could fill a book, so I'd just worry about me for now. I was always willing to tell someone why I went to Church if they asked, but they had to ask.

I did get pissed, though when people had to tell me why they quit the Church, which 99% of the time was based on some slight by a priest or nun. I would generally just nod and then drop the subject, but I wanted to scream *You don't follow a faith because of what some human does or doesn't do, you follow it because you believe in the faith!* The logic of the quitters, if followed, would have every cop in the world quit the profession because sooner or later a commander or fellow officer was going to step on it. No, good cops stuck with the job no matter what because their faith was the oath they took when they got hired: An oath to the laws and the Constitution of their state and nation. I had the same loyalty to my Church regardless of the mistakes of the people who ran it.

CHAPTER 66

There was another reason that I liked living on the west side of town: Bloomfield Park. Bloomfield was a city park located on West Michigan Avenue. It wasn't much bigger than a City block; however, it had outdoor basketball courts where the best players in the area showed up to play pick up-ball in the summer. I fell right in to the mix at the park and many times would jog over to get warmed up and walk home to cool down after playing, as it was less than a mile from my house.

I got a kick out of the fact that the majority of the players at the park were black and it was an all-white neighborhood. Twenty years before a black man likely wouldn't have dared to drive through the neighborhood, let alone hang out in the park. I never did find out how it happened to end up as the place for some of the city's best street ball, but I loved going over there just the same. I was no Larry Bird, but I could play some ball. I was quick and in good shape and, in games where speed up and down the court got you easy baskets, I had an edge. I also could shoot and wasn't afraid to take it to the hole. Playing against the fellas in college had sharpened my one-on-one skills, and so I was recognized as a guy with some "game." The fact I was white and left-handed made me just a little easier to recognize. No one had any idea I was a cop--and I wasn't telling either. I preferred just to play ball and, leave my personnel life out of it.

I got to know quite a few of the young black men who played at Bloomfield in the casual manner guys knew each other in gyms and on courts all over creation. I knew some first names, nicknames, or sometimes just recognized the guy enough to greet him with a nod, or a handshake and, a "What's up man?" I got the same thing in return and, every so often some ribbing about being a white boy. Every now and then a guy might toss out "Bird" along with a laugh or curse when I hit a long jumper or tough driving shot, and things were cool. In fact in all the time I played down at the park, I never saw an actual fight. Any pushing or shoving got quickly broken up with a "fuck that man, play ball."

There was guy that I would see at Bloomfield fairly often who always left me a little creeped out. He was a young white guy with a mechanical arm who would try to play in the games with the best players. At first I admired his courage, but after talking to the guy a couple of times I began to think 10-13 for sure. The guy had a kind of far-off stare and I just figured the less I talked to him the better.

CHAPTER 67

I was working B-22 one afternoon when I took a minor fight complaint. It was alleged a Mexican kid who lived a couple of blocks off Milwaukee on Pearl Street was involved. I had heard the family name before and they had a reputation for being good, honest people, so I was sort of hoping the kid wasn't involved.

I showed up at the house and, as I walked up, several older family members were on the porch. I guessed one to be the mother of the kid I wanted and the other to be a grandfather. I decided to try greeting them in my limited Spanish, and I also took my hat off before putting it back on. This scored me some major points right away, and so when I explained why I was there the kid was produced post haste. One look at Junior and I knew the kid had been involved, as he looked everywhere but at me.

Initially the boy didn't "know nothing" but once I laid a little, "You're shaming your family and your name" on him and, I added "I can help a guy who makes a mistake but not a liar." The kid cracked and admitted he had been involved in the fight. He said he was sorry and really was done doing this kind of stupid crap. I told him since he had been truthful with me I wouldn't petition him into the juvenile court system, but there was always a chance some of the other participants might press charges. (I knew they wouldn't but threw it in to keep the boy a little nervous.) The kid was only 14 or so and so could not be charged in criminal court as someone 17 years or older could be.

I explained to the family that I was willing to stick my neck out since the kid admitted his involvement and said he was done with this kind of stupid behavior. I also said since the family had a good reputation, I knew I could trust their word. The family thought I was one el grande hombre for that. They believed I had shown them respect and taken them at their word, and they could not thank me enough. They also vowed not to let me down, which I figured meant they'd beat the kid within an inch of his life if he so much as spit on the sidewalk. Junior got the message and stayed out of trouble. Over the years, different friends would tell me about some Mexican guy or girl talking about what a great guy I was to anyone who would listen, and I knew it was one of the kid's family members. I also knew I didn't deserve the praise, but I took it just the same.

CHAPTER 68

The flip side of this "Kevin is a great guy" came from, of all things, my encounter with an Irish Setter. An English Pointer I could have lived with, but one of my own? It just wasn't right. Oh well, traitors and informers have always been the bane of Irish existence.

The trouble started when I was sent to a loud music complaint on East Franklin just off Jackson Street. I could hear the tunes blaring from the upstairs as I arrived, so I walked up on the porch and rapped on the front door but got no answer. Looking through the front door I could see there was a small foyer, and off it was a stairway leading upstairs, so I assumed the house was split into an upstairs and downstairs apartment. I opened the door and had just taken a step in when a real Irish redhead with a temper to match charged me with teeth showing.

I thought for sure the dog was going to chomp me so I instinctively grabbed my night stick and held it out in front of me to give the Setter something to bite besides my leg. About this time, the pooch got back up in the form of one pissed off woman who was screaming, "Don't hit my dog" followed closely by, "Why are you in my house?" She did, however, pull the dog back behind her and it quieted down even if she didn't. I tried to explain I wasn't going to hit the dog; I was just trying to keep from getting bitten. I also pointed out I was on my way to the upstairs apartment--I wasn't *in* her house.

Wrong answer. The woman immediately started yelling at me this was all one house and there was no upstairs apartment. I was thinking I would prefer dealing with the vicious dog but realized I needed to get back out on the porch to try and calm things down a little.

I stepped out on the porch and said, "Okay. I'm sorry I stepped inside, but it was an honest mistake. Most of the houses around here are cut up into a couple of apartments." The lady was still pissed and said, "I don't care about them. You still had no right to come in my house." I decided I'd had enough of apologizing for an honest mistake, so I went on the offensive myself. "Alright. Its your house so that means it is your stereo blaring upstairs, disturbing the neighborhood, so you need to get it turned down or YOU will get a ticket."

This bit of news went over about as well as my attempt to avoid getting bit. "Are you telling me my son can't listen to his stereo? What kind of bullshit is that?" I decided I wasn't going to waste any more time trying to kiss this woman's ass so she wouldn't bitch to the boss about me. "Look, lady. I don't care who owns the stereo. It is too loud and so it's either turn it down or face paying a fine. You decide because I'm done screwing around." The woman stomped over to the stairway and yelled up at her kid to turn down the stereo because the asshole cop says you have to. The stereo got turned down and I couldn't resist smiling and saying "thank you" as I left. My simple act of kindness did little to make the lady happy, and she was still yanging at me as I left.

Sure enough, about 30 minutes later I got called into the station by the sergeant working desk to explain what happened over on East Franklin. Luckily for me, the lieutenant was off so the situation was being dealt with by the Sergeant. The sarge seemed satisfied with my explanation and told me to go back on the street. He said he'd take care of the lady and nothing was going on paper. I was relieved because, like most young officers, I was paranoid about getting in any kind of trouble.

I was a little bewildered about the whole situation as I thought about it. On 99% of loud music/noise complaints all a cop had to do was ask for things to be quieted down and they got instant cooperation. Most people were happy for the opportunity to take care of things with no official action and were apologetic about bothering the neighbors. This woman went off on me worse than most felons I arrested. I decided that somewhere in her past she'd probably had a bad experience with JPD. I laughed thinking maybe one of the many hounds on the Department had done her wrong and I was paying for his bad deeds.

CHAPTER 69

I was still a relief officer filling in for whatever officer was on their days off so I worked just about every section over the course of a month but I ended up down in the D-24 district quite a bit. Sometimes when I was lucky, I got assigned an Adam 30 unit. Adam 30 cars were used primarily as backup and so got sent to all the hot calls. As a back up unit, they didn't have to do the report. That was a great deal any way you cut it. Having more cars than the minimum number was also a good thing in that officers could be more proactive and go out and dig stuff up instead of just running from call to call. It also meant officers could take an extra night off now and then. Of course that usually meant I went from an A-30 car to busting a hump around a section for the night taking calls, but, those were the breaks.

My least favorite area to work was A-21 because rarely did anything good ever happen up there. You spent most of your time taking accident reports or other bullshit complaints. Fitzroy described it best when he said, "Twenty-one is nothing but a bunch of white folks in cars driving all over the place."

I didn't mind working Frank-26 because it was right next to D-24, so you ended up being back-up on a lot of the good calls in that section. I had also made friends with a couple of families who lived in the section, so when I was assigned down there I managed to score a home-cooked meal every now and then. One of the families I visited was that of Ken Hunt, the Jackson firefighter who had been standing at the door when Roger and I showed up at the scene of Calpurnia's demise.

Ken was a big, friendly guy who lived down on Grinnell Street with his wife Judy and their 2 sons and 2 daughters. Ken's nickname was "Big Al" after the Disney bear whom he strongly resembled. I would stop by the main station for a break now and then and got to know Ken pretty well. His family went to Queens, too, so I would see them there quite often. Ken made it there any day he wasn't working even though he himself wasn't Catholic. I used to tease him that he was a better Church-goer than most baptized Catholics so he might as well join up. He finally did, but I doubt my busting on him about it had anything to do with his conversion. Stopping by the Hunt house was always a bright spot in my day, and I truly liked all 4 of the Hunt kids.

The other house on my "meal route" was the Ziolowkowskis, a big Catholic family on Thompson Street. Bob Z. was one half of the "Brothers Restaurant Supply" business that was right next to the police station. There were 8 kids and they were all great people and really made me feel at home. Pat Z. used to joke that most times she didn't notice I was at the table with all the kids, and that was how I snuck in for a meal now and then. I would be the first to admit, I missed being around my family. Single life was great but, at heart, I was a family guy and didn't really want to live my life alone.

Of all the Ziolowkowski kids, my favorite was Mike. Mike was developmentally disabled but still was pretty sharp when it came to a lot of things, one of which was what the police were up to at any given time. Mike had a scanner and enjoyed listening to the radio traffic of the various agencies, and so when I showed up Mike fully expected me to provide details. Most times I could help him out, but when I didn't know anything about a particular call he was interested in, Mike would invariably look at me like I was a complete waste of time. He would ask me in an exasperated voice, "Why don't you know about this call? You're a policeman and you're supposed to know what's going on." Hubris wasn't possible with Mike Z. on the case, so I would just say, "You're right Mike, I've got a lot to learn."

CHAPTER 70

Passing my one year anniversary meant a couple of things to me besides getting off probation and getting about a 10% pay raise. First, the pay raise was nice and really gave me some cushion. The raise was substantial because the Department paid step increases at 1, 2 and 3 years and in addition it was the time of rapid inflation so we had a contract raise of 7% that year. Little did I know black clouds were looming, and a year from now pay raises would be the least of my concerns.

Secondly, and more important to me than the money, was now that I was off probation I could become a member of the Fraternal Order of Police Honor Guard that was made up of Jackson Police Officers, and well as one guy from a township Department that was located just east of the city. The Honor Guard marched in parades, served as color guard for a variety of functions, and represented the State FOP at the funeral of any officer killed in the line of duty. They also would serve as the official honor guard at those funerals if requested, which happened a couple times of year because many agencies at this time did not have Honor Guards.

The FOP Honor Guard was started by Lt. Frank Miller, a legendary Jackson officer as the Jackson Police Department Honor Guard but things got ugly in the late 70's when the Chief tried to order them to attend a particular function but was offering no compensation for their time which didn't sit well with the boys. Being that they were all cops, they were all too stubborn to work out a solution and instead just got more entrenched. As a result, the boys quit representing the Department and instead cut a deal to represent the FOP. Not a bad fit since Jackson formed the first FOP Lodge in Michigan back in the early 1900's.

I loved the fancy dress uniforms and the prestige of belonging to such a unit. By nature, I liked to be part of positive things and groups and saw the Honor Guard as just such an organization, much in the same way I saw being a Jackson Police Officer. I didn't worry too much about the fact that it was the FOP Honor Guard because pretty much everyone on the Department, except maybe the Chief, viewed them as the Department Honor Guard. Funny enough, years later it would be my hard ass Lieutenant Johnson who, as the new Chief, would extend the olive branch to bring the Guard back into the Department fold, where it still is today. Amazingly, Lt. Miller, although long retired, is still part of the Honor Guard and provides direction, guidance, and a connection to the Guard's legacy that is priceless.

The uniforms themselves were made up of dark blue riding breeches, a long-sleeved shirt, black leather riding boots, a high shine gun belt and flap holster, a white ascot, a white pistol lanyard, white campaign cord, and a dark blue Smokey-the-Bear style hat. No doubt about it, the boys looked good when all scrubbed up. John Stressman, Ric Cedillo, Gary Hudson, and Steve Leider from second shift were all on the Honor Guard and helped me to become a member of it. The old basketball coach, Mike Tash, sort of ran the show, with help from Lieutenant Miller who had retired by the time I came on the department. Gary and fellow rookie Carl Rice joined up the same time as I did, so that was cool too.

Tash had gotten his job back when an arbitrator ruled the Department didn't have enough to fire him but, besides from going to work, I figured Mike had never really stopped being a part of the Department. For all his bluster to the opposite, I felt Mike wanted to be in, not out, of the Department, and really did miss it when he got the ax. I think he was happy to be back and not just because it meant a regular paycheck again. I just hoped I would never find myself in similar circumstances.

Chapter 71

That summer was going along fairly well with no one getting murdered, kidnapped, or robbed, and I was feeling better and better every day about my ability as a police officer. I knew I had a long way to go, but I was pretty sure I was where I should be doing what was my calling. Of course many of the folks I dealt with were confident I was just another stupid cop keeping them from doing what they wanted to, so there was a definite balance in my life.

One such person who held that opinion was Jerry Racine, a 17-year-old pain in the ass and the youngest member of a family of brothers who all pretty much matched that description. Going to jail was not a source of shame for them as much as it was a right of passage. The family lived down in D-24 and could be counted on for some kind of trouble several times during the year but especially in warm weather.

I got sent on a domestic just off Ganson Street one fine afternoon, and when I arrived I found Racine and his girlfriend, Sarah Jean Diamond, having at in the front yard. They were screaming and yelling at each other, but no blows were being struck when I pulled up. Still, if they didn't shut up when I told them to, I figured I had an easy disorderly arrest and both of these two "gems" had it coming. Prior to turning 17, Jerry was a juvenile so he could get away with a lot more since locking a juvy up for anything less than murder was not likely. The result was that a lot of conversations between people like Jerry and the Cops ended with, "I can't wait for your 17th birthday."

I wondered exactly how a 17-year-old kid ended up in the middle of the street in a full-fledged domestic when I couldn't get a date when

I was that age. It was just one of the many wonders that the country boy discovered when he came to the city. Not only did 17-year-olds get into domestics, they fathered children all over the place. Those kids would grow up to ensure that my profession would always be necessary, and the State Prison of Southern Michigan would continue to be one of Jackson County's best employers.

Jerry decided at one point that going out into the middle of Ganson Street and challenging me was a good idea, and that was where I decided locking the little goof up was going to be the best solution to this whole goat rope. Jerry came out of the street and saved me the trouble. I was still thinking that he would eventually build a very long arrest record for the same stupid stuff. I turned out to be wrong. Very wrong.

Several weeks later, back at the old homestead in D-24 one evening, Jerry decided he should come out on the front porch with a shotgun and challenge the officers who had responded to a disturbance call at his Mom's house. The officers at the house yelled at Jerry to drop the gun and in most every case that is what happens--contrary to what TV portrays. Jerry decided to be the exception and made the mistake of pointing his gun at one of the many veterans of combat in Vietnam who now were on the Department. Men like that tend to recognize immediately when their lives are in imminent danger and they know they must act with equal speed if they are to live. A single shot from a Department-issued 12 gauge shotgun sent 9 .32 caliber rounds of buckshot hurtling into the chest of Jerry Racine and he was likely dead before he hit the porch. Just like Paula Samuelson and Calpurnia Smith, one minute you're alive and the next you are dead. The difference was Paula and Calpurnia had done nothing to deserve being killed. Jerry chose actions that no reasonable person could be surprised would lead to the conclusion they did.

I heard the news when Gary came in the house at the end of the shift. I didn't know what to think. There were several locals I'd dealt with whom it would not have surprised me at all to have gotten in a fatal encounter with the police, but I never would have guessed Jerry Racine would end up like that. It just reinforced to me that you had to be on your toes at all times. You simply never knew who would pull a gun or knife on you. No, the only way to survive this job was to expect the worst and be ready to react to it at all times.

The thought of having to shoot someone or even shoot at someone was not taken lightly by any sane officer. A police shooting was not like war. In war you are trained to identify your enemy and destroy him. Pure and simple. Once you do that, you move on to find more enemies and do the same thing to them. No one talks about "overkill" or "excessive force" or being "too quick on the trigger." As big brother Stanley pointed out to me, in the Army if you sneak up on your enemy and shoot him in the back, that's being a good soldier. Cops, on the other hand, had to clearly announce to their enemies they were there so the dirtballs had a chance to turn and shoot them. Police shootings were rare and so were subjected to a ridiculous amount of scrutiny, media attention, second guessing, and very often a lawsuit.

Most rational people could not understand how the family of a guy who points a gun at a cop and ends up dead for his effort can sue the police. It makes no sense that taxpayer money is paid out based on the legitimate action of good cops. It just defies logic. Well, it defies normal logic--but not the logic of the American system of civil law. There the idea is that you file a multi-million dollar claim over a legitimate police action using a lawyer who works for a cut of your settlement and figure eventually the governmental unit you are suing will offer you something to go away and shut up. Generally, that is exactly what happens.

Since both sides are represented by lawyers, they do the negotiating and come up with an allegedly equitable solution, sort of like when two different wolf packs show up at the same elk carcass and work it out so both get their fair share. The city, or elk carcass, is of course faced with accepting a payment of 15 or 20 grand to someone who is completely undeserving of it, or it must endure going to court and paying more than that in lawyer fees, not to mention running the risk of a jury handing over a hell of a lot more to the dead guy's family. During all of this, which usually drags out for a couple of years after the incident, the poor bastard who fired the shot is put through the wringer and has to keep reliving the incident.

Next to getting shot, having to shoot someone is about the worst thing that can happen to a cop.

Of course, the neutral purveyor of the news in Jackson, *The Citizen Patriot* newspaper, came through as expected with a headline that read, "Police Shoot 17-year-old." I couldn't believe the paper could be that low crawling. Yeah, the guy was 17 but he was also ARMED with a fucking shotgun and he pointed it at a cop. Anticipating a headline that read, "Officer defends Himself against Armed Suspect" or "Police Shoot Gun Wielding Man" was apparently too much to expect. Back then, I had the mistaken belief that the media only sought to report the news, not "flavor it" for public consumption.

Almost every cop in America, myself included, just wanted to puke when the media tried to claim they had no bias against cops. The bastards could be counted on to slant a story or word a headline to make the cops look bad and all the rest of law enforcement and I could do was seethe, because you are not going to win a fight with people who buy ink by the tanker truck. The newspapers had always been this way and they always would be. As I got older, I accepted that and managed to get along with the media reasonably well when I became a commander and later a chief of police. Sort of a know your enemy approach.

After the shooting, the Racine family mistakenly thought the shooting had been done by Officer Gary Hudson, and so on a couple of occasions they shouted racial slurs his way. One of them even shouted at him as he left a call they were at that they were going to "shoot a nigger" to even things up. Gary wasn't exactly the easy to scare type and shouted back, "Good. Shoot'em all." Not exactly the response his antagonist expected to get from a black cop they were busting on. Hudson was one tough son of a bitch, and if you felt froggy, he'd tell you to go ahead and jump. He had something for your ass.

CHAPTER 72

I was shooting the breeze one day with Sgt. Zomer and found out he loved basketball. Hudson was standing there, and so a little trash talking started. The end result was the boys agreed to play some Saturday morning driveway basketball at Zomer's house. Mike Brunk was added to the mix so we could go 2 on 2.

Police work attracts a lot of people who are athletic and all sorts of theories abound about why that is. I figured at least part of it was there was a sense of belonging to a team and it did present more of a challenge than parking your ass behind a desk, which was anathema to someone who was athletic by nature. Of course, liberal cop haters would say it was because police chiefs went looking for testosterone-driven Neanderthals to become the newest crop of head bashers out there stomping on the rights of the oppressed. And they said that like it was a bad thing.

Neanderthals or not, the opening game at the Zome Dome, as we christened the driveway was a spirited affair if not a skillful one. It was a chance for all these grownups to go back to playing the game they way they began. On a driveway with no coaches, refs, or rules, especially no rules, as the "no autopsy, no foul" standard was definitely being followed. More than a couple of shots followed more steps than a square dance, but all in all it was a great morning of missed shots, trash talk, and enough good plays to let the boys and me think we still had a little something left in the tank.

Several rematches were played during the summer, and each one was as good as the last. Typical of big boys, however, other stuff got in the way and the tradition didn't last but it was sweet while it did.

I saw the games at the Zome Dome as another positive sign that I was becoming one of the guys. That was important to me because the transition from rookie to member of the Department was far more complex than just completing training and be able to work on one's own. You had to establish a positive reputation with the officers already there. Establishing your rep was based on what you did more than what you said. Telling people you won't let them down is fine, but it's better to make sure you handle all the calls in your section so no one else has to. You don't need to try and be Dirty Harry, but when the shit hits the fan you better show that you'll jump in the middle of it whenever or wherever it is necessary.

What you didn't say was also important. Keeping your mouth shut when you would be justified in bitching was a big bonus for a new guy. Nothing could grind a good veteran officer's ass more than listening to a new guy whining. Your rep was also about how you showed respect for the grey beards. It's okay to work harder than they did and make more arrests, but don't wave it in their faces. In fact, you needed to make a point of seeking their advice even when you didn't need it. You also needed to spend time bs'ing with them about their experiences. That'll have them telling people that new kid is okay because, if you don't, the word will be the new guy's a stuck up little prick.

How you acted off duty was also important. If you never went to any of the functions at the FOP or never stopped for a cold one at Evanoff's, it sent the wrong message--a message that you were too good to hang out with the people you worked with. Even if you drank a Coke, as long as you stopped in with the boys now and then, it scores big points.

I was working on all this and figured I was doing fine but I still knew I had a long way to go. Staying on second shift didn't hurt because clearly those guys treated me well and went out of their way to keep me on the right path. Since I admired them, it was pretty easy for me to do my best to try to meet their expectations.

The big summer social event for the area emergency services was coming up and I was looking forward to it. It was the annual Dispatch Pool Party at the Calderone Ranch out east of town. The tradition was that all the departments agreed to cover central dispatch one day a year so all the dispatchers could be off for an employee picnic. One of them had connections with the Calderone family who had a large pool, a grill, and an area for gathering on their "ranch," and the family graciously let the dispatchers use it for their annual party.

Julie and I were still dating, so naturally I would be attending the gathering. I enjoyed swimming and eating, so this was an event right up my alley. I also didn't mind seeing a wide variety of women walking around in bathing suits. Like the guy said, just because you have a brand new car it doesn't mean you don't look around when you drive by a dealership.

The party was a great time and the weather was perfect, hot with lots of sunshine. People from all the area departments and the State Police Post showed up at these events, so I got a chance to meet officers I had never met before. Julie knew most of them because she worked at dispatch. The fact that she was young, beautiful, single and that they were all dogs, might also have something to do with the fact that they all had introduced themselves to her at some point.

I was beginning to wonder where I was headed with Julie. A man couldn't be single his whole life, but I had never really had a serious girlfriend--at least not for more than 3 or 4 weeks--and I had promised myself I would not get married for at least two years after finding a job. I wanted to make sure I had plenty of opportunity to waste my money and time as I saw fit and live the single life to the fullest. I wasn't interested in "living together," as that was the same as being married as far as I was concerned. No, if I was ready for that step I'd make it legal; otherwise I wanted a place that I could retreat to by myself.

The problem for me, of course, was that I was in love with Julie and didn't see much changing in that regard. I also knew that at some point she was going to ask that most female of questions, "Where is this relationship headed?" I figured I had time before it got to that, but I was starting to weigh my options.

Kevin M. Courtney

.

CHAPTER 73

I was constantly frustrated with the inability to make arrests on domestic violence cases, which were a large part of my business. Many of the domestic cases I was sent on were simply verbal arguments, but a significant percentage involved the old man thumping on his woman. I had taken reports of everything from a slap, to a punch, to a kick, to a full out beating. The problem was most of these assaults were misdemeanors, and Michigan law did not allow a police officer to make a misdemeanor arrest unless he saw the offense committed. The only exceptions were arresting a drunk driver at an accident scene and possession of marijuana. (You couldn't say for sure it was marijuana until the lab report came back, so, technically the arrest was based on probable cause.)

The typical approach on a domestic was to get the parties separated and get their stories. Officers then would ask if the victim (99% of the time the woman) wanted to prosecute and, if she did, they would explain the warrant process to her. It was the same for her as it was for Uncle Jed and Jethro of Sugar Shack fame. Often times, all the women asked was that the male half of the situation be made to leave the house, which the cops had no authority to force him to do. That didn't mean they didn't do it, however.

I just couldn't understand how a woman would put up with getting beat on, nor could I fathom what kind of dirt bag you had to be to go around beating on women. Most of the time I kept my cool, but on occasion I just wanted to drag the male half outside and nightstick the stupid right out of him. Once in a while officers got lucky and the male half did something you could arrest him for while you were there--or had a warrant for his arrest somewhere and you could drag his ass out of there for that. You had to be careful, though, as occasionally the act of arresting the old man sometimes turned the house against you, and you might end up battling everyone in the house including the woman who made the original complaint.

Usually an officer took the approach of, "Come on, help me out here. Isn't there somewhere you can go for tonight until things cool down?" Most times that worked, but unfortunately it gave the impression that the officer and suspect were buddies. The truth was most cops had no use for any of the assholes they dealt with, but showing that got you nowhere fast. No, you had to learn to con people and get them to think it was their choice to do what you wanted them to do. Sometimes the soft approach didn't work, so you had to use the bluff of, "If I come back, I'm taking somebody to jail so my best advice to you, sir, is to find somewhere else to be tonight." That cleared up more than a few complaints, but there were still a couple of places a week where officers would respond two or three times in a shift. Of course, there were also "couples" that were frequent flyers with the Department and got multiple responses during the year.

We did have one old couple, Sarah and Otis, who lived off Milwaukee Street in 22's section and were constantly calling in domestics. Sarah would swear Otis was choking her, and it sure sounded that way to the Dispatcher. Officers would arrive and listen to the same old song and dance and tell the two to knock it off and behave hoping for once they actually would. My theory was the cops showing up was the only break in the monotony of their lives the two old fools had. On one occasion one of my smart-assed brother officers suggested to Otis that he choke his chicken instead of Sarah. Otis looked at his crotch and said "That old thing ain't worked for 15 years."

One night an officer happened to be right around the corner when Sarah called, and he made it to the house while she was still on the line with dispatch claiming Otis was choking her. The officer peeked in the window and observed Sarah holding her own throat, all the while croaking, "He's choking me, he's choking me." Otis on the other hand was sleeping on the couch. Sarah apparently planned on waking him up in time to get an argument started before the cops showed up.

CHAPTER 74

Marty and Sherry were two real gems I had to deal with in the domestic department. Marty was around 20 and Sherry was pushing 40. Not only were they a couple, but they were also aunt and nephew. That was just too weird even for me. I mean, were talking Jackson, Michigan, not Skunkbluff, Arkansas. Now this loving couple went at it about two or three times a week when the mood was on them, and it seemed like we were there all the time. Marty was a violent and dangerous person with a temper that might have been the worst of anyone I had dealt with. Even now, 30 years later, I haven't seen many others like Marty.

Sherry obviously had some issues if she was banging a nephew who was half her age. Not only that, she was never cooperative and everything was always the cops' fault. I wanted to ask her who it was that decided incest was best and got this whole shit sandwich started, but figured I didn't need any time off so I kept my mouth shut.

I wasn't thinking of them at all as I cruised through D-24 on a quiet shift in the middle of a week. D-24 was an older part of Jackson and full of big trees and some still-nice old houses, and it could look quite pretty in the summer time. Dispatch ruined the mood and sent me to Sherry's house for a UDAA complaint, that's police shorthand for Unlawfully Driving Away an Automobile. Someone apparently had ripped off Sherry's car. Well, at least the change in why I was headed there was a welcome one, even if I expected Sherry to be her usual self.

I walked up on the porch and knocked on the door. Sherry came and immediately upon opening it she said, "The asshole stole my car and I've had it." I was no rocket scientist but I could pretty well figure out who she was talking about, so I simply replied "What happened?"

Sherry explained that she and Marty were split up and that he showed up at her house pounding on the door. The next thing she knew he had kicked the door open and had come storming into the house. He grabbed her and smacked her around demanding the keys to her car then scooped up her purse and took the keys out of it. Marty then left and drove off in her car. I was smelling a stack of felony charges to drop on Marty's ass but at the same time recognized who my victim was, so I was going to make damn sure I had things right before I did anything.

"Let me get this straight. Marty forced his way into the house, assaulted you, took your keys, and then drove away in your car." Sherry said, "That's exactly what the asshole did and I want him in jail." I was still playing things safe and so asked her specific questions such as, did you let him in? Did you say he could take your car? Did you give him your purse? Sherry answered an emphatic "No" to every question, but I was still playing it safe knowing the history of the two. So I even asked her how Marty got the keys. "I told you. He beat my ass and took them." I was finally satisfied I had a pretty good case.

I ran through in my mind what charges I would go for and came up with Breaking and Entering with Intent to Commit a Felony, Strong Armed Robbery, (taking the purse and keys) and UDAA. Maybe, just maybe, I could put an end to one problem address by sending lover-boy-nephew off to prison. Warrants were issued and Marty got locked up.

In Michigan, anyone charged with a felony is first arraigned in District Court, where he or she has a chance to plead to the crime. The rare thug who pleads guilty at this stage would go straight to Circuit Court where he would be arraigned a second time in that Court and, after pleading guilty would eventually get a sentence. In almost all cases, the defendant at District Court arraignment either pleads not guilty or stands mute and the judge or magistrate enters a plea of not guilty on that person's behalf. The law in Michigan requires that a preliminary hearing be held within 12 calendar days of arrest to determine if there is sufficient evidence to provide probable cause that the crime charged was committed and the person charged committed it. If the State can show it has enough evidence in the hearing, the suspect is bound over and, if not, the case gets pitched. Rarely do cases get pitched because in order to get to this step the case has all ready been given the once-over by the Prosecutor, who isn't going to let a weak case past his or her desk.

Most individuals charged with felonies waive their preliminary hearing because a) they know they did it and b) their court-appointed attorney isn't interested in wasting his time on a prelim when he knows the outcome will be his client will be bound over for trial. The exception is when the defense attorney believes there's a weak witness who can be worked over a little, or that there is some evidence he or she might be able to get tossed out due to police mistakes.

I wasn't too worried when I got a subpoena for Marty's case; because of the 12 day rule few people waived their prelims until after the subpoenas went out. Many were not waived until the day of the hearing, so getting a subpoena or even having to show up on the day of the hearing didn't mean there would actually be a hearing. Typically it meant you would get told the case was cancelled the day before a hearing or after you got to court.

I realized this was not going to be the typical prelim when I walked onto the second floor of the court house where the four district courtrooms were located and saw Marty and Sherry all lovey dovey in front of one of them. In fact, they were so busy nuzzling noses they didn't even notice me walk past them on my way to the jury room where, unless a jury was using it, which was rare, the cops waited for their cases to be called and deals got worked out between the prosecutors and defense attorneys.

I took one look at the assistant prosecutor assigned the case and said, "We're fucked." I then explained what I saw and the prosecutor said, "Well we've got no choice but to go through with it, but I figured something was up when the defense was all fired up about having the prelim." I fully assumed that asshole Marty must have gotten out of jail on bond and, once he did, he went straight to Sherry and got things all smoothed over.

Sherry took the witness stand and completely recanted her statements to me. The prosecutor tried to get her to tell the truth but she said it was all a mistake and that Marty never kicked open the door, he surely never hit her, and she gave him the keys so he could use the car. I wanted to jump up and smack the lying bitch but decided that wasn't a wise thing to do in a courtroom. Finally the exasperated prosecutor asked her why would Officer Courtney write a report that said she had told him that Marty did all those things. Her answer was classic, "Well Courtney lied because he's out to get Marty and since

Marty hasn't done anything wrong he made all this stuff up." With that my case officially went down the freaking tubes.

It was anticlimactic when the judge dismissed the case and the happy couple left the courtroom. I was so mad and frustrated I couldn't speak. Finally, I ranted at the prosecutor, "I go the extra mile for her, lock up the guy who has been whipping her ass on a regular basis, and my thanks is she calls me a fucking liar in open court. Well, ain't that fucking gratitude." The prosecutor just shook his head and said, "What can you do? You do good work and sometimes you get burned by the very people you're trying to help." I replied, "Yeah, well you just saw the last time I stick my neck out for her. That fucking loser she left with can thump on her seven days a week for all I care. I ain't arresting his ass again unless she signs a warrant."

I left the court and was still pissed 20 minutes later after I had stopped and grabbed a Pepsi at the stop and rob on Morrell just down the street from our house. I couldn't decide if I was more upset about losing a good felony case or the fact that jerk Marty walked out of court knowing he had put one over on the cops. I decided it was having Marty be the winner. Well, I'd said I wouldn't stick my neck out to arrest him for crimes committed against Sherry, but that didn't mean I wouldn't jam his ass up for anything else I caught him doing.

I never got the chance to even things up with either one. Not too long after the love fest in the courthouse, I came into work and was told a couple of day shift officers had responded to Sherry's house and found her on the floor unconscious. Apparently the usual beating wasn't good enough this time. Marty had stomped Sherry to the point that she was not expected to live. She lingered in a coma in intensive care at Foote East for several days until she died from her injuries. Marty caught himself a murder charge, and this time he wouldn't be able to sweet talk Sherry in to not testifying. No, the pictures of her battered body would say all that was necessary and wasn't nobody gonna change that story.

It would have been natural for me to think, *Well she asked for it,* and write the whole thing off, but I just became more frustrated at the senselessness of Sherry's murder. Jesus Christ it didn't have to happen! I had the guy dead nuts on some heavy shit and all Sherry had to do was tell the freaking truth! What could that loser possibly offer her that she would risk and then ultimately, lose her life for him? It just made no sense.

At this point in my life I just couldn't fathom that women like Sherry had such lousy self esteem they figured the "Martys" of the world were the best they could do. I'd learn to understand the whole domestic violence dynamic as I progressed through my career, but it would still amaze me what women would put up with from a man who professed to love them. I'd also never buy into all the psycho babble about why men beat women. It was simply wrong to raise your hand to a woman and no amount of bullshit would ever change that. Men beat their women because they could get away with it and it got them what they wanted. That belief and my experiences in Jackson would set the foundation for my approach to setting policy on domestic violence when I took over in Big Rapids.

The law changed several years later to allow for arrests on probable cause in cases of domestic violence and many departments, including mine, instituted mandatory arrest policies. Laws and policies like that would have without a doubt prevented Calpurnia's murder that night in '79. Unfortunately, they wouldn't have helped Sherry because she, not the cops, let her killer of the hook.

Kevin M. Courtney

.

CHAPTER 75

The house was a great set up for my roommates and I except for the fact the Gary and I were slobs and Rick was not. I didn't think things were all that bad until Julie finally commented, one day that Gary and I lived like "retarded apes." Gary responded by itching his side like an ape, and asking "what do you mean by that?" As much as I enjoyed his response, I decided there might be room for some improvement. There was, however, little, if any, chance Gary and I would reform, so I decided a housekeeper was the answer. Cheap sucker that I was, hiring a regular cleaning service was out of the question. Instead, I offered the job to Ann Ziolokowski who was 16 and the oldest daughter of the family that had befriended me.

I told Ann I would pay her $5 an hour for up to three hours a week and she could keep the additional money from returning all the empty beer and pop cans and bottles. Those all had a 10 cent deposit on them. Ann jumped at the opportunity, but her mother was a little less enthusiastic about her sweet young Catholic daughter dropping by what was surely the Jackson branch of Sodom and Gomorra Inc. without an appropriate chaperone. Say the National Guard, for instance. I solved Mrs. Z's worry by having Ann come by on Friday afternoons when all of us were working.

Things went along fine until the week Ann came home and mentioned she made an extra $10 that week just in empty beer cans. I had to explain to her mom, Pat, that it was the aftermath of a rather social five days and not the typical intake of the three residents. She gave me one of those "my ass" looks all mothers have perfected and said "sure." I didn't waste any breath protesting but did pull Ann aside and explained that bragging had cost many a miner their claim so she better clam up about where she was prospecting.

Rick had failed to mention to Gary and me that he had a Doberman as a pet. The lease on the house did not allow for pets but Rick would bring the pooch over to visit from time to time. A friend of Rick's kept the dog, Max, for him. Rick often had a hard time getting his share of the rent money in on time and while Gary and I weren't really worried about getting our money we occasionally would put our guns to Max's head and say, "Pay up or the dog gets it." Max was pretty much the wimpiest Doberman ever, and I suspect if he were human he would have owned a flower shop and thought figure skating was a great sport. Max would just stand quietly while his life was threatened. Rick would yell at Max, "bite the fuckers, or at least run away" but Max was completely opposed to violence and would just stand there hoping sooner or later someone would pet him.

We had been in the house about two months when by a fluke we all had a Saturday off. This could only mean one thing. Party! The barbeque was hauled out, beer purchased, dates lined up and even the weather cooperated. Along about 6 o'clock in the afternoon, about an hour before the guests were set to arrive, our landlord, Lynn Matzen, showed up. He was a nice guy and stopped by every now and then to make sure things were going running smoothly but today he smelled a party and decided to yank some chains.

First, he asked for a beer and then relaxed, showing no inclination to move along. I was trying to be sly but since Lynn knew what I was up to he wouldn't cooperate. He even asked questions about why it looked like we were expecting guests when it was just the three of us at the house. Well, I finally caught on to what was going on, and I just told Lynn he had to beat it as no one over 40 was allowed on the premises at times like this--it just ruined the mood. Plus, if he didn't split, I'd rat his ass out to his wife, Jan, and tell her that he was hanging around trying to check out younger women.

Lynn finished his beer and walked away laughing. He couldn't resist one last shot, though, when he asked if we were having a hard time with transportation. "What are you talking about?" I asked. "Well, it seems like I see a different car here every night so I assumed you were having car trouble." One look on our faces told Lynn his shot had hit home. He left a happy man.

We had a pretty relaxing night and I had to chuckle thinking I was living the suburban life; drinking beer and grilling out with friends on a Saturday night. Poor Lynn's fears of his rental property being turned into party central never materialized. The truth was that, while we liked a good time, it was a whole lot more convenient to head to Evanoff's than to have a bash at our house. We had a few parties while we lived on Westwood and that was cool, but we weren't all that interested in the clean up detail on a regular basis so we kept it pretty low key.

Interestingly enough, that was not the impression certain wives of officers had, because the common excuse used by those guys when they got home late was they were at a party over at "Gary and Kevin's place." I wasn't all that happy being someone's cover story, but I sure as hell didn't like not knowing I was a cover story when confronted by some angry woman telling me it was fine for me to be a drunken degenerate but I didn't need to drag her husband down too. I was beginning to perfect a blank, stupid look for those occasions but fortunately, before things got too far out of hand for me, the officer in question usually got tossed out of his house anyway. That saved me a lot of grief even if it did cost the poor fool who got tossed, everything he had or would ever have.

It was crazy shit like that which made me think maybe there was something to be said for staying single and having my own house. I didn't, however, share that opinion with Julie. Comments like that seemed to have a negative impact on my squeeze.

Kevin M. Courtney

.

CHAPTER 76

I had accumulated two weeks vacation, the standard for all new employees after one year of service, and so I decided I would take a week off in the summer and maybe look up a couple of buddies. I wanted to head up to the small cottage my family owned in Clare County and just relax. I stopped at my parents' house first for a day and, while there ran into Dick Belill, who was laid off from the GM factory.

Dick wasn't doing anything so he headed "up north" with me to drink a few beers and play a little golf. Most people who had a summer place in Michigan had it in the northern part of the State, so going "up north" meant heading to some type of cabin, cottage, campground, or resort.

I enjoyed spending a couple of days with Dick and playing a little golf, even though we both stunk at the game. Fortunately the course we played was wide open with few hazards. We played several fairways twice as we hooked and sliced our way around. I really valued the friends I grew up with and worried that living in Jackson would likely make it impossible to stay in touch with them as the years went by.

Julie had made arrangements to come up on her days off and my old roommate from college was also going to come up so the two of us could head up to Kalkaska and look up a girl we both knew from Ferris. Both the girl and my ex-roommate were two years younger than I was and were still in the five-year pharmacy program at Ferris.

Julie still wanted nothing to do with Dick because of the infamous New Year's Day call, so he was on down the road before she showed up. Dick and I still laughed like hell about the incident, but of course I wasn't quite so jovial when the topic came up with Julie. No, that was a sore point that would stay that way for a few years more, so I tried to let that sleeping dog lie.

I showed Julie around the area and we also played a little golf, too. She was very good at the game and it took me a couple of years before I could beat her, more because her skills deteriorated than mine improved. I even managed to fix a passable dinner for the two of us. The cabin was small and pretty basic with three bedrooms, a bath room, and a kitchen and living room combination. It was mostly a fishing and hunting cabin but back in the early 60's, when my Dad built it, it was pretty typical of the cottages working people had. It wouldn't have made a storage shed on John Stressman's in-laws-place but I still liked it. Lots of great memories were in that old cabin, the best centered around deer camp with my dad, brother, and our friends, and summer fishing trips with my Birch Run buddies Henry, Tom, and Mark.

Julie split to go back to work around the same time my old roommate, Mark, showed up. Because he was a pharmacy major, I had nicknamed him "Drugs," which at first bugged the straight laced Mark, but he soon grew to like the name. I had joked that when Mark moved in with me, he didn't smoke, drink, cuss, or chase women. After a year, he still didn't smoke. Drugs had a huge crush on the girl, Debbie, we were headed up to visit, and I was hoping that maybe she'd start returning the feelings as Mark was a great guy who had no luck with women.

We rolled into Kalkaska and found Debbie at the drug store she worked at in town, and she was quite pleased to see us. She told us she had to be at the store for another hour so we could go goof off and then come back and meet her. Kalkaska was the size of town that an hour was more than enough time to look the place over, but we did buy a few provisions for the evening while scoping things out. Debbie's parents owned some small rental cabins at a lake not too far out of town and were going to let us stay there, so once Debbie got out of work she took us to her house first and then out to the cabins.

Drugs, Debbie, and I, along with some of Debbie's pals from the area had a great night sitting around a campfire talking about our school days, and I tossed in just enough "war stories" from Jackson that all were impressed. I would have made a great Sanachie, Irish for story teller, and I liked the attention being a cop brought in situations like this where people respected the profession and were even a little in awe of what I did.

I got Debbie off to the side at one point during the evening and tried to rep for my man Drugs, but she said the words no man wants to hear: "Mark's great guy and a really good friend but that's it." I pled my man's case but I could see it was going nowhere, so gave up so as not to ruin the night. Still, I wished there was something I could do to change my buddy's luck. I could strike up a conversation with anyone, and while I got shot down more than Snoopy in his Sopwith Camel, I also managed to date a lot of women way out of my league simply because I had the nerve to ask them out. Mark didn't have that, but I also knew he didn't have any of the multitude of bad habits and jerk tendencies I did and would be the perfect boyfriend for any girl, but it didn't seem to matter.

The last stop on the northern Michigan goof-off tour was Houghton Lake, where my buddy Tom was staying at his grandparents' cottage. We pulled in late in the afternoon and figured to hang around for a few hours before continuing back to my cottage and then home the next day. Our timing couldn't have been better because the people at the neighboring cottage were up for a visit. They were from my hometown and had an eighteen-year-old daughter named Colleen, who was so absolutely gorgeous and well built that a gay man would pimp slap a Hell's Angel just to see her in a bikini. Drugs and I, on the other hand didn't have to do anything but walk down to the beach and stare. Which we did.

Colleen was happy to see me and came up out of the water to say hi. I took the opportunity to introduce Mark and she visited politely with both of us for a couple of minutes before heading back into the water. I couldn't help but thinking to myself, why couldn't have she been my age instead of 4 years younger. Oh well, the breaks of the game. Besides, she likely would have put me on the curb like most all of the other women I hit on back in high school. Drugs could not have cared less about any of that; he was just very appreciative that he got a look and told me so after we left.

There were about seven or eight young people hanging around the water when Colleen's dad came over and greeted me. "You got your hog leg with you?" he asked. I laughed and said, "Yeah but it's in the car." The old man smiled and said I was probably safe without it.

Of course no one else in the group had the vaguest idea what had just been said, but I loved old westerns so I knew "hog leg" was slang for a cowboy's pistol. I had to explain the conversation before my dirty-minded buddy, Tom, made some other explanation for hog leg that wouldn't be pretty.

It was good to see some more home folks and I really enjoyed the time off, but as I headed back to Jackson, I realized that was now "home" and I was glad of it. I was a Jackson Police Officer and proud of what all that entailed. It was time to go back to my Department and city and to keep building myself into being a good cop like Roger, Ric, Dave, John, and all the others.

CHAPTER 77

Karl Ankrom, one of my fellow Pick Me Brothers, ended up on second shift with me, and he also had the view that good police work meant being proactive. Karl was patrolling along East Wilkins just west of South Jackson when he observed a male lurking in an alley alongside a house. The man was acting "suspiciously" and became a textbook example of what was known as a "Terry Stop." The U.S. Supreme Court in the case of Terry v. Ohio said trained police officers have the right to stop and detain people when an officer believes criminal activity may be afoot. The officers have a right to pat the person down for weapons and do a preliminary investigation into what the potential perpetrator may be up to. The detentions are typically short in duration, and the person is allowed to go on his way unless the officer discovers the person detained indeed is committing a crime. Many a burglar had their careers screwed up by exactly this type of encounter and many a gun and stash of dope was taken away by cops doing Terry Stops.

Karl called out his location to dispatch and the reason for his getting out of his patrol car. He then got out and made contact with the man. He did a quick pat-down of the suspect and then requested and got ID from him. The ID showed him to be one Sam Tilden and that he lived a block over on Franklin Street. Sam had a few under his belt, so Karl figured he was probably just wandering the neighborhood half bagged and not really up to no good. Karl went ahead and ran a check on Sam and figured he would be on his way once it came back.

The dispatcher called Karl and said, "Copy a 10-9," which was code for "there's a misdemeanor warrant for the person you just ran." Well, Sam was up on the codes too and once he heard "10-9" he decided it was time to break wide and get the hell out of there. He took off running down the alley with Karl in pursuit. However, since Sam was about 5'5" and 150, and Karl was 6'7" and well over 220 it was pretty much a mismatch. At one point Karl, who still had his portable radio in his hand from running the check, chucked the radio at Sam and drilled him in the middle of the back. Unfortunately, while it was a heck of a toss, it did not knock Sam down, and Karl figured the little sum bitch was going to make a clean break.

Luck was on Karl's side this night and when Sam tried to turn from the alley to go down Franklin Street, he went ass over nose and down to the ground. Karl saw his chance and pounced on him and the fight was on. Sam was wiry, strong, and slippery as a greased eel. Karl had his hands full and since he had used his radio as a projectile, he couldn't use it to call for help.

Fortunately that "Pick Me Brother" desire to get in the middle of everything paid off, as Howard Noppe had started over towards Karl's location after he heard him call out that Karl was going to be checking out a suspicious person. About the time dispatch started checking Karl's status and getting no answer, Howard was pulling into the area and saw the battle. He jumped right in after filling in dispatch and in pretty short order they had Sam wearing a matching set of JPD's finest bracelets and lying on the lawn screaming "Sally Tilden save me. These motherfuckers are beatin' my ass." Sam not had run without a plan. He was just a short distance from his house when he end up with one extra-large white boy draped all over his ass, so he figured his old lady would hear his cries for help.

Sam was pretty scuffed up for having the big ape Karl land on him, but overall he looked better than he should for having moved up several weight classes for this fight. Sam, however, did lose a handful of beard to Howard while the 3 of them were rolling around in the typical fur ball that most police/suspect fights are. Cops love watching all these clean two or three punch dust ups on TV or in the movies, which always left the suspect knocked out and the cop standing around barely out of breath. The truth was very few physical confrontations with suspects involved throwing punches, and on the rare occasions a cop threw a punch, he usually ended up with a broken hand.

Still, after rolling around fighting with some goof who is doing his best to injure you, it was natural to want to play a little catch up. Karl and Howard resisted that urge and simply quit once they got the upper hand. This police restraint impressed Sam to no end. He fully expected since he got the ball rolling by running off and then fighting with Karl that one serious JPD ass-whuppin' was his to enjoy once Karl got the upper hand. The fact that he didn't get anywhere near what he figured he deserved made Sam Karl's number one fan from that point forward. In the strange relationship that exists between cops and the people they interact with on a regular basis, this was a mark of respect. Sam, and a lot of guys like him, knew when they had earned being arrested and even when they deserved to be on the wrong end of police use-of-force, but they also had a keen sense of what was fair. As long as the cop met their standard, the two would have little problems in their dealings. This was the case with Sam.

Right after I got back from vacation, Karl and I were working side by side. Karl was in D-24 and I was in F-26. Karl's "act of kindness" would pay immediate dividends for us. We were handling a dispute in Sam's neighborhood and it was the typical neighbors getting after each other because of too much sun and alcohol. We weren't having any luck at all in getting either side to chill out, and it looked like this was either going to be one of those situations the cops got called back to two or three times in a shift or we would have to lock some folks up. That was until Sam came forward from the crowd and gave a testimonial on what kind of cop Karl was and that as such "ya'all need to quit causing all this confusion and do what the man says." Amazingly, things quieted down and there were no more calls back to the neighborhood.

I picked up this same goodwill because Sam identified me as one of Karl's boys, and over the next few years whenever Karl or I ran into Sam it was smooth sailing. Sam wasn't getting in trouble like he used to and things were pretty smooth for everyone. That all ended when Sam got stabbed by his girlfriend's ex-boyfriend in the small shopping plaza on the corner of Prospect and Francis. I didn't know it, but Sam was a Jehovah's Witness and as such would not allow a blood transfusion. As a result, he died in the hospital from his wounds.

I truly felt bad upon hearing the news. Sam always had a good word for me and a sincere handshake when we saw each other, and there was genuine respect between us. Now Sam, who pretty much minded his own business, had ended up dead. It just didn't seem fair that after the guy quit being involved in the foolishness that can get you cut, shot, or beaten, he'd ended up being killed by a senseless act of violence. The final indignity as far as I was concerned was when the man who stabbed Sam beat a murder rap because expert witnesses testified medical science could have saved Sam but he refused to allow it. The way I saw it was, if you go around stabbing people, it's your own bad luck that the person you cut is a Jehovah's Witness. If you don't want folks to die by your hand, don't stab them because, if they do die, you are guilty of murder. Unfortunately, the courts lacked that Irish clarity of thinking and Sam's murder went un-avenged from my point of view.

CHAPTER 78

I was handling a call on S. Milwaukee Street in D-24 when I saw a couple of black guys around 18 or 19 arguing back and forth and looking at me. I heard one of them say, "I'm telling you that's the dude," to which the other one said "No way, man." I recognized the guys' faces and just about knew what the dispute was about; no way the white dude from Bloomfield Park was a cop. Once I was done with official business, I walked over to the fellas and asked, "You guys gonna be at Bloomfield tomorrow?" This caused the guy I first overheard to shout triumphantly, "I told you that was him!" I laughed at the other guy and said, "I know it's hard to believe a white cop can run a little, but it's true." We all laughed and gave each other the typical hand slap of the era signifying that all was cool.

I stood around bs'ing with the guys for a while and then left. Long before all the experts discovered "Community Policing," I had been taught that to be a good cop folks had to know you and you had to know them. The best way to do that was on equal footing, just like I had just done. Of course, I was simply following the tradition of the best beat cops in history, who, of course, everyone knows were Irish.

The Pick Me Brothers were all doing well in their second year with JPD and all were making their marks on the Department. Scott Rogers and Tom Bernardon were doing a great job on the traffic unit. They enjoyed the work and some friendly competition. Bernardon even wrote 50 tickets in one eight-hour shift. Quota? Hell no. He could write as many as he wanted. Bad drivers were abundant, so it wasn't hard to find the violations if you were willing to do the work. Of course, a warrant hit or a suspended driver would slow you down considerably, but Bernardon got lucky and didn't run into any slow downs. Tom didn't write cheap tickets either. Speeding was never for less than 10 over the posted limit and red light violations were never the close calls.

Scott was just as hard-working, and he had a way of turning his head when listening to a motorist story that was mimicked more than once by his fellow officers. His deep baritone voice was also distinctive and had just a hint of the hills and hollows from where his Dad had come from in rural Appalachia. Scott and his wife made up the first husband/wife officer team on the Department, and I thought that was cool and I respected both of them. Many agencies got all worked up if you tried to hire somebody's second-cousin-twice-removed, but Jackson PD took the opposite approach. There were brothers, fathers and sons, cousins, and everything in between working for the department. The attitude was if you're a good person and make a good cop, there's a good chance other members of your family are just like you. Most of the time it worked out that way, and the once or twice it didn't was no worse odds than hiring anyone else.

CHAPTER 79

A second trip was planned up to Stressman's in-laws place at Burt Lake that summer and involved John and his wife, the Ankroms, the Bachmans, and Julie and me. It was a great time for all of us and really cemented the bond that was growing between us. I was finding out that lousy shifts and days off didn't mean as much if you shared them with good people. One of the many highlights of the trip was when John's brother in law, a 21 year old college student, flapped his mouth about how these old cops never saw the day they could drink with him.

Karl and I couldn't let that go unchallenged so we grabbed a bottle of McMaster's Whiskey from a kitchen cabinet in the cottage, and handed it the college boy, and said, "Let's go sit down by the lake." Ankrom had been a sailor so he was damn near a professional drinker, and at that time I was also a fairly practiced drinker. Plus, we both drank whiskey often enough that we had a little more tolerance than the new kid. Junior hung in the best he could, but after about an hour of sitting on the rock sea wall doing backyard Boilermakers by taking a big pull out of the McMasters washed downed with beer we had been retrieving from the cottage, Junior finally had enough and with the simple pronouncement of, "I'm fucked up," he staggered back towards the cottage. Even though his mind was fogged over and he was having a hard time keeping the cottage door in sight, he heard, "Come back anytime, Junior; school's always in session," followed by demonic laughter and other gibberish he was probably certain came from Satan himself. About 3 o'clock the next afternoon when he was functioning again, all he would mutter was, "You fuckers are crazy."

Clearly, though, his bravado was gone and he finally coughed up that he was not yet ready for boozing with the big boys.

We also got the competitive juices flowing by playing badminton — not exactly a manly sport until you modify the rules and create full-contact, killer badminton. A 6'7" man swinging a badminton racquet with all his might can truly be an intimidating sight. Add to that the fact that he, and all the other players are probably blowing about a .15 on the breathalyzer, and it is clear it was not a gentleman's game.

CHAPTER 80

Mike Brunk and I got along very well even though Mike was a huge University of Michigan fan and therefore suffering from a very serious character flaw. Being a good Catholic, I was able to forgive him this most serious of sins and so we talked a lot. Mike was also a big fan of the Tigers and sports in general, plus had just a great, off-beat sense of humor. Mike was also active in the Big Brothers/Big Sisters program in Jackson and one day suggested to me I should consider becoming a Big Brother. Even though I was living the good life as a single man with a fantastic job, gorgeous girlfriend, and plenty of buddies to knock back a few with, I wasn't completely self-centered. I knew I had a responsibility to give back.

I was a little hesitant to say yes as I really wasn't sure I was cut out to be a role model for anyone, nor was I sure I was up to the responsibilities. Saying no wasn't easy, however, either, because my upbringing and faith stressed that "doing for others" was a whole lot more important than getting fat and happy with yourself. My dad and mother lived that out for their children to see. Dad told stories about my Grandfather Courtney being dirt poor yet always willing to share with those less fortunate, even when he really didn't have enough for his own family. He even raised a niece from infancy after her mother died, and her father was too much of a drunk to care for her properly. Grandpa Courtney also had his nephew living with them off and on for several years.

Brunk was smart and let his request sit for a few weeks, and then he hit me up again, this time suggesting that I just stop by the office and talk to the ladies there about the program. I figured I owed Mike that much, so I agreed and set up an appointment. The ladies at the office were very enthusiastic about my interest and they weren't going to let me get out of there without signing up. I liked what I heard, so I went ahead and filled out the application. The staff explained that there would have to be a background check and then they would try to "match" me up with a little brother that had interests in common interests with me.

It didn't take very long before I got cleared and a match was arranged. The staff told me my "little" was named Tim and that Tim was 10 and being raised by his grandmother. Tim's birth mother had turned Tim over to his grandparents while he was still an infant and they raised him as their own child. In fact, Tim called them mom and dad. The grandfather passed away a year or so back, and the grandmother decided Tim needed some male influence as he moved towards the teenage years. I was pretty excited about getting matched up but also a little nervous about the whole thing, too. After all, the kid could turn out to be a little thug, or worse yet, a couch potato uninterested in anything I was.

An initial meeting between Tim, the grandmother, and me was arranged and overseen by the staff, and it went very well. Tim was a great kid and seemed very happy to get me for a Big Brother. Tim and his grandmother lived about 6 miles west of town on Sandstone Road and there weren't really any other kids around for Tim to play with. It was clear that he was all for a Big Brother and was majorly impressed by my being a cop. Grandma seemed to think I made the grade too, and even snuck in a question about whether I was a church-goer. I set up a visit time with Tim and that started what would be a three-year match between the two of us. It ended only when Tim and his grandmother moved to the northeast part of the State to be closer to her son.

Every week I spent at least a couple of hours with Tim on an evening when I was off. We also tried to get in some time on Saturday mornings. We'd go bowling, out to eat, and just generally hang around. Tim really liked playing football with me in the backyard and getting the chance to rough house like most boys like to do. I often ended up out of breath trying to match the energy of a 10-year-old boy, but I was having as much fun as he was, Tim got along great with my roommates and clearly enjoyed being "one of the guys" around the house. He really enjoyed it when all of us were there and collectively decided to "beat" on him at once. Tim ate up the extra attention and would fill the house with laughter when we gave him a "pounding." It would cause social workers, liberals, and New Age parents to faint, but it was good old male bonding when the rough housing started, and Tim loved every minute of the attention.

I got rid of the empty beer cans and bottles and made sure the supply of Playboys and other such fine literary material was out of sight when Tim was going to be around, and I reminded Gary and Rick that Tim would learn colorful language and other important information from his friends and on the corner, not from them.

Kevin M. Courtney

CHAPTER 81

Summer rolled into fall and, typical of Michigan it stayed warm during the days but the humidity was out of the air and the nights started getting cooler. The Department switched to long-sleeved shirts and ties on Labor Day and would not go back to short sleeves and no ties until Memorial Day, so the first few weeks of September could be a little uncomfortable until the sun went down. The Kevlar vests that officers wore under their uniforms didn't help matters either. In the heat of the summer you got pretty hot wearing the vest. I was not above unbuttoning my shirt and lifting up the front panel of the vest like a car hood in order to cool down while taking a break in the station basement.

The urge to get out hunting started hitting me the first time I felt that little chill in the air that foretells the end of summer. I was really excited about this year because I could get a little time off, and I had found that several of my fellow officers liked to hunt also. I had banked a fair amount of comp time and hunting season was the perfect excuse to make some withdrawals.

Howard Noppe, Bill Kennedy, Tom Bernardon, Al Combs, and I planned a trip up to my family's cottage the first week of October, after the archery deer season opened, and while the we didn't kill any deer we killed a fair number of brain cells each evening. We didn't just booze it up though. Although we played poker each night and tossed back the beer, Al and I were up and out in the woods before daylight each morning. Al wasn't a drinker, but he did stay up playing poker. The other riff-raff stayed in bed until mid-morning, as they didn't bow hunt. Al and I would roll them out when we got back at about 10:30

a.m. and then we would all head out for some small game hunting.

I loved the peace and quiet of being in the woods and trying to outsmart an animal on its own ground. Most non-hunters would never understand the whole experience and why anyone would want to shoot a poor little animal, and hunters just waste their breath trying to talk them into changing their minds. If I could get them out in the woods with me, though, I had a chance, as I had seen many a non-hunter get hooked on the sport after one "field" experience. Typically, though, I preferred to ignore the naysayers. Most of them were chomping down their fair share of Big Macs and running around with leather shoes on, so in my mind that sort of made their "save the animals" pleas a little two-faced. I figured other hunters and I were a little more honest since we didn't leave someone else to do our killing and we ate what we shot.

We didn't come up completely empty-handed as Bernardon managed to bag a couple of grouse and someone else whacked a squirrel. I tossed in a rabbit that I'd shot with my bow. The game made a great stew. I just loved the reaction of city people when you told them you ate squirrel. Most wouldn't believe it at first and ended up thinking you were right out of *Deliverance.* The truth was that squirrels were tasty little buggers and I might have capped a couple in town if I thought I could get away with it.

CHAPTER 82

It was a nice warm Sunday evening and I would be on duty in D-24 until midnight. The night shift's early cars came on at 11:00 pm, so for an hour there were both second and third shift units working. This overlapping was done to ensure that there were always cars on the street. It also allowed the night shift cars to take calls that might otherwise cause overtime for the second shift units. There were no calls on this night, so that wasn't a concern.

"Willie" Willinski worked F-26 and came on duty at 11:00 p.m.; since there were no calls waiting he started in on his usual routine of checking commercial properties for breaking and enterings. On most occasions, all anyone making such checks would find was a door an employee had left unlocked, but once in a while a break in was discovered after the fact, so generally no one got too geeked up checking buildings.

Willie pulled into the parking lot of Robinsons party store on West Avenue just in time to see one of the Garrett brothers (of my first-day-on-the-job-fame) loading up a bunch of returnable containers he and his brother had just stolen from Robinsons storage building. They saw Willie, jumped in their ride, and the chase was on.

Now, normally, Willie could be a little hard to understand on the radio because of the way he talked, but not this night. I wasn't sure whether it was adrenaline or, that he just decided to make the effort to be understood, but old Willie sounded like Casey Kasem calling out the pursuit. The chase was weaving its way through the south side of Jackson and Willie was doing his best to keep up, but he had an older patrol car and was losing ground. I was the closest backup and so was designated the secondary unit in the pursuit.

I was trying to anticipate where the chase was going so that I could intercept it and help Willie out in the event the thieves bailed out or God-knows-what happened. I was running hot with lights and siren and that just added to the rush I was feeling. I concentrated on my driving and was glad it was late on a Sunday night and there was no traffic to speak of on the streets. My guess work wasn't bad and I jumped in behind Willie on Prospect Street and he requested I take over the pursuit as he just couldn't keep up. The adrenaline was flowing pretty good when I passed Willie. About this time, Tom Bernardon advised me that he was coming south on Airline Drive from the station just about the time the pursuit turned south on Airline and headed out of the city. Airline would turn into M-50 and then US 127, so I figured these yo-yos were really going to make a run for it. I wasn't all that excited about that fact since I really didn't know the out-county area very well.

I checked my speedometer as I got onto 127 and it read 115 mph. I was staying back off the suspects far enough to give myself some reaction room but also keep them in sight. I guessed they were maybe eight mph faster than I was, by this time Bernardon caught up to the pursuit and advised he would go around me. He was driving a brand new Plymouth equipped with all the extras a police car could use, and he blew past me like I was peddling my patrol car a la Fred Flintstone. I got a good look at Bernardon and instead of seeing madman like intensity, he waved at me and looked as relaxed as a guy taking his family out for ice cream. I remembered that image years later when Tom, who had left JPD and joined the Navy, flew into Battle Creek in the backseat of an F-15 fighter jet. The boy had a need for speed.

Once Bernardon got in position, I was able to slow down a bit and that didn't bother me in the least. By this time other units from the county had joined in and the suspects were starting to figure out they were in a no-win situation. They had also crossed the Lenawee County line and I guessed the little idiots had no idea where they were. No matter why, they slowed down before heading east on US-12 where they only went a short distance before losing control.

The suspects' car spun out, and as they tried to make a u-turn, raised a huge cloud of dust along the 2 lane highway. I was jumping on the brakes but was, in effect, driving blind into the cloud. Fortunately,

I stayed on the roadway and avoided the other cars that had come to a stop. By the time I exited my car, the two suspects were on the ground and being cuffed with not a lot of concern for their comfort. I figured the two had a serious ass whipping coming for putting my life and a lot of others' lives at risk, but all they got was tossed to the ground with a little extra vigor and that was it.

Once the two Garrett brothers were stuffed in the backseat of a patrol car, the officers involved stood around and took stock that they were still alive and the patrol cars were still all in one piece. The banter between us allowed us to come down off the emotions that a pursuit creates. It was incredible to think what was expected of these 22- and 23-year old men in situations that most people wanted nothing to do with and, even more incredible that they most always met the highest of expectations.

Still, it was easy to understand how a suspect who leads police on a high speed chase can get the occasional thumping. The mixture of fear and excitement that officers experience in a chase seriously overloads their systems and then, just as suddenly the chase comes to an end. All that energy has to be bled off, and if a suspect is dumb enough to offer resistance it is ridiculous to be surprised that the excess energy is directed at them. That's where a cooler head has to prevail and keep things from getting out of hand. Sometimes that voice of reason is the initial pursuing officer himself--or more likely a backup officer—who realizes his buddy is all geeked up and about to rearrange the suspect's landscape, and who steps in and gets things cooled down.

Liberals love to get their shorts in a knot over the fact that a police officer would actually consider such violence, but since the most fear inducing event they face is another Republican appointment to the Supreme Court, they have no idea what an officer goes through. There is a moment that you realize that your life truly was placed in peril and the idiot responsible is standing right in front of you. It is then and there it truly takes a herculean effort not to go medieval on the perp, which is what most normal human beings would do. Such is the lot of the police officer, as what any normal person would do is usually a no-no for the cop on the beat.

Kevin M. Courtney

CHAPTER 83

Things settled down as the fall wound on and I was looking forward to the start of the city league basketball season. I was also starting to figure out it was time to make some decisions regarding Julie. My plan had always been to give myself two years of being single after graduating from college and not getting serious with any one girl. Well, I was still single but the other half of the plan was in the toilet. I knew that she expected some kind of commitment or my sorry ass was going to get the gate, and I didn't want that. In fact, I had no real objection to marriage and had always looked forward to it and to having a family. I was no genius but I finally figured out that if you have a girl you love and who loves you it isn't exactly illogical to ask her to marry you.

I wasn't into that "living together" nonsense. I figured if you are married then you're married and you live under the same roof. If you're not, then you live in separate residences and maintain separate identities. Part of my outlook was based on religion, but it was also based on my belief you don't do important things half-assed. I looked at living together as a half-assed marriage and I wanted no part of that. Now it's almost a step in the courtship process prior to marriage, but it still wouldn't fit me.

Once I decided that I was ready for the big plunge, of course I would go the traditional route. I would buy the ring without any input from Julie and propose at Christmas. That would give me time to come up with the money and allow for any second thoughts. That she might say "no" wasn't a concern because she had dropped enough hints that even I could figure things out. About the only thing she didn't do was put up a billboard in my front yard, but I guess she decided I wasn't quite that dense.

I had been thinking that most all of the social gatherings at our house on Westwood Street were of the drunken riot variety and that it might be nice to try having a normal dinner gathering. Of course the time we'd tried that at the apartment complex had turned into a night of alcohol fueled debauchery, so Gary and I were 0 for 1 in the "trying to be normal" category. I talked it over with Gary and it was decided we would have a Pick Me Brother Thanksgiving dinner a week early. We picked a night that everyone could make it and announced we'd do the bird and everyone else would bring a dish to pass. How much more domesticated could we get? Everyone would also be bringing a date or a wife, so that would also help keep things under control. Or so I hoped.

It all worked out as planned and the dinner went off without a hitch. No bottle rockets in the driveway, no neighbors pissed off, and no one had to go to work the next day with a hangover that made them contemplate suicide. It was just a nice relaxed evening. It was the first such evening in my adult single life, and while I was headed for marriage and stability, I wasn't going to change completely after just one night. There was far too much stupid behavior left to be involved in.

The only real dark cloud in my autumn involved my little brother, Tim. Tim's biological mother had moved back to Jackson and was living in D-24's District. The staff at Big Brothers/Big Sisters had told me about it when I was matched with Tim. Apparently, Tim knew who his biological mother was and there had been some preliminary reintroduction going on. The staff, figuring I was black and white on issues like this, told me to keep my opinions to myself. I innocently asked, "Why? Do you think I have a problem with women who abandoned their children?" That got me a roll of the eyes and another "behave," which I agreed to do and did. I was always very neutral when Tim mentioned his "Mom" and let the boy talk about the whole situation. I agreed to behave, but I didn't agree to become a freaking cheerleader for the woman.

That all changed when I was sent on a domestic involving Tim's mom and a well known south side loser named Steven Edwards. I was civil to Mom and didn't mention who I was although I figured she knew. I did, however, tell Steven what went on between him and his woman was between them, but if Steven so much as sneezed in Tim's direction when Tim was at the house visiting, I would hunt Steven down like a rabid dog. Steven said he and the boy were cool and I responded, "Good. Keep it that way. Cause I ain't talking about locking you up if any harm comes to that boy." We reached a street level understanding of what cause and effect would be and there were no problems for Tim. I was not at all happy that Tim was going to be in an environment that rat bag Steven inhabited, but there wasn't much I could do. It would be a reoccurring theme in my career; not only couldn't I save the world, I was going to have a hard time impacting just one life some days. Still, dumbass mick that I am, I never quit trying.

Kevin M. Courtney

.

CHAPTER 84

Gail Rogers was the kind of person people are always glad to meet. She was very pretty, had a great personality, and generally was just a good cop to get to work with. I liked her a lot and enjoyed teasing her, and she gave as good as she got. Oddly enough, her birthday was the same day as Julie's and they got along great also. Gail and I got sent to Foote West Hospital on Lansing Avenue for a trouble-with-subject call in the ER one evening. At that time, Jackson had a Foote West and East Hospital because the Foote Hospital Group had purchased the former Mercy Hospital from the Catholic Order that established it. Eventually, Foote West would be torn down and everything would end up at a new Foote Hospital Campus along Michigan Avenue.

Gail's maiden name was Sturgill, and as she and I walked in the rear door of the ER I noticed a Jackson regular named Billy Lee seated in the waiting room with his main squeeze, Sue. Billy and Sue were a little slow but relatively harmless. Without missing a beat I greeted Billy with a big "How you doing Billy?" Billy smiled and said "fine," pleased at my interest in his well being. I followed that quickly with, "How's the rest of the Sturgill family?" to which Billy replied, "They're fine too." I said "Great" and went on into the ER with Gail cursing me under her breath and her face turning bright red. Once we sorted out the problem, which involved telling a drunk to shut up and get treated or go to jail, Gail admitted I pulled the whole family connection thing off pretty smoothly. I got more mileage out of the gag than I probably deserved, but Gail was a good sport and took it pretty well.

Christmas was coming up and I had hit it big again and ended up with Christmas Eve off, which would allow me to return home for my family's big get-together. I looked forward to going home for a variety of reasons, not the least of which was stuffing myself with my mother's cooking. Julie was a good cook and had fixed me dinner a number of times, and only once or twice did I almost make the fatal mistake of comparing her cooking to my mother's. Julie had one advantage, though, and that was I was pretty much eating nothing but fast food, so she didn't really have to whip up any masterpieces to beat the alternative. Besides, I was already plotting how to get her to learn some of my mom's specialties.

The onset of the cold weather created the usual slow down in calls for service overall, but second shift was still busy, if not quite as crazy as it was in the summer. I had been looking for engagement rings for about a month when I settled on one at Zale's in Westwood Mall. The salesperson was telling me three months salary was about the right amount to spend on a ring, and I nearly stroked out when I heard that. At my wages, a quarter of my salary would be about $4,500, and there was NO FREAKING WAY I was spending that much on a ring. I went with a more modest model and thought that was a boatload of money, but since I only planned on buying one this lifetime I swallowed hard and handed over the cash. My plan was to take Julie out to dinner and then propose to her back at my house on Westwood. (That way, if she turned me down, I could just throw her out the door and not have to suffer any public humiliation.)

Julie said "yes" so no evictions were necessary, and I was sure I had made the right choice. I knew I was far too set in my ways and a real pain in the ass some days, so to find a woman who accepted me for who I was and didn't try to change me was truly a blessing. No Irishman with a lick of sense wastes his blessings, and I kept up that tradition. Besides, Julie ended up with a fairly good deal herself. I had a job, a few bucks in the bank, was disease free, and had been the target of more than one young woman's attention.

My family was all very excited about the engagement when I announced it to them at the Christmas gathering, but my dad was still not sure poor Julie knew what she was getting into. I finally had to call the old man on his views and all he would say is, "You're gonna have to change son, that's all I can tell you." Well, maybe a little sanding of the corners wouldn't hurt but I figured Julie could do a lot worse based on the wide variety of idiots I had seen in my first two years as a cop.

It wasn't too long after Christmas that I was working a quiet, cold Saturday night. I had been assigned to the E-32 car, or "bar car," and was supposed to make a point of getting in all the dive bars in the downtown and East Michigan Avenue area. I was expected to get out on foot as much as possible and try to prevent trouble before it started by being a visible presence. The E-32 car also provided back up to the section cars when necessary.

I was headed west on Glick Highway and had just gone past Jackson Street when Dispatch called and advised of a stabbing that had just occurred in the parking lot of Scotty's Pub on Pearl. My lousy luck was back because the pub was only a block from Jackson and Glick, but because of the one way streets I would have to go up to Blackstone Street and backtrack the two blocks to Scotty's.

I acknowledged the call and stomped on the accelerator. Dispatch had sent Roger as my backup and advised he was coming from the south side. I hit Blackstone Street, went the wrong way to Pearl, and then headed back east the block and a half to Scotty's. I was flying with lights flashing and siren blaring. The theory on the siren was you wanted to scare the attackers away so as to save the victim. Catching the thugs was secondary at this point; the main focus was trying to keep your victim from getting killed.

I pulled in the lot next to Scotty's no more than a minute after the call and saw a man down in the parking lot. As I got out of the car, bystanders were hollering "They're running down the alley," while pointing south towards Michigan Avenue. There was a huge pool of blood around the victim and I could see his throat was cut almost from ear to ear, creating what in the black humor of law enforcement is known as a "permanent smile," Nevertheless the victim came first, so I couldn't go running off chasing suspects down an alley. I quickly called out on my portable radio that the suspects, a man and two women, were running south from the scene. At the same I told dispatch to have the rescue and ambulance "step it up." The truth was those guys were coming "lights and siren" to the call and didn't change their driving no matter what some cop on the scene said, but at least they knew it was a serious situation before they got there.

It wasn't five seconds after I made this radio transmission that Roger called out he had the suspects on Michigan Avenue. They had gotten exactly one block when they exited the alley and ran straight into Roger, who had them sprawled out at gun point faster than they could say "hard time." The 3 were Sandra Cotton, Alisha Williams, and James Mason. All three were hard cases and not first timers in the felony parade.

I was figuring I had a murder for sure because the guy who got his throat cut was an old wino named Ezekiel Worth, and he sure didn't look sturdy enough to survive the parking lot surgery the suspects had done to him. It never ceased to amaze me how much blood could leak out of a human body. I figured based on what I was looking at, I better go for the dying declaration before Ezekiel left the scene and maybe this world. The motive for the attack was robbery, so I had missed being on scene at an armed robbery by one block for the second time in my career. Roger, however, had bagged three armed robbers one block from their bloody attack on an old wino. Oddly enough, this scene was only a couple blocks from Amanati's where I'd missed my first armed robbery in progress.

I got a big break in the case when the bartender at the downtown gay bar ratted out that the three suspects had been in the bar together early in the night. I had developed a halfway decent rapport with the patrons and bartender in the bar since taking over the downtown beat, and it paid off with the bartender giving me some good information on a robbery. I figured what people did to whom was their own business, and I treated the patrons of the bar accordingly. I wasn't going to be joining any gay rights parades, but I wasn't looking to have them lynched either.

Ezekiel, proving that the winos of Jackson could probably survive nuclear war, pulled through getting carved up and was back out boozing quicker than most people who sprain an ankle.

The only problem with the case was the bartender changed his mind about the male robber, James Mason, being the guy he saw in the bar. I guessed someone got word to the guy that he'd get a scar to match Ezekiel's if he didn't change his story regarding James, and so he lied to save his ass. I didn't like it but figured you couldn't expect a lot of toughness from a swish bartender. The other two however went to trial and were convicted.

The highlight of the trial was when Ezekiel was asked to indentify the person who stabbed him and he pointed at Cotton and said, "It's that half man half woman dagger bitch right there." That brought quite a response from the people in court and the Judge had to chill things out with a little gavel work, but I figured it was just about the most singularly direct identification I'd ever heard.

Ezekiel was not the most lovable victim you could have in court, and it looked like the defense had beat him up pretty good where the jury was concerned. I was thinking the case was likely in the tubes as all those nice people on the jury would not want to send someone to prison on the word of a street alcoholic. I was wrong. The Assistant Prosecutor, David McClory (aka Radar due to his resemblance to the MASH character of the same name) did a masterful job on his closing argument to the jury and pointed out while not too many people would invite Ezekiel over for dinner, he still deserved to walk the streets of Jackson without getting his throat cut--and it was the jury's job to see that he could. The jury came back guilty on both defendants, and while I knew a guilty man was walking free I was still happy with the convictions. Besides, sooner or later, James Mason would be back in court and end up in prison where he belonged. Either that, or like a lot of other street thugs he would get what he had given.

In another twist of fate several years later, Ezekiel was thrown down a flight of stairs in A-21 section during a robbery handled by Gail Rogers, with me as shift sergeant. This time his luck ran out. Ezekiel died as a result of his injuries. Everyone thinks crime victims are always some clean cut person from a nice neighborhood and suspects are "bad guys" from the wrong part of town. The truth is those with the least seem to get preyed upon the most, and it was those people my fellow officers and I spent most of our time with, and with whom we built rapport. I found most affluent people looked at me as if I were the equivalent to their freaking gardener whenever I had contact with them.

Kevin M. Courtney

.

CHAPTER 85

In the late 70's and early 80's, Jackson had several memorable street winos that I dealt with fairly regularly. Each one was unique and made for some interesting situations. Chuck was a sawed off little drunk with a gravely voice who's nickname was the "Chelsea Kid." Rumor had it that he had been a fighter in his early years and that is where the name came from, but no one could ever quite confirm that.

Chuck would shovel a little snow, sweep the occasional sidewalk, or do other odd jobs for drinking money, but one of his favorite ways to get it was to bum it off the cops who crossed his path. He'd start out with "gimme a dollar" but figured if he was a big enough pain in the ass he could get at least a quarter from an officer sick of listening to him. Six quarters would buy a bottle of rot gut wine and Chuck would be happy. I was parked just north of the railroad tracks on the west side of Milwaukee Street, working on a report one afternoon, when Chuck trained his radar on me.

I saw Chuck coming and was expecting the usual financial request but instead Chuck said, "Arrest that son of a bitch over there." I looked up from my paper work and asked who he was talking about. Chuck pointed out another wino seated on the base of one of the railroad control boxes and holding a jug in a paper sack. "Why do you want me to arrest him Chuck?"

"Cause he's got whiskey and won't give me any."

I cracked up. "Well, Chuck, I don't think I can do that but here's a dollar so you can get something of your own." I figured the laugh I got was worth a dollar.

Apparently Chuck had a little money of his own because he beat feet straight across the street to White's Drug Store, which sold more booze than pharmacological products, and went right inside. I went back to my report writing and after a few minutes saw Chuck come out carrying a brown bag. I watched as he walked directly across the street and then headed right at the other wino while clutching his bottle in one hand. I thought, "Oh shit, he's gonna beat that guy with the wine bottle." I was just getting ready to make a run for Chuck when he stopped, opened up the jug he had in the bag, and took a long deep pull off it right in front of the stingy fucker that wouldn't give him any whiskey. Chuck put the cap back on, gave his antagonist the finger, and turned and walked off. It was the most entertainment I had ever gotten for a dollar.

Chuck met his end during a vicious cold spell in January with temps constantly dropping to -20 at night. He froze to death after being on about a three day binge. The sad thing was Chuck was only three blocks from his apartment. Seems he had an adult guardian through Social Services, who made sure that Chuck had a place to live, that the rent and utilities were paid, and that he had groceries. The guardian only gave Chuck two bucks a day spending money, which is why he worked odd jobs and bummed money from the cops. Two dollars wasn't near enough drinking money for Chuck, and the help of a guardian wasn't enough to protect Chuck from Chuck either.

Robert was a local whom I always seemed to find sleeping somewhere. He could be a real pain to deal with and never just moved along peacefully. I woke him up once from a nap in the little park-like area at the corner of Jackson and Michigan at 1:30 in the afternoon by whacking the bottom of his shoes with my nightstick. Worked better than an alarm and had him on his feet in record time. I suppose "wino whacking" would raise an eyebrow or two in our enlightened times today, but it worked.

Robert did pull a good one though. One Friday night in the winter he went into the Rose Room, which was the restaurant in the Fields store located in the block between Cortland and Michigan just west of Jackson Street. Robert strolled into the restaurant and proceeded to order three boiled dinners and one fish and chips dinner, which he managed to eat with no trouble. He then ordered pie and, after finishing it he sat back to relax. The waitress brought him his bill and Robert told her he had no money. She said if he didn't pay she'd call the cops, which he said was fine--he'd wait. When I got there Robert confessed to the whole thing, and when I said if he didn't pay I would lock him up, he was pleased. He pointed out to me that he'd started the day out hungry with no place to stay. He was now no longer hungry but still needed a place to stay, so he was hoping I would lock him up. Drunk yes, stupid no.

Then there was Orville. His claim to fame was burning down the Stowel Hotel on the corner of Michigan and Milwaukee: a dive if ever there was one. The Stowel had a bar on the first floor and all of the rooms were occupied by down-and-outers like Orville. On a bitterly cold January night, the Stowel caught on fire and all of us on duty thought for sure there would be multiple fatalities. Amazingly, even though it was a Friday night, not a single one of the old boozers who lived there died. The loss of a major cockroach habitat, however, was devastating to the city's ecosystem.

The blaze was spectacular and resulted in a multiple alarm response by the fire department. It was so cold that ice was forming on the back of the building from the water firefighters were pouring on it while the front was still fully engulfed in flames. I could see it all very clearly as I was stuck directing traffic in the middle of Glick Highway south of the railroad tracks, freezing my ass off. I never drank coffee, but when a guy brought me a cup I was so cold I actually drank about half of it. It is still the only time I've ever touched the stuff. Of course, had it been warm motor oil I probably would have given it a shot at that point.

While I was sipping my one and only cup of Joe and contemplating what would fall off first from standing out in this goddamned Arctic cold, John Stressman was doing crowd control out front of the hotel. After a short time, John went into the train station across the street to warm up a little when he was approached by one of the Stowel residents whom John tried to ignore until the guy said, "Officer, that guy over there is the one who set the fire."

John was thinking "right," until he looked over he saw Orville standing there with his hair smoldering and his eyebrows singed off. Turns out, Orville was making soup on a hot plate and knocked it over into a box of newspapers, which ignited and started the fire. Orville tried to put it out, and when he couldn't he boogied. We always told John it was his tremendous powers of observation that cleared the case. Nope, you couldn't slide nothin' by a guy like John.

Orville was a familiar sight around Jackson for years after that walking the streets with his head down, looking neither right, nor left, and stopping only to pick up cigarette butts big enough to smoke.

J.P. was another regular. He was once locked up in the station holding cell at the same time Chuck was being held. Officer Melvin Hartman made the mistake of trying to be nice to J.P. offering him half of the cheese sandwich Melvin had brought for his lunch. J.P. started screaming he was a man not a mouse. This got Chuck riled up and he told J.P. to "shut the fuck up or he'd whip his black ass." J.P. countered with a "well come on over here then you sawed off white motherfucker." Melvin left the booking area with the two winos hurling threats of violence back and forth. Neither one moved a step closer but they sounded tough.

My favorite experience with J.P. occurred when I was driving northbound on Francis Street and could see all the traffic in front of me turning left onto Mason Street. I couldn't for the life of me figure out what was going on. Once I got close enough, I could see J.P., drunk on his ass, hanging onto a sign post along the curb, waving his arms, and yelling some kind of gibberish. Drivers apparently thought he was directing traffic and so dutifully turned in the direction he was waving. I started laughing, thinking, I could stand in the middle of the street, in uniform, with the overheads spinning on my patrol car and people would still ignore my signals--but let a wino wave and they were all about watching him. I ended J.P.'s career in traffic and chased him back to his nearby residence.

We were an equal opportunity community in regards to street folks, and Marcia was one of my favorite ladies. Jackson's Marcia had some definite mental health issues but she also liked to drink. She would walk the streets of Jackson having very loud conversations with herself, and that of course worried the hell out of anyone who previously had not seen her. The cops and firefighters who saw her regularly paid no attention, and since she managed to take care of herself and not pose any danger to herself or anyone else, she stayed clear of Ypsi.

One day she was in the post office ahead of me in a rather long line ranting and raving like always. I was in plain clothes and thought about doing something until I realized the line was suddenly getting a lot smaller. I decided this was a good time to NOT get involved, and as a result Marcia and I both got in an out of the post office a lot faster.

Drinking was tough for Marcia, though, as she was generally banned from every bar in Jackson including "Jeff's," which was a real hard-core drinkers' bar and the closest thing Jackson had to a "skid row" establishment. I'm convinced she was probably the only person in the history of Jeff's to get a lifetime ban. She used to complain of being "debused" by the bars and wanted me to do something about it whenever I'd see her. Clearly, in her mind, Jeff's had debused her.

One Saturday when I was working the desk after having been promoted to sergeant, Marcia came into the station complaining loudly of "debusement." I wasn't real interested in having her in the lobby for an extended period of time, and I happened to know that my buddy Mike Lazaroff was on desk at the sheriff's department, which was just 3 blocks away, so I told her the new "Debusement Investigator" was at this very moment at the sheriff's department. Marcia asked his name and I told her I would only give her the name if she was serious about going over there and making a complaint. She swore she was, so I told her the fella's name was Lazaroff and she hot-footed it out of my station, thereby restoring my peace and quiet.

My tranquility was disturbed about 20 minutes later when I answered the phone and heard Mike saying, "Which one of you rotten fuckers sent this crazy bitch over here?" I could hear Marcia hollering in the background that she wanted to see Lazaroff. I told Mike I'd like to help him out but "debusement" was out of my jurisdiction. He colorfully advised me what kind of piece of crap I was, even though I was laughing the whole time and denying any knowledge of his situation.

I made a point of telling my family about Marcia at one of our Christmas gatherings. I pointed out how talking to her helped my home-sickness because it was just like talking to my own big sister, Marcia. Three out of four of my siblings thought that I was pretty funny.

Oddly enough, one of the other local winos was named Stanley, so I wondered if there was a pattern of some kind emerging regarding my big brother and sister. Stanley-the-wino had a habit of using the word "really" about 400 times per conversation. An example of a conversation with him would be, "Really Officer Courtney, I really wasn't pissing in that doorway, really I wasn't. Really, I'm really not feeling well and so really I just stopped to catch my breath. Really, officer, I'm really a good person, really I am." Five minutes of that shit and you REALLY didn't want to hear any more from Stanley. He was once put on a bus to Lansing through some form of flimflammery that I believe the courts may have been involved in, but I'm not sure and even if they were, they'd deny it like anyone else involved.

Stanley was MIA for quite a while after his relocation. That was until one night when I saw what I was sure was an unmarked police car speeding north on Lansing Avenue away from Foote Hospital. I didn't recognize the car as we had no dark blue unmarked cars, nor did any of the other local agencies. I had a pretty good suspicion of what happened a minute later when I found Stanley's sorry ass in the parking lot of the hospital. While I could never prove my theory--at least not without hot lights and cattle prods during questioning--I'm pretty sure Lansing PD, which used unmarked cars just like the one I saw, probably got sick of old Stanley and gave him a quick ride back to his old stomping grounds. Make that Lansing 1, Jackson 0.

Stanley was a big fan of Gail Rogers' and would come into the station every now and then and ask for her by saying he wanted to talk to that "bootiful" officer. I think he meant "beautiful" but Gail always had a nice "booty," so who am I to say for sure?

Elmer was a regular who would get so drunk he would just pass out where ever he happened to be. I was sent to a "man down call" on E. Biddle on a Saturday afternoon and when I pulled up in front of the address I didn't see anyone "down" anywhere. I did see the complainant, a black man of about 30, standing in the yard, and so I got out and asked him what was up. He told me there was a guy lying in his shrubs. I walked over, and sure enough Elmer was in there sleeping one off. The complainant asked, "Is he dead?" I replied, "Nope. Just bombed out of his gourd." I then called dispatch and requested an ambulance to haul Elmer in for detox.

While we were standing there, the complainant started grinning and said, "Well, if he ain't dead I got to ask you something." I said, "Sure, what is it? He said, "Take a good look at that guy and tell me he don't look like the Rev. Jim from *Taxi*." I took a second look and damned if Elmer wasn't a dead ringer for the Rev. Jim. I started laughing and before you know it, the complainant and I were really yukking it up. One of the neighbors came over, obviously curious about what the hell was so funny. My man and I finally controlled ourselves long enough to give him the story, and with one look he was also busting up with us. All 3 of us were still chuckling when the ambulance came and took Elmer into the hospital for an overnight detox visit.

I'm sure I probably didn't look all that professional, but in the job of a Jackson police officer you got to laugh when you can because God knows you'll have plenty of chances to cry.

Joe was a Mexican immigrant and a real pleasant drunk to deal with. Not a mean bone in his body and always very respectful to the officers with whom he came in contact. He was also some relation to Bachman's "squeeze" from my first year on the job.

One fine January day in Jackson with the temps around -18 at 4 o'clock in the afternoon, we got a call of trouble with a subject just west of Francis near Morrell. Steve "Fozzie Bear" Leider and I went on the call, and when we got there we found Joe on the porch of the residence. He told us he was having heart trouble and apparently when he pounded on the door to get someone to call an ambulance for him, the resident wasn't sure what Joe wanted and wasn't going to let him in to find out, so the homeowner called us.

We knew Joe really did have a bad heart, so we called for an ambulance to come normal traffic to take him up to Foote East. Besides that, we liked Joe and since it was twice as cold as a well digger's ass we figured he could use a little warming up. As we stood waiting for the ambulance laughing and talking with Joe, Steve told Joe he had to check his pockets for anything dangerous, which Joe didn't mind a bit. The only thing Steve found was a pint of cheap whiskey about three-quarters full. Joe looked heartbroken when Steve said, "We'll have to pour that out." Fozzie, being just as friendly as his namesake, relented and told Joe to go ahead and take a pull before it got dumped. Joe was so happy he swallowed down about five ounces without blinking an eye. Steve took the jug and, without thinking, capped it and stuck it in his pocket. A reflex action, I'm sure.

A few minutes later we saw the meat wagon coming up the street, and Joe asked if he could have one more for the road. Steve handed over the hooch and Joe knocked back another five ounce pull without so much as a burp and gave Fozzie back the remainder and he dumped out the last 2 ounces from a bottle that had about 12 in it when we showed up. Joe walked right over to the ambulance and got it without the slightest stagger.

The EMT's confirmed Joe was having some type of heart issues, so he was transported to the hospital. Later that night, in an effort to warm up, check out the ER nurses, and see how Joe was doing, I stopped in at Foote. The nurses said Joe had been admitted but it was nothing too serious and he would probably get out in a day or so. They asked me if I had any idea what his ETOH was. That was hospital talk for blood alcohol level. I said Joe probably never was below .10, the legal limit for drunk driving at that time, so I guessed twice that since he was a professional drinker. I was told to guess again. He was at a .44, over FOUR TIMES the limit for drunk driving and a level that was in many cases fatal! Yet, Joe had been talking and laughing and anything but falling-down drunk.

There are some happy endings in police work. Joe moved back to New Mexico, I think, and quit drinking. I saw him in Jackson several years later and was shocked when he introduced himself to me. He looked good and was living a good life. Sober. Another small miracle witnessed first hand by Officer Courtney.

CHAPTER 86

Most nights I got home from work around 15 minutes after 11 if I didn't hit Evanoff's. Typically, I would watch the monologue on the "Tonight Show" and if the guests were good I'd stay tuned; otherwise I'd watch a *Benny Hill* rerun or movie and check out the newspaper, usually going to bed around 1am. This night I was just tired and was in bed and sound asleep at 11:30, only to be woke up by Gary and other unknown voices yakking away in the kitchen and living room.

I dragged out of bed, and tossed my robe on, and I headed out to the kitchen looking to jump some ass. I met Gary in the hallway and started out with a pleasant, "Hey, I'm trying to get some fucking sleep while you drunken bastards are whooping it up." Gary said, "Man, Howard shot a guy tonight and so we figured once Evanoff's closed we'd better bring him over here instead of letting him go home alone." I thought that was an original excuse for ruining my sleep and said as much. Gary was dead serious, though, and after I got over the shock I could see the only reasonable thing I could was to get a beer and join the debriefing.

It seems Howard was checking businesses in the 600 and 700 block of E. Michigan Avenue and saw a guy skulking behind a building on the south side of Michigan just past Perrine Street. Howard's radar locked on the mope and figured he was up to no good of some kind, ducking in among the shadows of a closed business late at night. Howard pulled up so as to shine his headlights and spotlight on the guy and called out to him to stop. The suspect had both of his hands in front of him in his waist band which, short of pointing a gun at a cop, is just about the fastest way you can cause a cop to think you mean him harm. Howard called out to the joker to put his hands where he could see them, and that got no response. By this time, Howard had pulled his gun and was pointing it the man. He again told the suspect to put his hands where Howard could see them. This time the suspect answered with, "What if I don't?" Howard answered him, "You're liable to get shot" at which point the suspect said "Good" and spun around on Howard with a gun. Howard fired and the suspect went down.

"Shots fired" was the next thing anyone heard, and every cop with a radio on in Jackson County experienced such a jolt to their systems that it was surprising none of them had the big one. One minute it is a quiet weeknight and the next you hear one of your brothers or sisters has been involved in gunfire. Not only that, you may within minutes be drawn into it or be part of a manhunt to find a gunman so bold he would shoot at a police officer. Fortunately, the shots fired were followed quickly by "Suspect down I need rescue and ambulance."

Just like in "Humpty Dumpty," all the Kings Horses and all the Kings Men on duty flew to Howard's location. The suspect had suffered wounds to his arm and chest, but he was saved by some odd body armor. Turns out he was the one armed basketball player from Bloomfield Park and the framework of his mechanical arm deflected a shot that likely would have done serious damage to anyone else. He was quickly stabilized and taken off to the hospital under guard, but so far no gun had been found. Howard was about to stroke out at this point when Mike Tash stopped everyone and organized them into a search pattern. It only took a minute for them to find the gun behind where the suspect was hit. Apparently when he went down the gun ended up a few feet behind him. It turned out the gun was a starter pistol and the suspect had a suicide note in his pocket, absolving the officer who shot him of any wrongdoing. He in effect had plotted creating a confrontation with a JPD officer and knew slinking around buildings on Michigan Avenue was a good way to do it.

It was a syndrome that would later be officially recognized as "suicide by cop." Someone who wanted to die but couldn't cap himself would force a police officer to do it for him. The fact that the officer would have to face ending a human life under such circumstances didn't seem to enter into the equation, but what the hell do you expect from someone who wants to die?

I responded with a "You gotta be shittin' me!" when I heard who

Howard had dumped, and of course the gathered officers all gave me a look. I explained about the basketball and they all just shook their heads. Gary, of course, with his quick wit and sick humor said, "And you though he was talking about basketball when he'd yell at you to Shoot! Shoot!" Everyone laughed, but I was more than just a little creeped out by the whole thing. I wondered if I would ever have to shoot someone or if I myself might get shot. Both ideas gave me pause. I felt I was prepared, trained, and ready to deal with anything, but that didn't mean I wanted to. Carrying a gun was cool; having to use it was a whole different ballgame.

I hung out with the boys for another beer and then wandered off to bed with them still yakking away. I was glad to know that none of my buddies got hurt and that it was the bad guy who was in the hospital. At the same time, I was a little unnerved about knowing the guy who got shot and there was a part of me that felt a little sorry for the dope. The guy might be a little goofy, but damn, life is too precious to go getting yourself killed.

This whole situation also affected Julie. Things like this made her think about what could happen to me someday. However, her job actually helped her deal with that whole issue, because she knew what I, as an officer, got involved with and the quality of the people I worked with and counted on. She also genuinely liked Howard and felt bad about him being involved in a shooting.

I use to tease her that I wouldn't change my life insurance over to her until after the wedding so she needed to wait before she started sending me on all the dangerous calls if she wanted to "cash out" on my demise. She did not find that funny at all.

Kevin M. Courtney

CHAPTER 87

May rolled around and it was time to head for Ireland with big sister Cheryl, who was four years older than I. Going there had been a goal of mine for several years, and since Cheryl had already gone over once, I figured having her along as a travel guide was a good idea. We had spent a year planning the trip and I had squirreled away the requisite amount of money and vacation time. I would only be over there for eight days due to my lack of vacation and an upcoming wedding, but Cheryl would be staying on after I left. I figured with that amount of time I could still cover a fair bit of ground. My sisters were a force to be reckoned with once they got their minds set on something, so I knew I was strictly along for the ride and would not be involved in any decision-making, and I was fine with that.

We landed at Shannon Airport mid-morning like most flights from the East Coast. It was a typical Irish day with a bit of clouds and rain but fairly mild temps. The first thing we had to do was pass through the screening point, which was manned by a member of the Garda Siochana, the Irish National Police. The name translates to "Guardians of the Peace," which I have always thought was cool. The middle-aged Garda asked the usual questions about length of visit and who we were as he looked over our passports. After learning Cheryl and I were both police officers, he commented, "Now isn't that grand. Two fine Irish police officers from America come home to Ireland for a visit." I still count that as one of the best welcomes I have ever gotten anywhere.

Cheryl and I wandered around the west side of the country and I had a grand time. The only dark cloud on the horizon was that Bobby Sands of the IRA was entering the last stages of his prison hunger strike in Belfast for political recognition for IRA prisoners and literally could die any day. The majority of the Irish might not approve of the current version of the IRA or their tactics, but their memories of the English government's cruelty and own senseless violence against the Irish did not make it easy to avoid feeling some sense of loyalty to Sands. The Irish war for independence from England was only 60 years past, and the IRA was the means by which the Irish had achieved that independence.

Sands did pass away while we were on the trip and it was headlines in all the papers, and so many comments were along the lines of some things never change. It was clear, however, that the Irish we spoke to were pretty guarded with their comments to us as Americans. On a couple of occasions, however, they let a few more pointed remarks slip. One older woman said, after learning Cheryl and I were of the correct blood, "Would you expect the English to ever do anything but what results in the death of another Irishman?"

Cheryl and I were in a pub in Limerick where we got quite a lot of stares from the locals when we sat down. I got the same reaction from the bartender when I went up to get a couple of pints. I made small talk about who we were and what we were up to and that seemed to help. There were two very good traditional musicians in the place, and we had a nice time sitting there relaxing. I'm not so sure that we weren't seated with some of the local IRA folks waiting to have a bit of a chat, and that is why we got the stares. That or maybe they just didn't get many tourists in that pub. Either way, we still had an enjoyable night.

My own heart was torn over the whole "Troubles." As a police officer I could not condone the killing of innocent people and police officers, which the IRA certainly had done with their bombings and other violence. At the same time, I knew the English had created the mess in the first place by invading and occupying Ireland and repeatedly brutally repressing the native Irish, evicting the Irish from their lands in the Province of Ulster and giving the land to Scottish immigrants, idly watching the Irish starve during the potato famine of the 1800's, and creating a situation where generation after generation had to leave Ireland in droves for America, Australia, and elsewhere to survive. The English then doggedly hung onto the six counties making up the province of Ulster long after they should have given it back to the free and independent Republic of Ireland.

I also knew the English Army and the Royal Ulster Constabulary had shot more than one unarmed Irish protester and locked up more than one innocent Irishman, so I wasn't about to suddenly become one of their cheerleaders. I couldn't in my own mind say what I would do if I was faced with British troops patrolling my streets every day. I could only pray that somehow, some way, the government in London would finally allow the six counties to be returned to their rightful owner, the Irish people. Little did I know it would be another 25 years before that process actually commenced.

I now have numerous friends in England, including a current and retired chief of police, or chief constable as they are known there, so I don't have quite the same view of the English as I used to. I even spent five weeks studying there for my Master's degree and have gone pheasant shooting on an estate belonging to a cousin of the Queen. (Fortunately, no background checks were conducted or I would have got my Paddy ass tossed out of there for sure.) I have to say I really have enjoyed my visits to England and the friendships I gained. All of those experiences made me a little less militant about England and a bit more open minded. I still think their government's policies towards Ireland were terrible for far too long, but I no longer hope the United Kingdom sinks into the ocean. Way too much good beer there to allow that to happen, not to mention all those crazy Welshmen and Scotsmen that also drive the English nuts.

An interesting side bar to my shooting trip was that one of the places I went shooting at, Weston Park in Staffordshire, served as the location for high level negotiations between the IRA and English government as part of the Good Friday Accords that U.S. envoy George Mitchell helped broker under the direction of then-President Bill Clinton. Further proof the Good Lord does have a sense of humor.

One of the highlights of my trip with Cheryl was to look up the uncle of Lieutenant. Jim Henley, who lived in a small village south of the town of Castlebar. Pa was his name, and he was the postman in the village of Partree. Jim's dad had emigrated from Ireland, but his brother Pa had stayed behind. Cheryl and I hired a hackney to drive us out to the house, and the driver was a great guy. We explained what we were up to and he seemed quite impressed. Once we found what I thought was the right house based on Lieutenant Henley's directions, Cheryl waited in the car while I went up to the house to see if anyone was home.

I gave the white-washed door on the neat little cottage, a couple of really good knocks, but there was no answer. About the time I thought we'd struck out, I heard a voice ask, "Can I help you?" I turned to see the most Irish of-looking-men standing ramrod straight, wearing muck boots and the typical Irish cap. I told him I was looking for Mr. Henley to which he replied, "Which one? The road's full of them." I said "Pa," and he said, "You found him. I told him I was sent by my boss, Jim Henley in America, and that seemed to confuse him a little so I tried again and said I was a policeman from America and his nephew Jim was my boss in Jackson, Michigan. That struck home and his face lit up while he exclaimed "Jimmy. You work for my nephew Jimmy? Well come in the house. Any friend of Jimmy's is welcome here." I explained my sister was along and waiting in the car and he immediately waved for her to come in.

I went out to the car to get Cheryl and told the driver I didn't know how long we'd be. The driver said to not give it a second thought. He'd head over to the pub in the village and we should just ring him there when we were ready to go. I had to admit a little shock at his attitude and figured we'd have to pay up when the time to leave came, but whatever the cost it would be worth it.

Pa made sure Cheryl and I were seated comfortably in the kitchen before he opened the back door and yelled to his wife "Nora. Come in here. We've Yanks in the house." Pa and Nora were just wonderful people, both in their late 60's (although they looked 50,) and eager to hear news of their nephew Jimmy who they had visited in Jackson a few years back. I, of course, pointed out he was the star of the Department, and they said how they were amazed a man so young could be in such a high position. I told them that obviously the cream, i.e., the Irish, always rises to the top, which they enjoyed immensely. (I didn't bother to tell them Jimmy wasn't all that young compared to some of the other commanders.)

We had been visiting for about 30 minutes when suddenly Pa exclaimed, "Jaysus, Mary and Joseph, where's me manners? Would you two like a taste?" Now, it might have been my first visit to the old sod, but I surely knew I had just been offered a bit of whiskey and of course accepted, as did big sister. Pa pulled out some eight-ounce water glasses and a bottle of John Powers Whiskey. I thought it was typical of a farmer not to have regular cocktail glasses, so I wasn't too concerned about the size of the glass--that is until Pa poured them three-quarters full. I must have looked a little startled because he asked, "Would you like a little something to wash that down with?" I answered, "Sure, how about Galway Bay?" This got quite a laugh from Pa and Nora, and Pa quickly produced some 10-ounce bottles of Guinness and I was off. Cheryl was a little more reserved, but she didn't shame the Courtney family at all.

We stayed about an hour and a half, laughing and visiting and learning a great deal about everyday Ireland. These two fine people accepted us sight unseen into their homes and treated us like family simply because I worked for their nephew. I found it amazing, but the more I have traveled in Ireland the more I have come to realize this type of welcome was common and truly defined Irish hospitality. We finally had to leave and were sent off as warmly as we'd had been received. I made multiple promises to tell Jimmy all about our visit as soon as I got back.

We'd rung the hackney and he was waiting in the drive, very pleased to hear we had a grand visit. He enjoyed hearing the details, and I think he was impressed with the fact that we weren't the average tourists who seemed only to take pictures and ask stupid questions. I was figuring on a pretty good bill when we got back to Castlebar and was floored when he said it was "5 pounds," which was the equivalent of about eight bucks American. He had taken us on a 12-mile round trip and then waited an hour and a half for us. I told him there was no way he could charge so little for so much time and trouble. He replied, "Now what kind of man would I be if I took advantage of you when you were taking the time to visit your friend's family all the way from America?" We gave him a good tip but I still couldn't believe how cheaply we had gotten off. (You'd think that attitude would be long gone in these modern times, but a friend of mine just related a similar experience he had with a cabbie in Ireland in 2009, so Irish hospitality isn't dead by a long shot.)

I managed to see a lot of Ireland and the inside of several good pubs along with making the trip to see the Courtneys, so all in all I was quite pleased when I headed back to America at the end of my trip. I picked up several gifts for friends, relatives, and my fiancé and I even managed to get my roommate Gary a tie from Millar's of Connemara. He seemed to like it and would point out to people this truly was his tie since it had his name on it.

Kevin M. Courtney

.

CHAPTER 88

I got back to Jackson and went right back to work. I was starting my third year on the force and really beginning to feel like a full-fledged cop. I was never too shy, nor did I lack confidence, but the job of a police officer is pretty complex and as much art as science. Unless you are a complete ass, you realize that pretty quickly. The only way to become a good cop is to put in the time like every other craftsman does in order to learn his craft.

I was sent up on N. Elm to back up Bachman and Stressman on a domestic. It was Friday night and that meant lots of drinking and fighting in parts of Jackson. Normally only two cars were sent on these calls, but Dispatch sent a third because of all the hollering and carrying on they could hear in the background when the call came in. The combatants were one fat hillbilly and his rather tiny wife. This pissed me off right from the start as I had no use for wife beaters in the first place, and this asshole outweighed the woman by at least 150 pounds. Things weren't made better by the fact that the male half was a real cocky bastard and figured out quickly he was getting under my skin. I minded my manners as best I could; knowing it wasn't my call, but I still dearly wanted to cuff and stuff this idiot.

Dave and John did their best to settle things down in the house and get me out of there before I violated myriad laws and several Department policies. It was obvious to Bubba what was going on and he wasn't smart enough to leave it alone. The three of us were in the driveway when Bubba stepped out on the porch, shook his fist at me, and said, "Hey, boy, you're lucky your friends got you out of here when they did." No NASA rocket ever got a more complete ignition.

Kevin M. Courtney

I went absolutely nuts and was climbing the chain link fence that surrounded the yard when Dave and John grabbed me and kept me from going up to discuss the matter further. Dave said, "Let it go. We're leaving." I pointed at Bubba and said, "I will get you, you fat son of a bitch," and I meant it. I did have enough sense, though, to leave the scene, all the while praying for the chance to catch that bastard doing anything wrong. Even if it was jaywalking, I was plotting all sorts of police brutality I was so mad. The thought that gave me hope was that sooner or later people like Bubba would give you the chance to get even. It was in their DNA to keep crossing paths with law enforcement.

The next day at the start of the shift, the sergeant advised there was a domestic assault in progress in the 100 block of W. Morrell and I needed to go on it. He told me he would get a back up as soon as possible. I grabbed my stuff and the keys to a patrol car and ran out the door. I jumped in the car and headed south from the station, lights and siren. It was just eight blocks so I was there quickly and I pulled to the curb on the south side of the street. I went up the steps to the porch, and through the large oval glass window in the front door, I could see good old Bubba from the night before slapping the crap out of his wife, who he had pinned against a wall with one hand while he wailed on her with the other.

I knew at this minute that God truly did love the Irish because a) I had now observed the assault myself so Bubba was fair game and I didn't need Mrs. Bubba to sign no stinking arrest warrant, b) a person's safety was in immediate danger so I didn't need a search warrant to enter the house, and c) there was no way Bubba was gonna be able to run away before I could get my hands on his sorry ass.

I didn't give a shit where back up was or if any was coming. I just yanked open the door and hollered "POLICE." Bubba looked up and realized at that moment that what started out pretty good, slapping his woman around, was suddenly going very bad. He knew not only was there a cop charging at him, but it was the cop he had called out less than 24 hours earlier. It also didn't appear the cop was worried about Miranda, Constitutions, or habeas corpus. No, it appeared the only worry was Bubba's, and it centered primarily on whether he would still be sucking air two minutes from now. Bubba tried to square up to me but, even though he outweighed me by a good 100 pounds, I knocked him right on his ass as I charged into him.

Bubba went down across an overstuffed chair with me on top of him, looking to beat a couple of Irish jigs on his head. Just then Bubba Junior appeared from another room and decided he needed to save his daddy. Junior was about 18 and when I saw him coming I took a swipe at him with my night stick and missed. Junior didn't anticipate I might look dimly on his intervention and jumped back like he had seen a rattler. About that time, my back up, Elaine Mason, came charging in the house. I pointed at Junior and said "Lock that little fucker up." Elaine complied and Junior was down for the count before the fight even started. I turned Bubba over and got cuffs on him but resisted the overpowering urge to give him the beating he deserved. Junior had managed to "save" his daddy since his intervention created just enough distraction that I recovered my "professionalism." Had Junior not jumped in, Bubba would have certainly gotten some souvenirs and I probably would have gotten some days off on suspension. I'm not sure the time off without pay wouldn't have been worth it.

I was still mad when I brought Bubba and little Bubba into the booking area, and when Sergeant Zomer asked what I had arrested Bubba for, I replied, "Because he's a fucking hillbilly." That apparently was not covered in either state statute or local ordinances because Zomer went white and dragged me out into the hallway adjacent to the booking area and chewed me a new ass. I explained the assault and Zomer said fine but told me to knock off the other comments. I took the chewing and nodded my agreement. I mean I had it coming so what was I gonna say?

Once back in booking, things were calmed down until Bubba mentioned to Zomer, "You know that boy (pointing at me) said he was gonna get me, but I didn't think it would be this quick." Back to the hallway we went with Zomer back in ass chewing mode, but this one I wasn't going to take without offering a defense. My explanation didn't exactly thrill Zomer, but he more or less let it slide figuring one ass chewing per hillbilly offender was sufficient. Besides, while he might be a sergeant, he was still a cop and understood we were dealing with a wife beater.

The topper of the whole day was when Bubba Junior started to bitch about me and how I behaved. Bubba Senior jumped right in and told him to shut up or he wouldn't go his bail. "Me and that officer there was fightin' man to man and you had no business jumpin' on his back. That's a coward's move and I'll whup your ass if you ever do it again." Bubba then looked at me and said, "I'm sorry officer. I should have taught the boy better."

This was a little too much; a guy who beats his wife in front of her children and is more than willing to fight with a cop is suddenly concerned about what kind of role model he is? All I could do was shake my head and think, people wouldn't believe this shit if I told them.

CHAPTER 89

The house on Lansing Avenue near the City's northern border looked like all the rest of the houses and if not for the people usually on the porch or in the yard, no one would know it was an adult care home. I was sent to the house on a possible 10-13 with Tom Bernardon as my back up. I was thinking to myself that if it is an adult care home doesn't that mean everyone there is some type of 10-13? I was making the mistake many people do in confusing intellectual disabilities with psychological disorders, and I figured that out once I arrived at the house.

The lady in charge pointed to a 20-year-old black man, of about 5'2 and maybe 120 pounds who was standing in the front yard by himself. She explained to us that his name was John and he was having issues and seemed fixated on giants. He kept saying the giants were going to get him. She said John had never had any problems like this and was normally pretty high functioning. Tom and I walked over to John who was very cooperative but kept saying the giants were going to get him. I was very low key and told John we could help him and he just had to get in the patrol car. It was interesting in that people could be having all sorts of visions and other mental disturbances and yet usually could answer basic questions and follow simple directions. Tom and I were able to get John to come along with very little fuss.

Department policy was to handcuff all prisoners behind their backs, as well as people picked up on mental health orders, but I put John's cuffs on in front and it seemed to help keep him calm. The procedure was to take John up to the ER at Foote East where the Doc on duty would make an evaluation of John and decide if he needed to go to the state hospital at Ypsilanti. By this time I had made several such trips and gotten over the shock my first visit with The Viper had caused. I had not, however, volunteered for any more tours of the wards at Ypsi.

Typical of most ER's on a Saturday, Foote was busy so Tom and I were directed to a treatment room where we could wait with John. I took John's cuffs off and had him sit on a short stool in the room. John asked for a drink of water and I got a Styrofoam coffee cup and filled it up for him. John sat sipping his water, continually talking about the "giants," while Tom and I stood around the room waiting. Finally the Doc came in and made a pretty quick decision that John was going to make the trip to Ypsi, so I called and advised the desk sergeant what was up. The Sergeant decided to send Gail Rogers with me because she was a back-up car that day and Tom was assigned to traffic.

Gail showed up a few minutes later and when she got to the doorway of the treatment room, I reached down and touched John on the shoulder and said, "Time to go," but John didn't move. At this point I took a light grip on John's upper arm and said, "Come on John, we got to go," thinking John was just a little scared. Tom had moved over next to John and about that time John looked up and without warning jumped up, screaming, and flailing around. Tom and I both grabbed onto him but in all the commotion the cup of water got spilled so all three of us went ass over apple cart and on to the floor. I quickly tossed my glasses off to save having them broken. Gail jumped right in and in just a few seconds a quiet treatment room was turned into a real WWF cage match. After what seemed like a half hour, but what was only maybe thirty seconds of rolling around trying to get a grip on an ungodly strong and wet crazy man, we finally got control by pancaking poor John under the weight of all three of us. He was still managing to lift himself slightly off the floor like he was doing a push up. This, even though we all were bigger than the man and in the case of Tom and me, larger by over a foot in height and 50 to 75 pounds in weight.

As we were lying on the floor talking to John to calm him down, as well as catching our breaths while making sure all important parts were attached and working properly, it suddenly dawned on me that maybe having two officers over 6'2" inches tall standing around looking down on a guy with "giant" issues wasn't the smartest thing we could have done. Once we got the cuffs on John and things were truly under control, I mentioned this to my fellow officers and Gail chimed in with a quick, "No shit, Sherlock." Apparently she was not particularly pleased to have a quick bout of crazy wrestling on her Saturday. I tried to point out that she also had the chance to get a couple of free gropes on Bernardon and me but she didn't seem to think that was any kind of valuable opportunity.

The ER Doc was kind enough to hand me my glasses while pointing out that when the fight started, with no concern for his own safety, he jumped into the middle of the brawl, snatched my glasses up, and then ran out of the room like his ass was on fire. This gave everyone, except John, a good laugh, and reaffirmed that cops and ER Docs have a pretty good relationship. John got a room at Ypsi and Gail and I were still chuckling about the whole incident when we got back into town.

Kevin M. Courtney

CHAPTER 90

"Unknown wild animal" was not exactly a typical call for a Jackson police officer. Michigan certainly had its fair share of wildlife, but I couldn't really think of any of it that would be unknown in Jackson. That was, however, the type of call that Dispatch had sent me on, directing me down into the neighborhood just north of Prospect east of First Street. Having spent most of my youth hunting and running around in the woods, I was going through all the possibilities and decided it must be a case of misidentification. Maybe a German shepherd cut through someone's yard and they thought it was a wolf, city people being a little weird anyway.

I pulled into the driveway and was met by a fairly animated woman who said, "I appreciate you getting here so fast, officer. It's still in the back yard." "Good," I replied and I actually felt a little of the excitement a hunter does when he senses his quarry is near. I was scanning the backyard like a hawk but couldn't see a thing out of place. The woman excitedly pointed and said, "There it is!" I felt like an idiot because I didn't see a thing, so I had to say, "Where?"

"Right over there!" I still didn't see the unknown animal, so I asked, "Is it near that woodchuck?" As soon as we'd walked in the yard, I had seen the little rodent chomping away on some grass, but that was about as common as seeing a fly on your window so I paid no attention to it while looking for the "unknown animal."

The woman suddenly relaxed and said, "Is that what that is?" I couldn't believe it. She lived in Michigan and had never seen a woodchuck, aka, the "groundhog" of February 2nd fame? She immediately asked me if they were vicious and contrary to my normal inclination, I did not give her a smartass answer. I explained the little bugger was basically a rabbit with a different frame design and coat. I started to walk over to it when I noticed it had an open wound on its back and wasn't running away like a wild animal should. I figured a local mutt probably had chomped on Woody, so I decided I better give it a quick exit and explained to the woman what I needed to do. She nodded her assent and I asked her for a shovel. This would give me the means to bury the body and have her gone when I capped the little rodent.

I pulled a target load out of my shirt pocket, a la *Barney Fife,* and replaced one of my duty loads with the cheap round. I then quickly gave "Woody" a Mafia sleeping pill in the back of the noggin. The lady came back and I did a quick burial along the edge of her garden. She thanked me profusely as I left. I again had to laugh about city people. I could not think of anyone I grew up around who would have called the cops to whack a woodchuck. In fact, I had a hard time thinking of anyone I'd known growing up who didn't have a 22 rifle or a shotgun in the house for just such occasions.

The smartass in me returned when I sat in my car writing the report on the incident. I threw in a line about finding a subject named Woody Chuck knocking on death's door and helping him over the threshold with a well placed .38 round and figured it would be good for a laugh or two. It was for several people, but not the Captain who read it and sent it right back to me with "Save the Comedy" written across it in big red letters. I wasn't too upset by the literary criticism and rewrote the report straight to keep the boss happy. Still, it was worth a laugh for most of the officers and sergeants who read it so I was glad I did it. I took my job seriously but I still liked to laugh. Of course this same Captain once chastised Loretta Merrill from records and me for laughing out loud while walking in the hallway. He said it wasn't dignified. After he left, Loretta said, "well neither are we so what the hell did he expect?"

CHAPTER 91

It was late spring of 1981 and there was a storm brewing, but it wasn't one of the typical thunderstorms experienced in a Michigan spring. This was economic in nature. Jackson had taken two major kicks in the teeth with the closing of both Clark Equipment and the Goodyear Tire plant. This meant substantially less tax revenue for the city, which meant cuts in staff would have to be made. I wasn't particularly worried about it because like most 24-year-old single men, I had the attention span of a four year old and a "What, me worry?" attitude.

All that changed when the Chief of Police called a Department meeting at City Hall and announced that 10 officers would be laid off. The first eight would be all of the officers hired in 1980 and the next 2 would be the last 2 hired in 1979: That was Dave VanSteempvort and me. Suddenly I cared a great deal about economics and tax revenues. I might be a child of the 60's, but I viewed a job like my Depression era parents. Losing one was some serious shit! There was lots of buzz in the room when the Chief made his announcement, but I wasn't really paying attention. I was just trying to digest the reality that I was going to lose my job as a Jackson police officer. The problem was it wasn't just a job. It was a major part of my identity, like it was for most good cops, and now it was going to be stripped from me.

I left the meeting in a state of shock. I had all sorts of thoughts running through my mind: Would I have to move back home? Could I find another cop job somewhere? Did I want to work somewhere else? Then there was the big one: If I didn't have a job, could I afford to get married? It was one thing to go leech off the parents for a while, but a man couldn't get married and leech off his wife. No freaking way any

Courtney would be pulling that shit in this century. You could call us chauvinistic pigs if you wanted, but we were just old school in our belief that a man needed to be able to take care of his family, and how the hell would you do that without a job?

The discussion about this little matter was not something I was looking forward to. I had a sneaking suspicion that Julie, like most women, would not see postponing her wedding as a good thing. No, she would suspect that I, being a man, was up to something and conveniently got my no-good, sneaky ass laid off just to get out of getting married. That'd be just the kind of weasel move a man would pull. I was right. Julie welcomed my economic news and related cold feet about as much as Nixon did finding out his aides were ratting his ass out as fast as reporters could write it down.

This was turning out to be a real perfecta for me. Not only was I going to lose my job, it appeared I was also going to lose a fiancée. It also dawned on me that I had two months left to work before July 1 when the layoff would take effect, meaning I might just get my Irish ass killed for a city that was putting me out with the trash in 60 days. Somehow that seemed the most distasteful part of the whole layoff. It's one thing to risk your life as part of your job; it is quite another to do it knowing the city really doesn't care what you do because they're gonna put you on the curb no matter what. I thought, "Shit, send me out the door now. At least then I won't end up dying for you ungrateful bastards."

The first Saturday after the lay off notices were made official, I was so pissed off I called in sick and just sat around the house sulking. I knew in my heart I should be at work, but the natural stubbornness that my clan was born with boiled up and that whole "loyalty" thing was in there, too. Goddamn it, I worked hard for the city and did what they wanted, so they had no business tossing me aside like an empty freaking beer can. By the next day, the fury was gone and was replaced with resignation. I decided if this was the way the city wanted it, so be it. I'd go to work, do my job, and when the time came, I'd shake the dust from my sandals and head down the road. Julie would have to understand that until I could find a job, I could not get married.

Big time salt got poured in the cops' wounds when it was pointed out that the city, while laying off police officers, would be hiring firefighters. It seems the firefighters' union contract mandated

15 firefighters on duty at all times, and to accomplish this and avoid paying ridiculous amounts of overtime, the city would have to hire additional firefighters. "Ain't that just wonderful? The fucking hose draggers don't do a freakin' thing and the city is going to hire more of them," was one of the more polite things heard around JPD when that news broke. I didn't buy it. I figured the firefighters were entitled to whatever they negotiated. I also saw no benefit in the police and fire unions being at each others' throats. No, the enemy was the worthless assholes in City Hall who were putting me on the street, not the guys down at the Fire HQ on North Jackson Street.

It suddenly dawned on someone that it would be a good idea to offer the fire fighter jobs to the cops set to be laid off instead of some goof from off the street. Well, the command staff at the fire department didn't like the idea of just being told "here's your new firefighters" without some say so. The result was that job interviews were scheduled for each of the police officers interested in transferring to the Fire Department instead of taking a lay off. Around this time, a couple of senior cops asked if they could be interviewed also. I was excited by this prospect, since if someone higher up the seniority list than I was transferred, I would be able to stay at JPD since I was the most senior of those slated to be laid off.

The interviews for the firefighter positions were pretty professional and I did my best to convince the panel that I truly was interested in coming over to the fire department and not just looking to keep a paycheck, even though the latter was the truth. At the end of the interview, one of the assistant fire chiefs who I had run into on a few calls basically called me out by saying, "You know, Kevin, I've seen you out on the street and it seems to me that you're a cop by nature and it's what you were meant to be. How are you going to handle losing that to become a firefighter?" I thought about lying but figured the guy called it straight and deserved a straight answer. "I guess I don't know, but I don't really have a choice in the matter so I'll do my best and give you a fair day's work everyday I'm over here." The assistant chief smiled and said, "Fair enough."

The next month was pretty stressful for all the officers on the pink slip list, but I was saved when Detective Jim Conant, a 12-year veteran of the Department, accepted a transfer to the fire department, thereby saving me from lay off. I don't know if I was more relieved or happy but no matter, I was still a cop with a job. Everything after that would take care of itself. I was, however, surprised that Jim took the transfer because he was not dead wood at the Department. He was a good cop and a good investigator. He had played a major role in several important cases, including the Tastee Freeze kidnap and murder the summer of '79. I guess he just decided to try something new. He took full advantage of the new job and eventually started a very successful chimney sweep business. He was a lot of things but lazy wasn't one of them.

The rest of the officers slated for lay off all took transfers to the fire department and did their best to fit in. The truth was aside from Conant and VanSteempvort, they were all square pegs in a round hole. I found it very odd to see them at fire scenes or around the fire stations. Eventually, as openings in the police department occurred over the next year or so due to retirements, they all came back except for Jim and Dave who made the fire department their careers. Both did very well as fire fighters and, as far as I could tell, never looked back.

Nevertheless, it was very hard to watch the transition of my fellow officers to the fire department. In a department like Jackson PD where you knew everyone, layoffs weren't an anonymous proposition. I also had the distinction of being a "survivor," so I felt a little guilty watching my friends have to give up being an officer while I didn't. Granted I was staying by the skin of my teeth, but I was still staying.

Needless to say, Julie was also pleased that I had a job and no longer could attempt to pull some kind of low-crawling weasel move to get out of getting married. I was also happy about that but troubled that she could even think such a thing about me. Oh well, it was not my fault she didn't understand.

To compensate for the loss of the ten officers, the department eliminated the Youth Services Unit, which had been staffed by a sergeant and several patrol officers, and returned those folks to regular patrol duties. Their job had been to work in the schools and deal with juvenile crime in general. Pretty progressive for the 70's and proof that the whole school liaison craze of the 90's was another example of law enforcement history repeating itself. Needless to say, none of the youth services officers were real excited about the loss of their special assignment, but the department had little choice.

Interestingly enough, the traffic unit was not disbanded because it was funded in large part by a federal grant which required a commitment of three years on the part of the Department or the city would have to pay Uncle Sam back. That made no sense, so the unit stayed--which didn't do a lot to please the youth services unit folks. I figured at least the traffic cars were out on the street and available for back up should they be needed. Definitely selfish, but I was more concerned about the thugs out on the street than those in the schools.

Kevin M. Courtney

.

CHAPTER 92

I was working A-21, in the northwest part of the City one warm Saturday afternoon when Al Combs and I were sent on a "fight in progress" call on Van Buren Street across from the Van Buren Street Apartments. I was closer than Al but heard his location and knew he would arrive right behind me based on our relative distances from the call. The fight was reported to involve several individuals in the upstairs apartment.

I pulled into the driveway believing Al was coming right behind me, and so I headed for a door at the back of the house that lead to the stairway to the second floor. I walked up fairly cautiously as I could hear lots of yelling, and when I reached the top I found a full-fledged battle was underway. There were four people involved, including one nitwit who had a chain binder commonly used to tighten chains that secure loads on flatbed trailers. Since there were no semi trailers in the apartment, he used the binder to go upside the head of one of the other participants, an Ernie Rodney by name. There appeared to be blood all over the walls, and all the people in the room were sweating like pigs and trying to catch their breaths. I yelled at the goof with the chain binder to drop it, which surprisingly he did. Ernie then saw this as his chance to get even and charged his nemeses, so I had to grab him to stop the fight from getting rolling again. I shoved him back into a chair and was holding him there when the other three suddenly became his best buddies and were looking to jump me. As on many other occasions, I yanked out my lumber and let the other team know the first one in range was going to get smacked.

While all this was going on, I was beginning to wonder where the hell Combs was. Just then I heard radio traffic that he had been involved in a crash at Jackson and Glick and was unable to respond to my location. Not a good feeling.

I realized at that moment I was confronted with four people who wanted to kick my ass and three of them were between me and door out of the apartment. Ernie was certainly doing his best to encourage them to jump in and save him. I was giving serious thought to letting Ernie go and fighting my way out of the apartment until Combs' replacement, coming from where I didn't know, showed up. I knew the idiots I was dealing with and finding and arresting them later would be no problem if I did decide to beat a hasty retreat.

Ernie was still struggling to get loose, so I had to look back down at him and just as I did, I heard a deep baritone voice that made Barry White sound like a member of the Vienna Boys Choir. The voice said, "State Police, Back the fuck up!" All heads in the room looked to the door and there stood Trooper Walt Strothers in full uniform. Had I not been otherwise occupied, I would have kissed him. Walt, who was an athletic looking black man of about 28, took a step towards the idiots who were looking to jump me. The little assholes wanted no part of him so they did indeed "back the fuck up." I was able to get my man cuffed and we also put the grab on Mr. Chainbinder. Shortly after Walt arrived additional city units showed up because I was not answering my status checks; hence dispatch had figured something was wrong and they were right.

Once things were under control and we had finished putting the habeas grabus on those who needed it, I went up to Walt to thank him for saving my ass. I asked him if he had just happened to hear the radio traffic and decided to respond or if dispatch had alerted him. Walt said no, he wasn't even on duty, to which I replied, "Then how the hell did you get here?" Walt explained he lived at Van Buren Apartments, and he was on his way into the Post to go to work when he saw my car in the driveway across the street. He knew the house was occupied by idiots so he thought it odd there was only one patrol car present. He decided maybe he better just walk over and check to see what was going on, and that is how he ended up walking into the middle of my mess. I was dumbfounded, yet Walt's willingness to extend himself for a fellow officer without being asked, or it even being expected of him, was a perfect example of how most all cops see other cops as their brothers and sisters, regardless of who they work for. I know I sure didn't give a rat's ass that it said "State Police" on Walt's shoulder patch when he bailed me out. I thanked God I worked in a profession that let me associate with men like Walt. The only thing I could think to say to him was "thanks" and that whenever we were in Evanoff's together, I would buy all his beer.

Not long after that, Walt backed Howard Noppe over on East Michigan Avenue and some white trash asshole decided he would ignore Walt and try to push his way into the situation at hand. Walt proceeded to put his finger on the guy's chest and back him up with a clear explanation of, "When the Michigan State Police tells you to back up, you back up." The explanation and finger tap took the guy about 50 feet away from the situation he wanted to stick his nose in. Howard said Walt was so forceful and convincing, that Howard started to leave until he remembered he was a cop and it was his call.

Ernie was in need of stitches from the binder so I had to haul him up to Foote East Hospital. Roger Ramirez came along as my back up since I'd already had one go-round with that mental midget, Ernie. At first things were fine and the dope sat quietly, waiting to be treated. Foote was busy that afternoon so we had him sitting on a stool in the hallway, and a short distance away was a young mother and her five or six year old daughter.

When the Doctor came in the hall to treat Ernie, we took his cuffs off of to assist in his treatment, Ernie decided he didn't like the way things were going so he started cursing and being the jerk he really was. A big surprise. Roger and I told him to pipe down on several occasions and, finally, after the Doctor said he couldn't treat him while he was carrying on like this, it was time for Ernie to vacate the hallway. Roger reached down and grasped Ernie by the bicep and said "Let's go," intending on taking him somewhere less public. Ernie responded by lunging up and taking a swing at Roger. Roger stiff-armed him which kept Ernie from connecting.

I was standing to Ernie's left and a step or so farther away than Roger, which put me in a very advantageous position. I was in a perfect spot to punch Ernie with my left hand, and since I just about totally left handed I took advantage. I started my punch in Mississippi, picked up speed through Arkansas and Illinois and landed it right in the eye of that sorry little bastard Ernie as he stood in Jackson, Michigan. It was without a doubt the best punch I have ever thrown or landed and it knocked Ernie right on his ass. I was headed in for a quick follow-up when Roger stopped me and quickly put the cuffs back on Ernie. I didn't care; Ernie had one coming and praise Jesus, I got to give it to him.

My punch further opened up Ernie's chain binder cut so we still had to get him treated. The Doctor made a quick job of it, and slapped on three or four butterfly bandages, and sent Ernie on his way. Roger and I booked, printed, and photographed him before chucking him in the cell. The mug shot showed up in detail a month or so later, when a warrant was issued for Ernie for failing to show up for court. I took more than just a little crap when my fellow officers saw Ernie's face and read my badge number on the booking photo. I tried to point out all the damage was done pre-arrest, but no one was buying that story at all.

CHAPTER 93

The next thing I knew, the week of my wedding had arrived. Julie and I had found an apartment to live in out on McCain Road past Sandstone about six miles west of Jackson. It was an old farmhouse split in to an upstairs and downstairs apartment and very well kept. It also sat on 160 acres of excellent hunting land, and my mind was all ready racing with visions of trophy deer dancing in my head. It was also only a mile from where my little brother, Jeff, lived so that was an added bonus.

The lease on our house had expired in June, and Lynn, our landlord, had agreed to let us extend until after my wedding date on the 29th of August. Ultimately, Gary and Rick decided not to keep the place and were headed their separate ways the first of September, so our timing worked out pretty good. Rick was going to get married to Dave Bachman's sister-in-law Georgia, so Gary found an apartment of his own. I would miss living with those guys as it was a real easy, comfortable arrangement and they were both great friends and good people. Fortunately, they have stayed my friends throughout my life.

Poor Lynn. His next tenant was a nice, quiet lady with a child who never paid her rent on time and caused more damage in six months than we did in fourteen. He sold the house shortly thereafter and his only profitable period as a landlord was when the three single guys, who he so feared would tear his place up, were his tenants.

My buddy, Henry, from Birch Run, who was in the Air Force, would be standing up in my wedding, so he rolled in on Thursday. We thought we'd get some dinner and just kick back that night. I needed to stop by the landlord's and pick up my damage deposit so I'd have a little extra pocket cash for the honeymoon in Toronto. Henry and I stopped on our way to dinner, and Lynn and Jan were very gracious to us--in fact too gracious. Jan started pouring us whiskey like it was lemonade and neither Henry nor I had ever turned down free booze, so we left there after an hour a lot happier than when we arrived.

Suddenly drinking more alcohol seemed a good idea, so after getting a couple of burgers and more booze, we headed for the Sheraton in downtown Jackson, which had a pretty good bar with music and dancing. We meet up with Dee, the lady who worked in the evidence room at JPD, and one of her pals, and we had a great time drinking and dancing with them and several other lovely ladies in the place. The music knocked off at midnight, so Henry and I immediately cut across the street to Evanhoff's which was only a block away on Cortland.

We'd no more sat down in there than the owner, Jordan, was announcing last call, so Henry and I each ordered three drinks since we clearly weren't bombed enough all ready. There were several of my colleagues from JPD, the State Police, and County in attendance, so we had a great time and finally headed back for my house when Jordan told everyone it was time to go. That I shouldn't have been driving is an understatement, but I managed to get home in one piece. I was aware of my condition so did my best to be careful, but clearly I should have found an alternative to driving. Back in those days, however, things were different and, right or wrong, my actions were not out of the ordinary for most of the drinking public. It was not uncommon for cops in those days to tell a drunk to park his car and walk or to let a sober passenger take over. That all changed for the better in the 90's but it took some time.

Henry and I made it home in one piece and I crashed. The next morning Henry had to be up early, as he had made a promise to a dying uncle in Saginaw, a little more than 100 miles northeast of Jackson, that he would let the uncle see Henry in uniform before the uncle passed away. Henry looked like he was dying when he left, and I'm sure I wasn't much better but at least I could sleep for another few hours. Poor Henry got about half way back to Saginaw when his stomach demanded he stop. He pulled off to the side of M-13, a two lane State Highway, and was upchucking in the ditch when he heard a voice from above ask, "Are you all right?" The voice could have been God's for all

Henry knew, but alas it wasn't. Henry turned his head to see the shiny shoes and light blue pants with a dark blue stripe of a Michigan State Trooper. Henry's response to this concerned inquiry was, "NO, and it's you fuckers that did this to me!" The Trooper got quite a laugh out of that and Henry's explanation before going on his way.

When he told me about his experience, I explained that we called those situations a "citizen assist." Henry said, "If the guy really wanted to assist me he would have shot me right there and put me out of my misery instead of leaving me in the ditch." Fortunately for me, Henry recovered later in the day and made it back in time for the rehearsal.

When I finally rolled out of bed just before noon, I had the mother of all hangovers, and it made the one from the spaghetti dinner debacle look tame. The mere sight of food caused me to turn away, and between my stomach doing spins and my pounding head, I was not in good shape. A long afternoon nap after loading up on aspirin might have cured things, but that wasn't an option. I had promised Julie that I would pick her up just after noon so we could run last-minute errands in preparation for the wedding. At the time we decided that, it didn't sound like any big deal, but then again I didn't plan to be hung over like a sailor after four days of shore leave.

Julie and I had decided to cover most all of the costs of our wedding and reception, and so we were quite cost conscious. With that in mind, we had decided to have our rehearsal dinner outside at the new apartment since the weather would still be nice. My roommate Rick agreed to grill chicken for us and we bought bulk potato salad, beans, etc. Neither of our families were fancy-dinner kind of folks, so they would be quite satisfied with what we served up. Much of what we were doing on Friday was picking up the supplies for the rehearsal dinner.

I was really having a hard time in my condition since the sun was both bright and hot, and that just made matters worse. Even my hair hurt. Julie, who was justifiably stressed, was not overly happy with Henry's and my choice of behavior just two nights before the wedding. My strategy was to be quiet in my misery and hopefully this too would pass. That tactic, and almost my wedding, went right out the window when after stopping at a party store for beer, Julie was upset about something, and going on about it, causing me sensory overload. I probably only had about one circuit operating, so it didn't take much to overload me. I asked Julie if she could just not talk to me for a while, and for whatever reason she did not take it in the "a small request from a dying man" vein but rather she felt it inappropriate for the time and place. I knew this when she replied to my most innocent of requests by snapping, "Fine. I don't have to ever talk to you again if that's what you want."

I was in such bad shape I decided to not seek forgiveness right away and instead enjoy the silence. I was sure that 15 minutes of no reply would not fatally damage my ability to crawl back into her good graces but rather would do wonders for my massive hangover. I was right. Not only did I get forgiven, I managed to snag a lifesaving hour-and-a-half nap after dropping her off with the assurance I would be completely recovered in time for the rehearsal.

The rehearsal went smoothly and Rick did a fine job preparing the dinner which was very good. My brother Stan and the other groomsmen, along with Julie's brother-in-law, Peter, and his brother who happened to be visiting from Germany decided to go out for a beer after the dinner. Julie gave me a look that made it clear I had used up my fatal hangover recovery days for the next six months, so I really was going for just one or two. Besides, no way my system could do another night like the last one.

CHAPTER 94

We all headed down to Evanhoff's and the place was pretty quiet for a Friday night. There was a pool table in the bar at that time, and we decided we'd should play some pool. The only problem was the table was currently occupied. My brother, Stan, was a quite a good player and so he came up with the solution. He would challenge the winner of the current game and the rest of us would put a line of quarters on the table so that we would, in effect, control who played after that. Someone asked what happens if you lose and Stan replied, "I've watched those guys play. I ain't losing."

The guy holding the table was a local named Tommie, whom I saw a lot during the course of my work. He was relatively small in stature and liked his alcohol but never really caused anyone any grief; so he was just part of the landscape of where I worked. He was easy to remember though, because he suffered from the syndrome that makes a person's eyes bug out like a frog's. I suspect that caused him to take a fair amount of grief growing up, but again he never really gave me any trouble so I viewed him as relatively harmless.

Stan's turn to play came up and, like he had directed us, we put numerous quarters on the table behind his so as to lock up the table once he won. We went back to our table and left Stan to his business. He gave Tommie a fairly quick beating and, of course, Tommie demanded a rematch which Stan politely declined since he pointed out the other players (us) had first shot. This didn't sit well with my man Tommie, who proceeded to offer to take my brother outside and whip his ass. Stan pointed out to Tommie that besides the fact there was no way Tommie could whip his ass, most of the people seated at the table Stan was pointing at were cops, and so not only would Tommie get HIS ass kicked, he would go to jail. Tommie looked over at us and gave up that "ass whipping" plan in a hurry.

None of us knew all this was going on, but I figured something was up when Tommie kept hovering around the table with a clear case of "pissed off drunk." Stan gave me the abridged version of what had transpired, so I suggested to Tommie he better chill out or boogie on down the street before he did get in trouble. He took the hint and wandered off while we continued to shoot pool. It was a good night and I kept my word; having only a couple of beers. Peter's brother from Germany seemed to enjoy himself and managed to get along pretty well despite the language barrier, even without his big brother Peter translating.

I went to bed that night with a strange sense of foreboding and excitement. I was truly looking forward to being married, but I also was concerned about it being my only wedding day. Divorce was rampant in law enforcement, and from what I had seen it never seemed to be an enjoyable experience for the people going through it, so I had no desire to join their ranks. Sadly, John and Beth had split up early that year and it really hurt both Julie and me. Beth was in the wedding and while I tried not to take sides, I suspect I hurt John's feelings by not having been more of a support to him. Fortunately, John and I stayed friends. Unfortunately, Beth moved away and out of our lives, although we still think of her often and have great memories of our friendship in our first two years in Jackson.

CHAPTER 95

Things went very smoothly at the Church, although I did have to step off the altar and stand on the end of the white runner so it could be rolled down the aisle. My cousin, Michele, got quite a kick out of that, so even then I was providing entertainment to the members of my extended family. I also noticed two occupied JPD patrol cars at the back of Church before the service started and figured Julie had them there with orders to shoot if I tried to sneak out. She later claimed they were day shift officers just sneaking in to watch the ceremony on duty. I didn't buy it then and still don't.

The reception was held at the bowling alley on Wildwood out by the airport and it was a great party. Lots of relatives, friends, and cops from all the area agencies. The fact that Julie was a dispatcher meant she knew as many if not more of the area officers as I did. Common practice in those days was to post an invitation on the bulletin board of the Departments to let everyone know he or she was welcome, and so turnout was usually pretty good. Julie and I ended up leaving the party around 11:30 p.m. although we had paid for the DJ to play until midnight. Just for good measure, we purchased an additional keg of beer just before we left because the place had a liquor license allowing it to stay open until 2:30 a.m.

I later would learn when the DJ announced at midnight that he was playing the last song; Ric Cedillo took up a collection and presented it to him so he would keep the place jumping as it was still half full. The DJ politely declined until Cedillo pointed out all the people who would be disappointed were cops and they would remember both his name and face. I suspect Ric was also using his best Mexican bandit stare while negotiating. The DJ told Ric he would be happy to keep playing and that the money provided was more than enough. The party rolled on until everyone had to clear out because of the 2:30 am closing time, at which point Mike Lazaroff, the Jackson county deputy I'd later sic Marcia on, invited the diehards to his apartment a short distance away on Robinson Road.

Several hours later, one of my sergeants staggered into his house at 6 am, whereupon his wife lit his ass up about where the hell he'd been. The Sarge muttered, "At Courtney's reception" which got a "Till six in the morning?!?" response. All Sarge could offer was, "It was an Irish reception," before he passed out on his bed. Unconsciousness was only a temporary reprieve because the Missus went for the jugular the moment he woke up.

As for my new wife, Julie and I had spent the night downtown in Jackson but only after I had told everyone we were going to drive to Ann Arbor to spend the night before heading to Toronto on our honeymoon. That bit of subterfuge was to prevent my car from being impounded or some other similar fate to befall me. I knew the senses of humor of the people I worked with and what they were capable of and took reasonable precautions based on that knowledge.

The next morning, as Julie and I headed out for Toronto, I realized my life had dramatically changed in a relatively short time. Not just because I was married but because in a span of two years I had gone from being a college student from a small town with little clue about being a cop to becoming a married man getting his grip on the profession of being a police officer. I was excited at what lay ahead of me and amazed at what I had all ready experienced. No doubt about it, all those dreams I had back in Birch Run had come true, and I thanked God every day for my good luck.

Driving north toward Canada with Julie by my side, there was no way I could imagine what the next thirty years would bring. Our lives ultimately would be blessed by four children who filled our home with love and laughter. Yet, great sadness would befall us, too, as just 3 years after our wedding I would lose my dad and as a result my children would never know the man who I loved and respected so deeply. Julie's Dad would pass in the late 90's and my mother in 2008. The hardest blow however, was the death of our precious five-year-old son, Kevin, in 2002. Time, faith and love heal a lot but that is a pain that never quite subsides.

I eventually would become the Director of Public Safety for the City of Big Rapids, Michigan, and would "retire" to the farm I'd always dreamed of – aptly named Four Green Fields Farm – complete with Belgian horses.

I couldn't have known all this as a young cop on the morning after my wedding so many years ago; back then, I knew only two things for certain: I was in the right job, and I'd married the right woman. Through all my personal triumphs, failures, and all that life brings, I have been eternally grateful for that.

And as for those wide waters that exist between our lives as we know them and our dreams as we envision them, I'm still swimming that chasm with faith in God and the luck of the Irish on my side.

The water is wide
I can't cross over
and neither have
I wings to fly
build me a boat
that can carry two
and both shall row
my love and I.

ACKNOWLEDGEMENTS

I want to acknowledge my wife Julie who kept after me to "do it" every time I mentioned wanting to write a book. Her confidence might be misplaced but I still appreciate it and without it, likely wouldn't have gone through with the project.

Equally important to me was my editor Susan McNamara who not only made tremendous improvements in my work she, with the typical directness of an Irish woman, made me "get off my arse, and get published."

I need to also mention the staff at 2 Moon Press who were so great to work with and helped this book become a reality.